D1264826

Psychology

The Science of Behavior

A volume in the series

INTRODUCTIONS TO PSYCHOLOGY

edited by

Eugene L. Hartley and Frances P. Hardesty

Psychology

The Science of Behavior

KURT SALZINGER, Ph.D.

Professor of Psychology,
Polytechnic Institute of Brooklyn,
And Principal Research Scientist, Biometrics Research,
State of New York Department of Mental Health

Springer Publishing Company, Inc., New York

Springer Publishing Company, Inc.
200 Park Avenue South, New York, New York 10003

Library of Congress Catalog Card Number: 71-78916

Printed in U.S.A.

To Suzy

ACKNOWLEDGMENTS

The figures used in this book came from many sources, which are given in the figure-captions. For explicit information, please refer to the *References,* beginning on page 279. We are grateful to the authors and publishers of this material for giving us permission to use it. The following is a list of the copyright holders of these figures (the figure numbers are those used in this book):

Academic Press: Figure 10-7.

American Association for the Advancement of Science: Figures 5-2, 5-7, 6-9, and 6-10.

American Medical Association: Figure 9-12.

The American Physiological Society: Figures 5-5, 5-6.

The American Psychiatric Association: Figure 9-1.

The American Psychological Association: Figures 3-1, 3-2, 3-5, 3-7, 3-8, 3-11, 3-12, 3-13, 4-1, 4-7, 5-1, 6-7, 6-11, 6-12, 7-1, 7-2, 7-3, 7-9, 7-10, 9-2, 9-3, 9-4, 9-5, 10-2, 10-5, 10-6.

American Scientist: Figure 3-6.

Appleton-Century-Crofts: Figures 3-3, 5-3, 5-4, 8-1, 8-2, 8-3, and 10-3.

W. H. Freeman and Company: Figure 10-4.

Grune & Stratton: Figure 9-8, 9-9.

Harper & Row: Figure 6-3.

Holt, Rinehart and Winston, Inc.: Figures 6-1, 7-7, 7-8, 9-11.

The Journal Press: Figure 7-5.

Charles E. Merrill Books, Inc.: Figure 6-13.

New York Academy of Science: Figure 9-7.

Pergamon Press, Inc.: Figures 7-4 and 9-6.

The Psychological Record: Figure 6-8.

The Society for the Experimental Analysis of Behavior, Inc.: Figures 3-4, 3-9, 3-10, 4-8, 6-5, 7-6, 8-4, 8-5, 8-6, 8-7, 8-8, 8-9, 9-10, and 10-1.

The University of Chicago Press: Figures 4-3, 4-4, 4-5.

The University of Illinois Press: Figure 6-2.

Williams and Wilkins Company: Table 10-1.

The Wilson Ornithological Society: Figure 4-6.

Yale University: Figure 1-1.

PREFACE

The purpose of this book is to present a consistent approach to psychology. Its central concept is that the proper study of psychology is the study of the behavior of organisms, including the behavior of man. I will let the book speak for itself on how successful such an approach is.

In writing such a book, I have found myself to be influenced by my reinforcement history and I should like to give credit to those most responsible for it. The informed reader will notice first my indebtedness to B. F. Skinner. His systematic approach to psychology was conveyed to me not only through his books but also through the personal contact which I had the good fortune of having with Fred Keller and W. N. Schoenfeld. The reader will also find that I have been influenced by C. H. Graham and C. G. Mueller in the area of psychophysics and by Otto Klineberg in social psychology. To all these men I give thanks. My debt to Joseph Zubin might be described as being in the area of abnormal psychology but this would grossly underestimate it, for he has been the psychologist who for most of my career supported my research and my thinking even while he disagreed with parts of it. My thanks to him.

I wrote this book while teaching at the Polytechnic Institute of Brooklyn. I give thanks to Helmut Gruber, Chairman of the Department of Social Sciences, who made possible my trying out on students many of the ideas found in this book and who facilitated the typing of the manuscript. This book has benefited greatly from the thorough editing done by Mrs. Dorothy Lewis at Springer.

My most important debt is to my wife, Suzanne Salzinger, who, in addition to all her wifely attentions, found the time and the patience to read this book and improve its contents. Thanks Suzy.

Kurt Salzinger
New York City
July 3, 1969

CONTENTS

FOR THE STUDENT

By the time the student has learned the contents of this book he should be able to see the basis for the advice which will be given in this section. Since the information will be helpful at the beginning of the book, however, I will make an attempt to impart it at the outset and ask that he trust its correctness before understanding the basis for it.

Perhaps the most important principle of effective learning is that it is an active process. Learning does not take place just because the learner exposes himself to material. Since most students who reach college have learned to read in what is essentially a passive way, such reading does not result in learning. Furthermore, those responses which are active often consist of inappropriate responses, such as underlining, a response typically made when reading material for the first time. Not only is such a response unrelated to learning, since underlining is not the response the student is trying to acquire, but, in addition, the underlining which a student is likely to do on first reading a book is often incorrect in that it calls attention, in future rereadings of the material, to aspects which are not particularly important in and of themselves or which are understandable only if taken in the context of other material which has not been underlined.

The way in which a student may learn adequately is by making the reading of the book serve as a response to the kinds of questions he, or the instructor, is likely to ask about the material. Thus, the first task the student must set himself before he reads is the formulation of the questions to which the book provides the answers. This book was written in such a way as to make this task relatively simple. At the beginning of each chapter there appears an outline of the contents of the chapter and at the end there is a summary. The questions may be formulated by determining which of the words, expressions, and paragraphs present new material and therefore require learning. After the student has read both the outline of the chapter and the summary, he should keep thinking of the questions to which he is finding answers by reading each particular section. After having read the chapter, he should reread the summary and thus test himself to see whether all the terms are now, in fact, clear to him. He should determine his understanding by writing the explanation on a piece of paper or by answering subvocally, without having the book available to him; merely saying to himself that he understands might simply mislead the student into believing that he understands when in fact he does not. Should the student discover that he does not understand, then he must reread the section appropriate to the question. The point of the procedure is that the student must give himself the opportunity to respond in the same conditions under which he expects to be asked the question. If the student finds himself peeking when he is supposed to be constructing the answer without having the book available for reference, then he might just do what one psychologist has suggested for this kind of situation, namely, sit on the book while he is trying to construct the answer. The combination of the discomfort, to be terminated only after writing the correct answer, and the unavailability of the text for reference when constructing the answer, will allow the student to learn to make the response most desirable, e.g., defining terms, describing processes, explaining experiments, their procedures, their results, and their implications, thus showing an understanding of the text which would obviously be useful in a test situation as well.

K. S.

1

The Scientific Study of Behavior

GENERAL CONSIDERATIONS IN A SCIENTIFIC APPROACH

Psychology as a Science

The man in the street thinks of psychology as a subject that everyone knows something about, as a study of the mind and the heart, or simply as psychotherapy. In fact, however, psychology as an official science dates itself from Wilhelm Wundt's establishment of an experimental psychology laboratory in 1879, a laboratory which could not have been founded without the previous work of such investigators as Johannes Müller, Fechner, and Helmholtz in Germany. In Russia, Sechenov, the forerunner of Pavlov, published his work on reflexes in 1863. It seems reasonable to say, therefore, that the science of psychology is at least a century old.

A scientific approach to a given subject matter can be distinguished by a number of characteristics: precise and objective conditions of observation, control over the conditions in which the behavior is being observed, planned manipulation of the conditions influencing the behavior so as to do an experiment, control conditions to isolate the effective variable, followed by exact and objective statements of summary and interpretation allowing the new data to be fitted into a larger system of facts. A scientific approach also requires the scientist to have faith that his subject matter is basically amenable to analysis and that the events he studies are lawful rather than capricious in their occurrence. Some people, intent upon propagating what they think to be a more beautiful view of man, say that, basically, man (or at least enlightened man) does what he wants to do and therefore defies predictability. And yet even a superficial view of the condition of life around us makes it clear that man is predictable and that his behavior can be controlled. The very complexity of our civilization, with the extreme degree of specialization of labor skills and with the distribution of the necessities in our society, makes the predictability and control of behavior a basic requirement of survival. What, after all, would happen if you could not get food by simply asking for it in a grocery store? What would happen if you could not predict, with a very high probability of being correct, that a car would not run you over when the driver is confronted by a red light? These are everyday instances of the predictability and control which are characteristic of man. This book will provide many experimental examples of this predictability and control of behavior.

In 1952, Grünbaum refuted a series of common arguments against the notion of causality in human behavior. It might be well to recount these—with some modification in the light of behavior theory. The first argument used against causality is that each individual is unique. In point of fact, inanimate objects and other animals are also unique when one is looking at particulars. Cause-effect relations among inanimate objects hold between classes of events, not between unique events. The same is true of human beings: cause-effect relations hold for classes of people, classes of responses and classes of stimuli. The uniqueness of individuals is no more or less important in the prediction and control of the behavior of man than the uniqueness of physical events is in the prediction and control of the behavior of physical matter. A second argument often given against causality in human behavior is its ostensive complexity. This argument is refuted by simply pointing to the course of the history of science. Would not these same indeterminists have argued against the possibility of ever reducing the large variety of motions on earth and in the heavens to a few simple laws? Would they have seriously considered all matter as being made up of about a hundred elements? Clearly this argument is one based on a prejudice, not on fact. A third argument suggests that man's behavior is caused by his seeking a goal, the point being that human behavior is caused by events in the future, a kind of causation quite different from that found in physical events. In fact, what controls the behavior of the individual are past reinforcements (rewards) for similar behavior and current stimuli which in the past were associated with behavior leading to that reinforcement. The path of causation in behavior is quite similar to that of causation in physical phenomena. A fourth argument states that determinism and moral choice are incompatible. This argument mistakes determinism for fatalism. Actually, moral choice allows the determinist to expose himself and/or others to those conditions which will evoke moral behavior from him and others. Skinner (1955–1956), in an article on freedom and the control of men, points out that a science of man is inevitable in a free society, and that with such a science it will be possible to maintain a democratic society.

Perhaps most basic of all the qualities of a scientific approach to psychology is the strict and explicit separation of the language of the subject, the organism being studied, from the language of the experimenter, the organism describing the behavior of the subject (Mandler & Kessen, 1959). The subject's verbal behavior must be viewed as data much the same as, for example, the subject's reaction time to a sound. Whereas the experimenter's statement that the subject's reaction time to sound is faster than it is to light is a summary statement based upon analysis of that subject's reaction times, a subject's statement to that effect must be construed as raw data. The experimenter must identify the variables of which such a statement (verbal response) is a function. The fact that under certain conditions the verbal response of the subject may be identical with the verbal response of the experimenter does not mean that one can simply ask the subject to describe or predict his response to a certain stimulus. Although it is tempting to use human beings as informants rather than as subjects, this procedure is fraught with danger.

The Rorschach test, a well-known projective technique, employs a procedure which utilizes the subject as an informant in the following way. The test itself consists of a series of ten cards containing symmetrical "inkblots" which vary, within and among the cards, in color and degree of shading. After the subject has described what he sees in each blot, the cards are returned to him and he is asked to point to the parts of the blot which stimulated him to say what he said. In a recent experiment, Baughman (1954) subjected the Rorschach test to empirical scrutiny by doing what should have been done when the test was first constructed. He modified the cards in such a way that the color and shading which had been implicated as critical variables in certain kinds of neurotic responses were present in some sets and absent in others, a control procedure clearly called for in any experiment that tries to isolate an effective variable. Then, by comparing responses given to the different stimulus sets, those with and without color, those with and without shading, etc., he was able to see directly by appraising the frequency of "shading" or "color" responses whether the responses were, in fact, correctly labeled. The study had a number of interesting results, but most interesting for us here was the fact that "shading" responses occurred in the absence of shading in the stimulus and that "color" responses occurred in the absence of color. The conclusion to be drawn is quite clear: The subject does not know what aspect of a stimulus is controlling his response. Only experimental variation of a stimulus allows one to conclude whether a given aspect of a stimulus is controlling a response or not. Despite the topographical similarity between the subject's response, "The color made me think of a clown's hat," and the experimenter's possible description, "The color made him say it is a clown's hat," the two statements are most definitely not interchangeable, since only the latter is based, or could be based, on an analysis of data objectively and precisely appraised.

Psychology as the Study of Behavior

It is often said that a theory is not displaced by contradictory data but rather by a better theory. Such is the case with scientific concepts. The already bankrupt concept of elementary sensations in introspectionism was displaced in behavior theory by the concept of behavior. From the vantage point of today, this hardly appears to qualify as an original concept. And yet, when Watson (1913) published his first paper on behaviorism, it was revolutionary. In his book, *Behavior,* Watson (1914, p. 27) stated: "The behavior of man and the behavior of animals must be considered on the same plane; as being essential to a general understanding of behavior." In the first chapter of the same book, Watson (1914, p. 1) said, "Psychology as the behaviorist views it is a purely objective experimental branch of natural science. Its theoretical goal is the prediction and control of behavior. . . . The behaviorist attempts to get a unitary scheme of animal response. He recognizes no dividing line between man and brute. The behavior of man, with all of its refinement and complexity, forms only a part of his total field of investigation."

Thus the concept of behavior as used by Watson stimulated the development of the field of comparative psychology. It meant that Darwin's great discovery, the theory of evolution, could be applied to the enhancement of knowledge in psychology. It meant that eventually the concept of behavior would allow psychologists to extrapolate their work on fish, rats, pigeons, monkeys, etc., to man. It offered the possibility of utilizing far more efficient methods of obtaining data for the purpose of gaining an understanding of the principles that govern human behavior as well as animal behavior. Finally, the concept of behavior is powerful enough to allow one to extrapolate, within a single organism, from one response system to another (e.g., from nonverbal to verbal behavior) or from one response class to another (e.g., from pressing a bar to pulling a chain).

We shall return to more careful consideration of the concept of behavior when we discuss the behavioristic approach. For the moment, it will suffice to say that Watson's rejection of introspectionism as a method, his rejection of the establishment of the basic elements of states of the mind as the subject matter of psychology, and his substitution of the study of behavior, both to improve the method and to provide psychology with workable subject matter for a science, prepared the ground for the development of more than fifty years of experimental psychology. It is the fruition of those years of effort which will form the basis of this book.

Operational Definition

When the psychologist rejected armchair psychology as a major method of investigation, adoption of the concept of operational definition was inevitable. The idea of the operational definition was first made explicit by Bridgman (1928), who stated that any scientific concept was no more or less than a unique set of operations. He illustrated this by specifying the operations involved in a concept as seemingly obvious as length. As the concept of length applies both to ultramicroscopic dimensions as well as to stellar distances, the concept of "tactual" length has to be given up. In order to measure distances at these extremes, it becomes necessary to perform different operations, e.g., optical ones, which may not give rise to the same measurements as the tactual ones. To the extent that both operations can be applied to a common distance, and to the extent that they give rise to the same measurements, one concept-name is appropriate for both. However, as Bridgman points out, if, in utilizing new and more accurate types of measurement, the scientist finds that the different operations yield different measurements, he must be prepared to adopt new concepts.

In psychology, the concept of intelligence poses the problem of operational definition in very much the same way as does length in physics. Is it reasonable to consider the operations we employ to measure "intelligence" in a two-year old child (type, speed, and dexterity of motor responses) to be equivalent to the operations we employ to measure the supposedly same concept in adolescents (memory span, current information, reading ability, word meaning, arithmetic problems, analogies, and so forth)? Empirical attempts to relate those two measures of intelligence show that it is very difficult indeed to predict the adolescent's "intelligence" on the basis of his "intelligence" at age two. Under those circumstances, "intelligence" appears to be not so much a scientific concept as an expression of a hope, or at best a statement of a program of research towards the end that the concept of intelligence is a reasonable way to describe the human organism throughout his entire life span. In this area, consideration of operational definitions suggests that one should, at the very least, talk of Intelligence_1 (for two year olds) and Intelligence_2 (for adolescents). Hebb (1966) recently suggested Intelligence A and Intelligence B, defining A as the innate potential, essentially not measurable, and B, as the actual intellectual functioning level, the measurable intelligence. According to Bridgman (1928), *A* is, technically, "meaningless." The problem of different "intelligences" comes up again when one attempts to measure it in other special populations such as in senile individuals, the physically ill, or in neurotics or psychotics, for the operations involved in obtaining a measure of intelligence vary from one group to another.

One must include, in the operational definition of intelligence, not only specification of the content of the test, but also the preparation which the person being tested brings to the testing situation. The operations for the measurement of intelligence are not equivalent when applied to Adolescent A, who is brought up in an environment where reading and problem solving are encouraged, and to Adolescent B, whose environment encourages development of other skills.

It should be obvious, then, that operational definitions are useful in clarifying discrepant findings such as those arising in the area of intelligence. It must be noted, however, as was suggested in the beginning of this section, that operational definitions are part and parcel of any actual scientific observation. They are used by the psychologist as soon as he decides to observe anything. Bridgman's contribution, then, stems from the fact that he proposed that the operations used to measure a concept be the total meaning of that concept. Spence (1956, pp. 13-14) described operationism in the following way:

> Accepting the requirement that all terms employed by the scientist, no matter how abstract, must ultimately be referable back to some primitive or basic set of terms that have

> direct experiential reference, these writers have suggested that a basic vocabulary for science is provided by the terms designating directly observable physical objects such as tables, chairs, and cats, their properties, e.g., green, hard, and loud, and the relations between them such as between, before, and below. Different members within the group refer to this vocabulary of basic terms differently, calling it variously the "observation vocabulary," the "observable-thing language," and so on.

Skinner (1961, at a symposium on operationism in 1945) noted that psychologists could have taken the old subjective concepts of psychology and redefined them in operational terms. He remarked, however, that by the time Bridgman's book came out there was no longer any reason to redefine subjective concepts operationally.

> The reinterpretation of an established set of explanatory fictions was not the way to secure the tools then needed for a scientific description of behavior. Historical prestige was beside the point. There was no more reason to make a permanent place for "consciousness," "will," "feeling," and so on, than for "phlogiston" or "*vis anima*" . . . What was wanted was a fresh set of concepts derived from a direct analysis of the newly emphasized data, and this was enough to absorb all the available energies of the behaviorists. (Skinner, 1961, p. 283.)

In another paper, Skinner (1956) argued that these new concepts derived directly from an analysis of data, and came from a deep-rooted respect for data, as well as from luck, laziness leading to better apparatus design, etc., but certainly *not* from the typical experimental design books or from setting forth detailed theories replete with predictions.

The operational definition can thus be applied to concepts which the scientist believes, on some basis, to be critical for carrying out his work and which, if operationally defined, will improve the course of science. The warning which must be sounded here is that many concepts derived either from common sense or from philosophy or history may well not be worth resuscitating.

On the other hand, operational definition may refer simply to replicable concrete description and manipulation of variables, both independent (what the experimenter changes) and dependent (what the organism does) variables.

The need for using operational terms in the course of an experiment, however, need not limit the scientist's initial thinking about a specific problem. He might start with a hunch, an accident, a mistake, or a theory. The theory might be grand or, as is more usual nowadays, limited; it might come from consideration of data in psychology or related fields, or from considering an area of research which overlaps two sciences. Some scientists suggest that all their successes stem from following up mistakes they have made which revealed to them the importance of a variable they were not even examining (or intending to examine) at the time. Yet there is probably an equally large number of scientists who have sworn that only those who are willing to keep at a given question, no matter how tempting digressions might be, are the ones who make important discoveries.

Such investigators as Miller, Galanter, and Pribam (1960) have suggested that behavioristic theories like those of Clark Hull were very much related to the machines around in his day, *viz.*, the relays forming a telephone switchboard; they suggest that the computer today should be embraced as a newer and more appropriate model for behavior. There is no reason to reject the computer as a source of research hypotheses or suggestions, but there is no guarantee that research generated in this manner will be more fruitful than research generated or stimulated simply by the experimenter's familiarity with the data in his field.

We are not suggesting that by using operational definitions research goes on in a vacuum or that the experimenter ought not to have concepts or be aware of generalizations which allow him to design related experiments. We will, in fact, present a system of ordering behavior which, we hope, will stimulate a better understanding and better experimental analyses of the phenomena which are regarded as peculiarly psychological. Thus, it should be clear at the outset that the empirical approach espoused here is not the unfortunate, unguided, and unfocussed research in which the computer has been unhappily involved, such as the search for all possible relationships within a matrix of haphazard variables. That recent development has made a farce of the concept of operational definition. This is the kind of dust-bowl empiricism which has defined intelligence as: "That which the intelligence test measures." No one of repute now holds with such a view. As we shall see later, such concepts as intelligence, if we decide to retain them, must be defined by a set of converging operational definitions, such as the relation of the test measure to genetic and environmental factors whose specific significance must be detailed. Thus a concept which has many connotations other than the ones allowed by the operational definition must either be renamed so as simply to describe concretely that which it measures, or it must, if it is more seriously directed at measuring more than what its operations relate to, be shown to be empirically related to other measures which also have been empirically specified.

Which course science will follow—a strictly empirical approach based on consideration of data, with a belief that the lawful relations which are revealed are meaningful, or an empirical approach based on data collected to test the validity of a preformulated theory—only time can tell. Today both courses are followed in psychology.

Observational Techniques

Introspectionism. This technique may well have more importance in terms of the history of psychology than in terms of current practice. Nevertheless, it still appears to have some adherents and therefore deserves at least brief mention. It was, of course, the technique of choice in both Wundt's laboratory (where experimental psychology was founded) and in E. B. Titchener's laboratory in this country at about the same time. Defining psychology as the study of the primary elements of conscious experience, introspectionism as a method appeared to be reliable, particularly as long as it restricted itself to the study of sensations. Transfer of the method to the study of such processes as thinking, however, revealed its unreliable nature, and resulted in the virtual rejection of the method. Today, the method has survived in three forms. Only one appears to have remained unchanged. It is still a critical method for phenomenology (the study of immediately given—not conceptualized—experience). Phenomenology and behaviorism constituted the subject of a recent symposium (Wann, 1964). A reading of that symposium, together with a recent article (Brody & Oppenheim, 1966) brings one to the conclusion that introspectionism in its old form might be worthwhile preserving only for purposes of examining that behavior of the scientist which precedes his actual observation and experimentation. As already suggested above, we do not yet know where the most fruitful ideas for research come from and this method, therefore, may be one such source. It should be pointed out, however, that this author is rather skeptical about it as a source of new ideas.

A second form of introspectionism has survived in the utilization of the psychophysical techniques. Among the responses a human subject may be asked to give are whether he sees a light, which of two weights is heavier, or to adjust the intensity of a tone until it is just twice as loud as another. These techniques have in some cases survived, almost completely unchanged, in much the same form as that in which they were originated during the nineteenth century by Weber, Fechner, Helmholtz, Plateau, and Wundt. In fact, Plateau's method, which proposed a power law instead of a logarithmic law of sensory intensities, was only recently revived by S. S. Stevens. The reason that this form of introspectionism has survived is that the psychophysical techniques are basically behavioral techniques in which a verbal response is evoked by a physical stimulus, a relationship which is conditioned before the subject enters the experiment and which can be conditioned, in comparable form, in animals.

The third form in which introspectionism has been preserved is as clinical insight. This will be discussed in more detail in the next section.

The Clinical Approach. The development of clinical psychology, psychoanalysis, and other forms of psychotherapy is more recent than that of experimental psychology. Despite this, the evolution of clinical psychology has unfortunately followed a path independent of that of experimental psychology. As we shall see later, behavior theory can be effectively applied to abnormal psychology (which is generally thought to fall within the province of clinical psychology) and a good start in that direction has been made. In the meantime, however, clinical psychology developed its own methods of observation and it is these which we will discuss here. The basic clinical technique appears to be quite simple and sounds very much like common sense. If you want to find out about a person, have him speak to you in a conversation, i.e., in an interview. Quite early in the history of psychology this technique was refined and reconstructed in the form of a test by R. S. Woodworth, the experimental psychologist. During the course of this early structured interview, the patient had to reveal things about himself by responding to such questions as, "Are you frequently depressed?" It is immediately apparent that such a response is another offspring of introspectionism. It also must be noted that, almost universally, clinicians are convinced that the most significant information about a person's behavior disorder is to be obtained from that person's reflections about himself. In later sections we will take up a more detailed discussion of this aspect of clinical psychology and some of its methodological difficulties when viewed within the general framework of a behavioral approach. Here we will confine our remarks to the clinical technique of observation. Perhaps the first point to be noted about such observation is that the clinician intends to observe "everything," i.e., essentially there are no limits set by the observation on what the clinician is going to attend to. This means that some things will inevitably escape the observer, introducing a source of error which precludes the method's use for scientific purposes. Studies of what the clinician observes during open-ended observations have shown that his introspective report of what he observes, or interprets to be the basis of what he observes, cannot, as might have been expected on the basis of other empirical results investigating introspectionism, be accepted at its face value. Despite the fact that much lip service is given to the importance of gestures and tonal aspects of speech during such observation, empirical studies (e.g., Giedt, 1955) have shown that the clinician pays most attention to the manifest content of speech.

As psychologists, it behooves us to ask what variables control the observing behavior of the clinician. An experiment by Holland (1958) is of great interest in this respect. He noted, in considering typical signal detection experiments (as in detecting targets on radar displays), that not all the relevant behavior in such situations is measured. What is measured is the percentage of signals detected, the latency of detection, or the threshold value of the stimulus necessary for detection to take place. But these are the effects of observing, i.e., only if the observer is viewing the screen will he be able to detect the signals. What about the observing behavior itself? Under ordinary conditions this is relatively difficult to specify, since it consists of a number of different responses, like scanning and focussing. Holland, therefore, modified the situation in such a way that the observing response was made quite obvious. Behavioral analysis of the typical signal detection experiment made it clear that it is the detection of the signal which constitutes the reinforcing event, i.e., the reward for making an observing response is the event observed. In terms of the technical language we will introduce later, the observing response is considered to be an operant, i.e., a response whose occurrence is controlled by the consequences (reinforcers) of its emission in the past. In Holland's experiment, subjects, while in the dark, were required to report deflections of a pointer on a dial. The dial was made visible for a period of .07 second for every key press made by the subject. By differential scheduling of the reinforcers (pointer deflections), the rate of observing responses was modified. Thus, as the rate of pointer deflections varied from, on the average, one every 15 seconds to one every 30 seconds, to one every minute, to one every two minutes, so the rate of observing responses decreased. We can infer from this experiment, then, that one variable which controls the clinician's observations is the rate at which the events he is looking for (the pointer deflections of Holland's experiment and therefore the reinforcers) occur. The events he looks for are likely to be those behaviors his preconceptions or his theory call for. On the basis of this argument, it becomes clear why clinical observations, no matter how many are made, cannot be accepted as a basis for the validation of a theory. Observations made under these conditions are especially subject to the biasing effects of the observer "seeing only what he wants to see," or, in more technical language, in the observer's attending only to those events for which he was previously reinforced.

Another paper (Chapman, 1967) provides experimental evidence for another observational problem in clinical procedures, which occurs in the absence of appropriate safeguards. This problem has to do with the fact that clinicians are often forced to take action before they have sufficient evidence. That insufficiency is due to the emergency conditions under which they must work. Consequently, the interpretation of a few facts, and their subsequent fit into the theoretical framework in which the clinician operates, make the observational error of an illusory correlation between events in their observations more likely. Chapman's task was quite straightforward; he briefly presented his subjects with pairs of words, some of which tended generally to be associated with each other and others which were generally unrelated to each other. In addition, most of the words making up the pairs were short, but a few were manifestly longer. After they had viewed the pairs of words, the subjects were required to report the frequency of co-occurrence of the various word pairs. The results showed that the subjects reported significantly greater co-occurrence of words having associative connections than was actually the case. What is perhaps even more revealing is the fact that subjects reported greater co-occurrence of the longer words than was actually the case. It seems, therefore, that not only the variable of past association of events (which one might certainly have predicted) but also the variable of distinctiveness produced a bias in reported observations of association.

There remains the question of why such faulty observations continue to be made. No doubt part of the answer was the absence, until very recently, of practical alternatives. Part of the answer most probably has to do with the demands that our society makes upon the clinician. But part of the answer is undoubtedly to be found in studies like the following one. Ulrich, Stachnik, and Stainton (1963) administered some personality tests to a group of subjects and about a week later privately presented each of the students with the same personality interpretation as was given to every other student. When these subjects were asked to rate their personality interpretations in terms of how well they fit them, the resultant ratings given were good to excellent in 53 out of 57 subjects. Furthermore, when subjects were administered the same tests and given the identical interpretation by testers identifying themselves as students, still as many as 59 out of 79 subjects rated the interpretation as good to excellent. The authors point out that not only were the clinical interpretations accepted as correct by the subjects, but that, in addition, they tended to reinforce positively the interpreter of their personalities by praising the accuracy of the interpretation in glowing terms. Thus, here we have evidence for the apparent gullibility of the people being observed by the clinician, as well as a suggestion for the mechanism which operates to maintain the strength of the interpretations given by clinicians.

In summary, we find that clinical observational procedures are unsuitable as a method of validation in the scientific study of behavior.

The Ethological Approach. The ecological approach to behavior comes from biology and treats of the general relations between organisms and their natural environment. Ethology, a branch of ecology, refers to the relation of the *behavior* of organisms to their natural environment. The emphasis in the ethological study of animals is biological and therefore the observations are based on adaptive behavior as defined in terms of Darwin's theory of evolution. Ethologists are interested in arriving at a taxonomy of behavior. The types of behavior they study are innate and species specific. Thus, while they study behavior primarily by simply looking at it, they use the following as anchor points for defining response classes: the releasing stimulus, the topography of the response and its universality in the species or a special segment of the species, its significance in the survival of the species (importance in reproduction), its significance in the survival of the individual organism (importance in obtaining food and warding off enemies), its evolutionary significance (a search for behavioral homologies and analogies, i.e., resemblance in behavior due to a common ancestor as opposed to resemblance due to similarity in function of the behavior being compared), and, finally, its biological mechanism of control.

Since observation of these behaviors takes place in the natural environment, automation for more reliable recording is not generally possible. Reliability of observation is therefore obtained by repeated observations by more than one investigator. Lawfulness of responses results from their relation to the anchor points mentioned above. In addition, the classes of behavior are made more reliable by the fact that they are defined, at least in part, by their very stereotypy. The stereotypy thus makes them even more easily identifiable.

The argument is often presented by ethologists that, unless the behavior being studied occurs in nature, it is apt to be trivial. The choice of behavior to be studied, even for the ethologist, depends upon more than simply its occurrence in nature, however.

Two other considerations might be mentioned here. First, study in nature makes it more difficult, if not impossible, to isolate the variables controlling behavior. Ethologists have, therefore, come to accept this factor in at least some cases, introducing experimental modifications of nature where necessary. Secondly, a behavior is sometimes chosen because it is most sensitive to the effect of variables of interest to the scientist undertaking the investigation. We will discuss the choice of behavior and animal at greater length later (Page 23 ff.).

Before closing this section, it might be well to mention an approach to the study of *human* behavior (Barker, 1965) which is very much like that of the ethologist's. In psychology, observation in the absence of some sort of intervention, whether by experimentation or by test, is almost nonexistent. Barker argues that T-data (which Barker defines as consisting of "transducer" data, where the psychologist changes the form of the behavior only in *recording* it) often give rise to generalizations quite different from those derived from O-data (what Barker calls "operator" data, where the psychologist provides the conditions under which behavior of special interest to him occurs). Although psychologists interested in using the O-data approach to behavior have claimed both reliability for their observations and lawfulness in their data, it seems to this author that many of the criticisms of O-data can be met by better, more ingeniously designed experiments, allowing T-data to occur under controlled conditions (See Page 20 ff.).

General Problems of Measurement. The ubiquity with which statistical procedures are discussed elsewhere makes it unnecessary for us to review them here, although they are appropriate to this section. Three points, however, which are frequently omitted from discussion of statistics will be mentioned in this context. The first concerns itself with experimental functions of statistics; the second deals with the properties of the numbers which are being manipulated statistically; the third is the problem of how much measurement is necessary.

The function of statistics is, first of all, simply to summarize data. This function can be carried out in a number of ways: by drawing graphs; by computing measures of central tendency (e.g., the mean, which is the sum of all the scores divided by their number); by computing measures of variability (e.g., the range, which is the largest minus the smallest score); or by measures of relationship (e.g., product moment correlation, which varies from -1, for a perfect negative relationship, through 0, no relationship, to $+1$, for a perfect positive relationship). Descriptive statistics, as these measures are termed, are, relatively speaking, quite easy to compute and often quite useful. At other times they can be misleading, however. Murray Sidman (1952), for example, pointed out the danger of accepting a learning curve (e.g., number of responses per minute as a function of trials) based on averaging the data of a number of organisms as representative of the learning curve for the individual organism. While for many years, psychologists had averaged over many animals to reduce individual variability and to "extract" *the* learning curve, recent research has shown that an average curve might be typical of the behavior of none of the individual organisms. Furthermore, for some experimental problems, variability of behavior can be reduced by training animals until their behavior has become more stable, thus obviating the necessity for averaging to reduce variability.

An additional function of statistics is to give the experimenter information on how much he can trust his results. The experimenter may want to know whether, if he did the experiment over again, he would get the same results. Statistics of inference allow one to estimate the probability with which the same or essentially the same results would occur in other samples of the population being studied. These statistics play an important role in the field of experimental psychology. On the other hand, whenever feasible, there is no better method of checking the reliability of an experimental result than actually repeating the experiment and measuring the replicability of the data.

The second problem of measurement relates to the properties of the numbers which are being manipulated statistically. Numbers are, after all, simply verbal responses. Although some numbers can be added, subtracted, multiplied, and divided, it is simply not true that all of them can. Take, for example, the numbers used to identify football players. Would it make any sense to average these and say that a particular team had a higher football player value than another? The answer is obviously "no." These numbers are simply names and cannot be averaged together any more than can the names George, Harry, and Gertrude. These names constitute what is called a *nominal scale.*

Suppose now that we were interested in summarizing and comparing dominance patterns in two differently treated groups of hens. In this species dominance patterns can be measured by noting which bird gets away with pecking which other bird. On the basis of these data a rank order can be established. Let us suppose, then, that the investigator finds a particular hen which changed, after a specific treatment, from a rank of 2 to a rank of 8 (the higher the rank the greater the number of hens that can peck that hen). Is he entitled to say that the hen is four times as low as it was originally in the hierarchy? It may not be as obvious as in the first case, but the answer is still "no." In fact, the investigator cannot even say that this hen changed more than one whose rank went from 1 to 3. Let us see why this is so. First, we must note that measurement consists of the assignment of numbers by a rule which in turn reflects the operations used by the investigator in his experiment. This rule must be remembered when manipulating these numbers afterward. When a given rank is assigned to a hen, all we know is that all hens with ranks lower than its rank can peck it, and all the hens with higher ranks can be pecked by it. We do *not* know whether it is as easy for the hen with rank 1 to peck the hen with rank 3 as it is for the hen with rank 8 to peck the hen with rank 10. If one were interested in whether these differences in ranks are equal, one would have to use a measure such as amount of time that the two dominant hens spent in pecking the submissive hens before the submissive hens pecked back. Since a rank tells us only which hen can peck another hen more, we can make no generalizations about relative differences between ranks. Ranks have the property of more or less and constitute what is called an *ordinal scale.*

Still another kind of number is characteristic of experimental data. Suppose that we were interested in determining whether, or to what extent, the height to which a rat can jump is genetically determined. We might inbreed separately all the rats that jump high and all the rats that jump only a small distance for a number of generations. By mounting a vertical scale on a wall and noting the highest point that the snout reached, we would then have a measure of the height of each jump. Suppose the scale attached to the wall started 6 cm above the ground, thus establishing an arbitrary 0 point. The readings we obtained would allow us to tell which rat jumped higher than another rat; they would even tell us by exactly how much one rat jumped higher than the other. They would not, however, permit us to tell how many times higher one rat jumped than another. A score of 6 cm for one rat would not be twice as much as a score of 3 cm, since in both cases we would have to add the 6 cm from which the scale begins. When we add the 6 cm above absolute 0, we find that one rat actually jumped only 1⅓ times as high as the other. We would, however, despite the arbitrary 0 point, be able to say that one rat jumped 3 cm higher than the other. A scale which has an arbitrary 0 point, rather than an absolute 0 point, such as the one we just described, is called an *equal interval scale.*

Many experiments give rise to numerical data which lend themselves to all the manipulations usually associated with numbers. Number of responses, physical threshold values (e.g., intensity of light necessary for a stimulus to be seen), latency, and duration of a response, etc., yield such numbers. All of these measures have in common the possession of an absolute 0 point. These numbers give rise to a scale called an *equal ratio scale.* Numbers constituting an equal ratio scale have all the properties of the other scales, i.e., property of equality and difference of the nominal scale, properties of "larger than" and "smaller than" of the ordinal scale, property of equality of intervals between numbers of the equal interval scale, in addition to their own special properties of an absolute 0 point and equality ratios.

The interested reader will do well to refer to a more detailed discussion of these scales in the *Handbook of Experimental Psychology* (Stevens, 1951). For purposes of our discussion here, it is important to note that the operations involved in making the observations determine what statistical operations can be imposed on the resulting data.

The third aspect of measurement in psychology requires only brief mention. Part of the legacy of psychology appears to be the unfounded belief that only trivial phenomena can actually be measured. At this point let it suffice merely to call attention to the fact that this is a prejudgment. A reading of the remainder of this book should dissuade a serious student of the field from such a position. An idea often associated with the belief that important psychological phenomena cannot be measured is that if all aspects are not measured, then the measurement process is inadequate. Yet measurement, like operational definition, is predicated on the fact that we cannot measure all aspects of a concept. There is, in addition, a good possibility that attempts at "complete" measurement are not even useful. A behavioral science must include all variables which are relevant to its subject matter; it must also, however, be able to exclude those which are irrelevant. Thus, the beauty of science stems as much from the parsimonious use of variables for prediction and control as from the number and variety of phenomena to which they apply.

Finally, as to the question of how much to measure, it is the resulting degree of lawfulness which constitutes the appropriate criterion.

The Experimental Approach

Although it has recently become less fashionable to speak of the scientific endeavor as a search for causes—we now feel constrained to speak of functional relations or controlling variables—it is nevertheless true that a science restricted to the observation of phenomena in nature, rather than one engaged in experimentation, cannot provide us with the compelling evidence necessary to conclude what controls or causes what. The correlation between the number of storks flying over Sweden and its national birth rate is well known as an example of the futility of the *post hoc, ergo propter hoc* (after this, therefore because of this) argument based upon mere observation. One argument against restricting scientific activity to observing behavior in nature is that it is impossible to arbitrarily decide at what point in the ongoing behavioral sequence to instate the suspected causal factor, thus precluding the possibility of discovering that some other factor might have produced the end result. In experiments, one usually refers to the hypothesized causal factor as an independent variable, i.e., a variable which an experimenter manipulates *independently* of all other factors, or in more sophisticated experiments, in systematic variation with a number of other variables, sometimes referred to as parameters of the experiment. The end result is referred to as the dependent variable, i.e., the variable which depends on the action of the independent variable.

Let us look at an example of this approach, namely, the learning curve which came from the experiments of Clark Hull (1943), of which a more up-to-date version is to be found in Spence (1956). Most formulations of a learning curve have shown that a negatively accelerated curve describes the acquisition of a response as a function of reinforced trials. The equation (adapted from Spence, 1956),

$R = D\,[A\,(1\text{-}10^{-i\,N})]$, describes learning in this way:

$\underline{R}$ = a response measure, e.g., proportion of correct responses, or rate of response

$\underline{D}$ = drive, e.g., number of hours of food deprivation

$\underline{A}$ = the limit of the increase in response strength

$\underline{i}$ = a constant determining the rate at which the asymptote of learning is reached

$\underline{N}$ = number of reinforced trials

Note that, if we accept this equation as an appropriate description of the variables controlling learning, the dependent variable $\underline{R}$ can, in any one experiment, be shown to vary as a function of the variable $\underline{N}$ with $\underline{D}$, $\underline{A}$, and $\underline{i}$ as constants. This formulation enables us to do an experiment in which we can answer the question of how fast, say, a given fish ($\underline{A}$,$\underline{i}$) might learn ($\underline{R}$) to hit a target requiring a certain amount of force ($\underline{A}$,$\underline{i}$) at a given level of food deprivation

(D). We assume that the constants A and i are influenced both by the individual fish (how large and bright he is) as well as by the task involved (how much force is necessary to activate the food magazine). If we vary the number of hours of food deprivation (D), that factor becomes a parameter, and we might expect a family of learning curves describable by the same equation but characterized by different learning asymptotes. Figure 1-1 shows an empirical fit of this kind of equation.

Given an experimental approach, we can slowly add the variables necessary to explain the phenomenon of learning and, because we have control over the independent variables, our results are

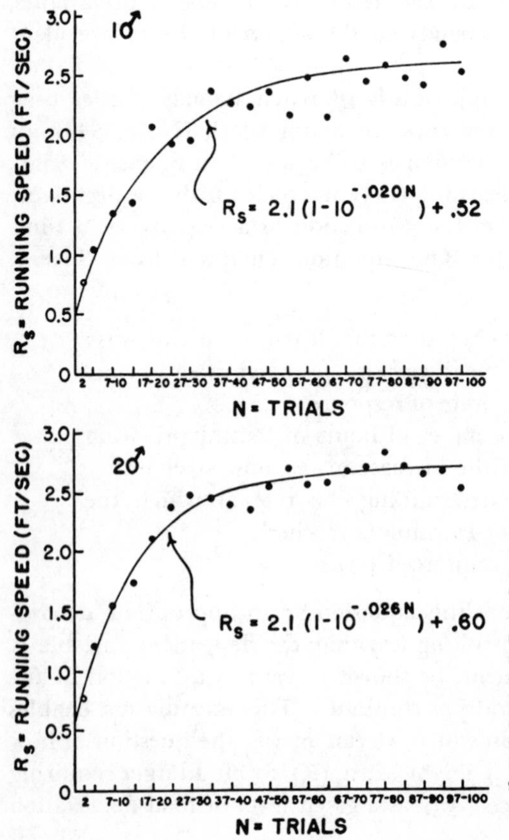

Fig. 1-1. Individual speed curves of conditioning of an instrumental running response for two male rats. The filled circles represent the mean running speeds for each daily session of five runs, first-trial speeds being excluded. The hollow circle in each graph represents the speed on the second training trial, i.e., the initial nonfirst-trial speed in the training series. (Stein, 1955, as seen in Spence, 1956, Fig. 35)

more cogent than they would be if we were lucky enough to find them in nature.

This leads us directly to the next point. While it is true that it is difficult to duplicate precisely in the laboratory the conditions found in nature, it is even harder to find, in nature, the conditions required by experimentation. The suggestion is often made that one can produce an independent variable by selection of appropriate occurrences of that variable in nature. In addition to the fact that such selection does not eliminate any built-in but concealed correlation with other events, it is most difficult, if not entirely impossible, to find in nature the kind of repetition required for scientific investigation, as, for example, delivery of the same size reinforcer for the same response. (The previously cited exception to this rule is the innate stereotyped behavior studied by the ethologist.) The reader should note that the well-known physical law, $F = ma$, which is obviously relevant to falling objects in nature is, in fact, found to work with precision only in a vacuum (a most "unnatural" medium).

It is sometimes argued that some variables cannot be produced at will in the laboratory. Examples of this kind of variable are sex, age, and genetically determined characteristics. The flourishing field of behavioral genetics bears witness to the fact that genetic manipulation of behavior is possible now by selective inbreeding and will, no doubt, eventually be possible by selective induction of mutations. Sexual characteristics also have been found to be amenable to experimental modification by means of injection of hormones. As to aging, it seems reasonable to suppose that this too will fall victim to the process of isolation of modifiable significant variables. It may even turn out that when the significant variables constituting the concept of age are separated into nerve degeneration, muscle deterioration, and other biological factors, that age will be eliminated as a concept of scientific import.

The Animal as Subject

Although Alexander Pope may have thought he was simply voicing a truism when he said, "The proper study of mankind is man," it turns out that the proper study of mankind is, in many circumstances, accomplished more efficiently by starting with other animals.

There are, of course, a number of reasons for studying animals, not the least of which is an interest in the animal itself. Other reasons for the study of animals are the use of the animal as a model for the study of human behavior (Page 24), the unsuitability of human beings for some experiments (Page 25), and finally, for purposes of accomplishing a comparative analysis (Page 26) based on Darwin's theory of evolution.

The Animal as a Model. In an age where models are so commonly used, particularly the computer model, it is somewhat surprising that animals are not more frequently used in the same way. In fact, a good deal of research done by psychologists consists of the study of that animal behavior which is considered to be analogous to human behavior and which appears to be simpler to study in the laboratory animal than in human beings. A warning must be heeded from Fred Keller, however, who hesitated in extrapolating from rat to man because of the complexity of the behavior of the rat. The implication, of course, is that while man may in many ways be a very complex organism, so are other animals.

One question which may be asked is what animal is the best model. For many years, American psychologists viewed the rat as the seemingly perfect model for learning experiments. Although in recent years some psychologists and many ethologists have scoffed at this approach to behavior, what they have forgotten is why the rat was used as a model in the first place. Related to the question of which animal constitutes the best model for man is always the question of which animal displays the kind of *behavior* which constitutes the best model for *man's behavior.* When Small (1901), the psychologist who established the maze as the learning instrument *par excellence,* studied the rat, he used the maze at least in part because it appeared to constitute both a controlled and, perhaps even more important, a natural environment for the rat. Furthermore, learning to run through a maze appeared to resemble learning processes in human beings. Skinner's turning his attention to the pigeon later on was at least in part determined by the fact that frequency of response or response probability constituted what he considered to be the best measure of response strength for pigeons as well as for man. Although rats were also conditionable in a situation in which the same response was repeatedly called for, it turned out that the pigeon was capable of much higher rates of response and was therefore more sensitive to differences in experimental procedures. The fact that the pigeon is further removed, phylogenetically, from man than the rat is not as important, when using an animal as a model, as the appropriateness of the specific behavior under study. The use of an animal as a model requires only that a significant aspect of it be like the aspect being modelled. There are, of course, many examples of such use of animals. Hirsch and Boudreau (1958), for example, studied an innate form of behavior in the fruit fly (*drosophila*), certainly not because of the closeness with which it resembles human beings, but because this particular organism had been examined in great detail with respect to its genetic make-up, and because the production of selected strains is rapid by comparison to other laboratory animals. Study of the flatworm, *planarian,* is another example of a simple organism used as a model despite the fact that it is very far from man phylogenetically. The flatworm lends itself to experimentation with what some scientists have optimistically called the memory molecule, namely, RNA (McConnell, 1962), since it can be ingested, without destruction, through the uncivilized process of cannibalism, and since the cannibal appears, in fact, to acquire a new response by means of this process. More recent research has questioned the exact nature of this finding with the worm, but it has given rise to similar research in mammals. What else can be asked of model research?

Unsuitability of Man for Some Experiments. It is, of course, quite clear that some experiments are too dangerous or too impractical to perform with man. Thus, for example, the genetic study of man can consist only of observational procedures. A great deal of neurophysiological work must be restricted in man to measurement of those effects on the brain that are caused by disease, accident or war. In animals, on the other hand, the experimenter can exert strict control over such variables as the physiological, genetic, developmental, dietary, and sensory conditions of the organism if the experiment calls for it. Thus Pavlov's great discovery of the conditional response can only be ascribed to the fact that his passion for exactitude in the conditions of the experiment and the behavior of the animal (which would have been impossible with humans) allowed him to notice a process which his distinctly unpsychological research of the digestive system in the intact dog did not alert him to search for.

A Comparative Analysis of Behavior. This approach is very much in use in zoology where the tracing of anatomic structures has been highly successful. The theory which has unified the facts uncovered in this area is Darwin's theory of evolution. In psychology, there has been a recent revival of interest in comparative work. Although some of the phenomena studied, such as animal intelligence, have been difficult to define properly, nevertheless it has meant that the presence of a particular type of behavior in one species might lead an investigator to look for that same kind of behavior in a phylogenetically neighboring species. Discovery of the same or similar classes of behavior in a phylogenetically close species makes it possible to postulate more general mechanisms for behavior. It puts the concept of the animal as a model into the frame of reference of the theory of evolution.

Special Considerations in a Behavioral Approach

The layman pictures the scientist as the cold, dispassionate observer of facts in precisely planned experiments. While scientists certainly try to live up to this model in the laboratory, it is good to remember that scientists are also human, i.e., that their behavior too is controlled by some of the same variables which control the behavior of laymen. Furthermore, in the analysis of a scientist's theory, it is as important to know what the theory opposes as what it espouses.

Watson's behaviorism was as much disenchantment with Titchener's introspectionism as it was an acceptance of a behavioristic view. Watson tried to show not only that his approach was appropriate but also that the other, the entrenched approach, was inadequate. A discussion of Watson's behaviorism must also take into account that, at the height of his career, Watson was forced to leave his academic position, and that many of his extreme and unscientific pronouncements were made while he was working in the business world of advertising, removed from the constraints of academic discipline. Among the statements for which Watson became well-known was the one expressing an extreme view of environmentalism, a view which never figured importantly in his or later behaviorists' experimental work. Now, with more knowledge about genetic effects on behavior, students of behavior are at last in a position to work with genetic variables in their experiments.

Hirsch (1963), a behavioral geneticist, has maintained that individual differences are the rule at least in genes, and this being the case, he feels that behavioral research ought to concentrate more heavily on such differences, utilizing methods such as introspectionism, which he believes have a greater chance of bringing out individual differences. It seems to this author that an acceptance of his argument about genetic variation makes all the more interesting those uniformities in behavior which have been located (many within a given species as well as among many different species). As to paying sufficient attention to individual differences, there is surely no more powerful approach for isolating and describing such individual variation than the single organism type of research on which present day behaviorism is concentrating. In essence, the student of psychology must learn to keep separate the lore which has become associated with the term behaviorism as a pejorative from the science of behavior, which consists of an experimental approach to the study of behavior.

Let us now look at some of the other characteristics of the current day behavioral approach, often known as descriptive behaviorism (Skinner, 1938, 1953; Ferster & Skinner, 1957; Keller & Schoenfeld, 1950). As we have already indicated, a scientific approach is as much known by its opposition to concepts as by its avowal of them. It might be well to state first what today's study of behavior opposes. It opposes anthropomorphism. In psychology, this consists of the attribution of human characteristics to the behavior of other animals. What is recommended instead is the application of the simpler and possibly more fundamental generalizations drawn on the basis of the experimental analysis of behavior of animals to man.

The behavioral approach takes a stand against subjective concepts like mind, consciousness, and the like, as concepts too vague to be amenable to experimentation and possibly also irrelevant to the study of behavior. Many subjective concepts turn out, upon behavioral analysis, to be verbal responses to private events. These concepts then require analysis themselves rather than being useful in the analysis of other behavior.

Current day behaviorism is known also for its opposition to theory, to statistics, and to physiology. We shall submit here that this opposition exists only with regard to certain kinds of theory, statistics, and physiology. Thus, behaviorism objects to theories which are explanations of observed facts at a level of observation different from that of behavior, particularly when that level is not measured. This applies, for example, to a description of a learning process in terms of such concepts as synaptic transmission when no data are collected on it; it also applies to theorizing which contributes nothing new (except a name) towards explicating the behavior being studied, as in using terms such as "expecting" food or finding a reinforcer "pleasant" in descriptions of the rat running down a maze. In his most important paper on the subject, Skinner (1950) does not in fact suggest that theory in this sense be eliminated; instead, he asks whether such theories do in fact contribute to the general development of a science. As indicated earlier, we know relatively little about the creative aspects of a scientist at work.

Before leaving the topic of theory it is important to show that behaviorism does not exclude, as some have mistakenly thought, all types of theory. Thus, theory is necessary for the reduction of data to a minimum number of terms and to enable the scientist to generalize. The choice of the most opportune time for constructing such theory lies clearly within the purview of the scientist, but it probably should follow, not precede, the identification of relevant variables.

The behaviorist's opposition to statistics and physiology lies in their use as a substitute for behavioral data collection. Both are clearly called for in many circumstances. Both are most useful to psychology when the study of behavior has been complete. In the same manner, it is possible to relate behavior to physiology most advantageously only when both are measured and when it is realized, as we shall show below, that there are causal relations possible in either direction.

What then does a behavioral approach advocate? First of all, behaviorism today views stimuli and responses in terms of classes and not as muscle movements or stimulus elements as did Watson and Guthrie. It is clear, at least for operant behavior (a full definition of this class of behavior will be discussed later; loosely speaking, we may refer to it here as voluntary behavior under the control of its consequences), that intact animals emit responses having in common no more than the fact that they are followed by the same or similar events. Thus, a dog which has been trained to depress a lever may from time to time make use of different parts of its anatomy to effect obtaining food, all such movements having membership in the same reponse class. Behaviorists today talk of classes of responses like bar pressing, target hitting, button pressing, plunger pulling, emitting plural nouns, paranoid speech, fighting, marble placement, writing, observing, and so on. In none of these cases is there an attempt to build up complex responses on the basis of simple muscle movement responses. Furthermore, the formulation S-R (stimulus-response) which has been so popular in learning theory in the past is relevant to classical conditioning (roughly speaking, involuntary behavior) but not as critical (in that form) to operant behavior. As we shall see later in the book, no exact stimulus-response sequence has to be posited for the acquisition of operant behavior.

Secondly, behaviorists are often described as viewing animals as "black boxes" or empty organisms. This implies that the occurrence of behavior should be explained at the behavioral level, i.e., the behavioral psychologist must look for controlling variables in the environment or in the past behavior of the animal whose behavior he is trying to explain. This does not imply that he must shun physiological study, but rather that he must use physiological variables only as he might use any other independent variable in the case of the establishment of an empirical relationship to behavior.

The third tenet of current behaviorism emphasizes study of the single organism because it is the behavior of the single organism which the psychologist must predict and control, rather than some mythical mean or average animal. This necessitates training an animal until his behavior is stable which, in turn, results in an emphasis on the study of the variables which control and predict the maintenance of behavior, not merely the acquisition of behavior. It should also be pointed out that the emphasis on the single organism makes it possible for the investigator to examine behavior in much greater detail than is otherwise possible in the treatment of groups. The study of the single organism has a long and respected history in psychology. Dukes (1965) recently reviewed both old and current studies of this kind, noting the fact that such studies are appropriate in all fields of psychology. He lists four rationales for single organism studies: (1) when the behavior being studied shows little variation among organisms, (2) when the study disproves a universal generalization, (3) when the phenomenon being studied is unique, and (4) when study of one organism allows better focussing on a problem (particularly in pilot work).

The fourth precept of the behavioral approach is that the data are always right. Theories may come and go, but if the experiment has been properly conducted, then any disagreement between data and theory must be resolved at the expense of the theory. The data must not only be decisive but they should also lead the investigator on to further research. Generalizations which are made should stay as close as possible to the data.

The fifth characteristic of the behavioral approach is the use of rate of response as the basic measure of behavior. This is considered to be the most direct measure of behavior, giving rise to the measure of probability of response which has the virtue of being very close to the intuitive notion of response strength. Thus, a man who is called abusive is generally one who frequently engages in abusive behavior; one who is called friendly, intelligent, stupid, talkative, etc., can also be described in terms of the frequency concept. Finally, the best argument for the probability of response measure of behavior stems from its success in actual learning experiments, which will be dealt with in detail in this book.

SUMMARY

This chapter defined psychology as the study of behavior of organisms, including the behavior of man. It then sketched out the characteristics of a scientific approach to the study of behavior, noting the arguments for and against the measurement of human behavior. It pointed out the importance of separating the language of the subject (data) from the language of the scientist (objective description). The importance of the concepts of behavior and operational definition in a scientific approach to psychology was stressed.

Observation is, of course, one of the basic activities of the scientist. First the chapter mentioned the pitfalls of the introspective approach and the forms in which it still survives. The clinical approach was described next and rejected as a scientific method of data collection. The ethological use of observational techniques was presented, including a listing of the reasons for its success.

General problems of measurement were discussed, including the functions of statistics, properties of the numbers obtained by measurement, and the degree of measurement necessary for the analysis of behavior.

Advantages of the experimental approach over the simple observational path were detailed. It was pointed out that, while the conditions in nature cannot always be duplicated in the laboratory, the conditions necessary for the conduct of a controlled experiment can only rarely be found to occur in nature.

Reasons for the use of animals as subjects were listed as follows: the animal's behavior can serve as a model for human behavior, human beings are unsuitable as subjects for certain experiments, and the use of animals has great value in a comparative analysis of behavior.

Finally, the chapter took up special aspects of a behavioral approach, listing the concepts it utilizes and those it opposes.

2

Basic Processes In Learning: Respondent Conditioning

Everyone is willing to concede that learning is an activity which takes place in school. The psychologist's claim for the concept of learning is much wider. According to him, the human organism learns not only academic subjects, but also to dance, talk, and play baseball; to make friends and enemies; to persuade people and be persuaded by them; to act like a model child or like a brat; to be the life of the party or a social recluse; to fear cats or love them; to be neurotic or well-adjusted; to be a precise observer or a poor witness; to be an artist or a plumber; and so forth. There is also an increasing amount of evidence, as we shall see, that learning is at least implicated in, if not the major cause of, hallucinations, delusions, stuttering, and psychosomatic illnesses like ulcers, hysterical blindness, bedwetting, and depression.

Some form of learning also appears to characterize a large segment of the animal kingdom and certainly becomes more important as we go up in the evolutionary scale. There is evidence for the conditionability (learning) in very young infants. Moreover, Spelt (1948) demonstrated that even the fetus in utero can be conditioned during the last two months of pregnancy. He presented a vibrotactile stimulus (conditioned stimulus) to the abdomen of the pregnant woman, followed by a loud noise (unconditioned stimulus), and showed that, after 15-20 paired presentations, the conditioned stimulus alone elicited the fetus's movement, formerly only elicited by the loud noise.

For more general treatments of the area of learning the student is advised to see Deese and Hulse, 1967; Hall, 1966; Hilgard and Bower, 1966; Kimble, 1961, 1967; and Prokasy, 1965. In accordance with our treatment of the subject of operational definitions in Chapter 1, we will not make an effort to define learning in a general and abstract way. We will define learning in terms of the two conditioning procedures used to produce a change of behavior in the organism. One of these procedures is called, variously, classical, Pavlovian, reflex, or respondent conditioning. This chapter will be devoted to this kind of conditioning. The other procedure is called instrumental or operant conditioning and will be dealt with in Chapter 3. The overlap in response classes, and those aspects that both experimental procedures have in common, will be taken up in Chapter 3.

Historical Background of Respondent Conditioning

All events have predecessors which can account for at least part of each so-called new development. Despite the fact that Pavlov's name has become irrevocably associated with respondent conditioning, he was not really the first one to consider the possibility of a conditioning process. It was Descartes, in the seventeenth century, who first constructed the term "reflex" as a basic unit of analysis for involuntary behavior. At the end of the eighteenth century, Erasmus Darwin, Charles Darwin's grandfather, was speaking of a phenomenon very much like the conditioned stimulus, namely, the pleasurable ideas which had in the past accompanied mastication of food. These ideas, he suggested, through their association with food, became capable of producing the salivation response (Verhave, 1966). Ivan Michailovich Sechenov, working in the middle of the nineteenth century, is the scientist often described as the father of Russian reflexology. He believed that both voluntary and involuntary behavior could be reduced to reflexes. Furthermore, he conceived of the study of psychology as the study of behavior, taking a stand in favor of an objective psychology which was to be a determining factor in the viewpoints which were held later by both Pavlov and Bechterev in Russia. In the United States, J. B. Watson, as already stated, argued for a science of psychology some 50 years after Sechenov, apparently without being acquainted with his writings. It should also be mentioned that Sechenov's work already contained a form of the ideas of the interplay of excitation and inhibition, the substitution of the reflex for the idea as the associated element, feedback in the control of reflex behavior, perception as learned behavior, and the orienting reflex. Finally, Sechenov also can be said to have formulated some of the concepts which C. S. Sherrington was to arrive at experimentally in 1906. (See Herrnstein & Boring, 1965, and Kimble, 1967, for further description of Sechenov's work.)

It is important to remember that the above-mentioned scientists were physiologists and that they all believed that an objective psychology could be arrived at through the study of the nervous system. The basic concept of the reflex is a physiological one. The simplest reflex consists of a stimulus which impinges on a receptor organ whence it is transmitted by sensory or afferent neurons to the spinal cord; there it is picked up either directly by motor or efferent neurons or indirectly by internuncial neurons. It then travels to motor neurons to stimulate the effector, which might be a muscle or gland. Generally, it is the pathway through the nervous system which interests the physiologist; it is the input-output relation and its strength and modifiability which are of major concern to the psychologist.

A few words about Pavlov's career are in order here. Before he began his work on conditioning, he had already done substantial and significant work on a number of physiological problems: circulation of the blood, innervation of the heart, and functioning of the digestive system, for which last he had won the Nobel prize. In 1902, Pavlov began his work on conditioning, reporting on it in his Nobel prize lecture. Thus, rather than reviewing at length the work for which he was cited, he embarked on a new field of endeavor in his usual whole-hearted and dedicated fashion. His research was of a nature to interest the Russian revolutionary government. Despite the fact that he criticized the Communist government, apparently until the early 1930's, he was consistently and generously supported by that government so as to be able to conduct his experiments under the exacting laboratory conditions he required.

It was Pavlov's work with chronic physiological preparations, consisting of conscious animals experimented upon over and over again, which made it possible for him to observe the fact that stimuli other than the food or even the acid or alkaline solutions which he had placed in the mouth of the dog had come to elicit the secretion of digestive juices. Thus, the sight and smell of food served to trigger the secretion; even the sight of the experimenter appeared to elicit the response. And this, it appeared to the observant scientist Pavlov, was worth following up. In his Nobel prize address, he spoke of the "psychical" stimulation as a miniature model of the physiological stimulation. Thus, he found that the sight of bread elicits more salivation that the sight of meat, just as bread in the mouth elicits more salivation than meat in the mouth. In that address, Pavlov also mentioned the fact that repeated presentation of the sight of the bread alone eventually resulted in the cessation of the salivation, while restoration of the salivation could be accomplished either by a few hours of rest or by allowing the dog to eat the bread. Pavlov also spoke of the unconditioned or unconditional reflex as opposed to the conditioned or conditional reflex. The unconditioned reflex, which he also labelled the physiological reflex, is caused by the actual placement of food or acid in the mouth; its occurrence is unconditional, i.e., independent of other conditions. The conditioned reflex, on the other hand, is conditional, i.e., a new reflex dependent on the co-occurrence of certain events which we will describe below.

The Basic Respondent Conditioning Procedure

The Classical Experimental Arrangement of Conditioning the Salivation Response

The first step consists of the preparation of the dog. This is done by minor surgery in which the saliva coming from the duct of the parotid gland is brought outside the body by means of a glass tube attached to the side of the dog's cheek. The amount of saliva collected in this fashion can then be measured in order to yield an estimate of the magnitude of the response. The dog is trained to stand quietly in a harness within a room which is isolated from that of the experimenter and from other potentially distracting stimuli. The dog is presented all stimuli by means of automatic devices, although the experimenter can watch the dog through a window. Before the conditioning experiment begins, the stimulus which will ultimately serve as the conditioned stimulus (CS) is first presented to the dog to establish that it does not by itself elicit the response that is to be conditioned. The experimenter then sounds a tone (CS) and some 5 seconds later powdered food (unconditioned stimulus—US) is placed before the animal. In an experiment carried out in Pavlov's laboratory by Anrep (1920) 50 pairings of such a tone and food over a period of 16 days resulted in the typical conditioning effect. The pairs of stimuli were separated during any given day by intervals of 5 to 35 minutes. As was suggested before, the presentation of the CS alone ultimately results in the ineffectiveness of that stimulus in eliciting the response. On the other hand, measurement of the effectiveness of the conditioning process can be accomplished only by presenting the CS alone, i.e., without the US. The procedure followed to estimate the strength of the effect of the CS was therefore a compromise, in which the CS alone was presented after 1, 10, 20, 30, 40, and 50 CS—US pairings, thus allowing the process to be measured on a continuous basis. The CS was presented alone for 30 seconds and the experimenter measured the magnitude of the response, in terms of number of drops of saliva secreted, as well as the latency of the response, in terms of the time in seconds from the onset of the tone to the salivary response. Both indices of conditioning showed the effectiveness of the procedure: the amount of saliva increased from 6 drops after

10 pairings to 59 after 50 pairings, having reached its maximum effect after 30 pairings, and latency decreased from 18 seconds after 10 pairings to 2 seconds after 50 pairings, also having reached its maximum effect after 30 pairings.

The Respondent Conditioning Paradigm

We can now represent the respondent conditioning paradigm for the above experiment in the following way:

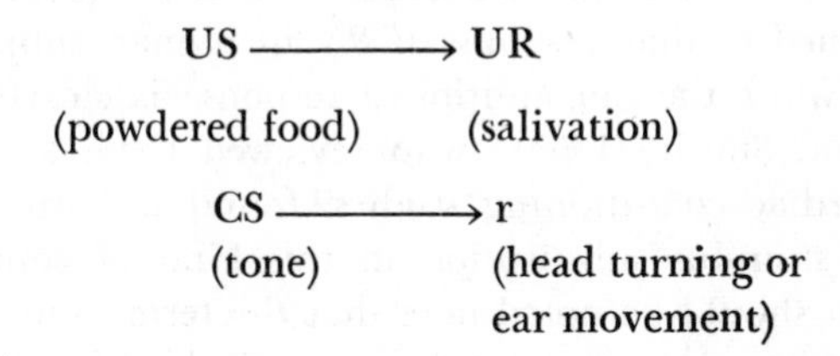

The above represents the pairing of the tone (CS) with the powdered food (US). The arrow between the US and UR (unconditional response) shows us the unconditioned salivary reflex; the arrow between CS and r (orienting response) shows the orienting or investigatory reflex. The orienting reflex results from the fact that any new stimulus will arouse some response from an animal. If the stimulus continues to be presented, the animal adapts so that the r drops out; if, on the other hand, the organism is required to make a response (usually an operant in human beings) to that CS, then the orienting reflex is relatively resistant to habituation, as is found in experiments in semantic generalization. Typically, the r does drop out so that it need not be considered further in the conditioning process. The repeated pairing of the CS and US results in the conditioning process which can be represented in the following manner:

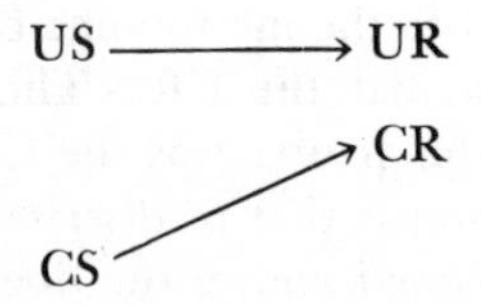

As already shown in Anrep's experiment, repeated pairing of an initially neutral stimulus (CS) with an unconditioned stimulus (US) causes the CS to elicit a conditioned response *like* the UR.

It is important to make clear that the degree of resemblance between the CR and UR varies from one response system to another. There is good similarity between the CR and UR in salivation, but even here there is a difference both in the amount and in the chemical composition of the responses. Other experiments have suggested that there may be larger differences still. A series of experiments performed by Notterman, Schoenfeld and Bersh (1952) have shown a conditioned cardiac response (CR) in human subjects to be decelerative while the unconditioned response is clearly accelerative. Zeaman and Smith (1965), who reviewed these as well as other human cardiac conditioning studies, found it hard to accept the notion of stimulus substitution in this kind of conditioning. In addition, it should be noted here that the term "substitute," which is often used to describe what happens to the CS in the process of conditioning, is inaccurate. The CS does *not* substitute for the US in eliciting the response, since the US continues as before to elicit the UR. The CR is also sometimes viewed as a "preparatory response" where the CS prepares the animal for the US.

The elimination of the CR (known as extinction) is accomplished by presenting the CS without having the US follow it:

Two other phenomena can be demonstrated with the respondent conditioning paradigm. The first is that of *generalization* of the CS. It is to be noted that the CR can be elicited not only by the CS to which it was conditioned but also, in smaller magnitude, by stimuli like it. Thus, it was shown in Pavlov's laboratory that if the salivation was conditioned to the metronome beat of one frequency, other frequencies also elicited the CR. The closer the stimulus frequency was to the CS the greater was the CR.

The second phenomenon is that of *discrimination*. Thus, using the same stimuli as mentioned above, the dog will gradually show less of a conditioned response to frequencies other than the one to which he was conditioned, by having only that frequency, and no other, followed by the US.

An obvious parameter of the respondent conditioning situation is the time relation between the CS and the US. When the CS is short and precedes the US by only a half second or overlaps it in time, the conditioning process is called *simultaneous.* When the CS starts well before (two to three minutes) the onset of the US—overlapping with it, or ceasing a half second before the onset of the US, or even going on beyond it—the conditioning is called *delayed.* Furthermore, either onset or cessation of a stimulus can act as a CS. The term *trace conditioning* is reserved for the condition where the CS is short and terminated well before the onset of the US. This is a paradigm like the delayed conditioning paradigm, except that there is an interval of no stimulus between the CS and US—hence the term "trace" to account for a proximal stimulus, presumably within the animal's nervous system, which functions to maintain the stimulus during the CS–US interval. Pavlov also used a *temporal conditioning* procedure in which the US was presented at regular intervals (e.g., every 30 minutes) in the absence of any external CS. All of these paradigms have produced effective conditioning. The only paradigm which has been manifestly unsuccessful is one called *backward conditioning,* in which the US precedes the CS. Despite the fact that Pavlov explored a variety of paradigms, the CS–US interval is still an active area of research in respondent conditioning.

The Scope of the Respondent Conditioning Procedure

Respondent conditioning procedures have, of course, been applied to animals other than the dog. They have been used with organisms as disparate as the planarian (flatworm) and the human being, and with fish, sheep, goats, rabbits, cats, and monkeys.

It should also be noted that responses other than salivation have been conditioned by this paradigm. Cardiac conditioning has already been mentioned; some others are the galvanic skin response (GSR—a change in the electrical resistance of the skin due to sweating), respiration, vocalization, eyelid response (blinking to an air puff), and vasodilation. The US's have also varied over a great range (electric shock, light, air puff, food, acid) as have the CS's—visual stimuli of all kinds, auditory ones, thermal, tactual, olfactory, proprioceptive and, most recently, interoceptive stimuli (Razran, 1961). Research on respondent conditioning has been extended into still another area in an attempt to explicate the process called *higher order conditioning.* In this process the CS, established in the usual manner, is then paired with a neutral stimulus much the same as a US might be paired with it. Such an experiment was done by Pavlov, using an auditory stimulus as the original CS; after the CR of salivation was established, a black square was presented prior to the CS (sufficiently before the first CS so as not to inhibit the first conditioned reflex, cf. *inhibition,* below). The black square then became the CS for salivation (albeit of lesser magnitude than salivation to the CS of the tone). Furthermore, such a *second-order conditioned reflex* could be used successfully as the basis for conditioning a third-order reflex, provided the conditioning process involved electric shock. Fourth-order conditioned reflexes could not be established at all in dogs. The tenuousness of these higher-order conditioned reflexes makes questionable their importance in respondent conditioning. In addition, the inability to establish higher-order conditioned reflexes has brought into question the significance of respondent conditioning in human behavior, which, in large measure, presumably depends upon some such process as higher-order CS's. On the other hand, language, which Pavlov calls the *second signalling system,* may be an essential ingredient of higher-order conditioning. One would therefore expect to find extensive higher-order conditioning only in a speaking organism.

As we shall see later, the importance of respondent conditioning in general is demonstrable in the area of psychosomatic medicine (cf. Chapter 9), and with respect to conditional reinforcers in operant conditioning (cf. Chapter 3).

Pavlov's View of the Role of the Nervous System in Respondent Conditioning

As a physiologist, Pavlov explained the process of conditioning in physiological terms. Despite his stress on the fact that anthropomorphism and other subjective explanations had to be shunned at all costs, he made use of some physiological concepts with no more objective evidence for their validity than the subjectivists had for theirs. In a recent collection of the basic writings of Pavlov, Kaplan (1966) pointed out that in some ways the writings of Pavlov are remarkably similar to those of Freud. Both men appealed to inferred internal events, although Pavlov's have the advantage of being at least potentially observable and therefore potentially amenable to experimental test. Furthermore, Pavlov's inferences were made at a time when it had already been shown that the passage of a small electric current through parts of the cortex (the outer portion of the cerebrum, which is the newest part of the brain from the point of view of evolution) produces movement in certain groups of muscles, thereby giving rise to the idea that different parts of the brain are centers of different kinds of activity. The acquisition of a conditioned reflex was explained in the following way (Kimble, 1967) : The US sets up intense activity in one area of the brain, causing the dominant *excitation* to attract, or at least to *irradiate* towards, the weaker excitation aroused by the CS in another part of the brain. This causes what Pavlov called a *temporary connection,* so that the presentation of the CS alone arouses excitation in the center corresponding to the US. He stressed the temporary aspect of the connection, and suggested that there were subcortical as well as cortical connections, with the second signalling system (Pavlov's reference to language) having connections in the frontal parts of the cortex.

In addition to the concept of excitation, Pavlov also invoked the concept of *inhibition,* a process which restrains the evocation of reflexes. He distinguished between two types, *external* and *internal* inhibition. External inhibition, also called *passive* or *unconditional* inhibition, can be demonstrated by the occurrence of a novel stimulus just before, during, or after the CS, but before the CR. Such a novel stimulus can be demonstrated to evoke an orienting reflex, the arousal of which is postulated to attract some of the excitation which might otherwise be attracted by the CS center. Internal inhibition, also called *active* or *conditional* inhibition, occurs (1) whenever the CS is presented without the accompanying US, i.e., during extinction; (2) in a discrimination experiment, to the negative stimulus (the stimulus which is not followed by the US) ; (3) in backward conditioning, where the US precedes the CS, resulting in essentially no US for purposes of conditioning; and (4) if the interval between CS and US is long, which would allow sufficient time for the internal inhibition to occur. It should also be noted that because it appears to accrue slowly after a number of CS presentations, the process of internal inhibition itself is considered to be conditioned.

Pavlov used other physiological concepts in his theoretical system for respondent conditioning. But we have here a good enough sampling to see that there is a discrepancy between Pavlov's objective operational description of his experimental procedures and the results and the physiological labels he has given these processes. Thus, when Pavlov says that the repeated presentation of a CS without a US produces internal inhibition, he is no longer simply describing a result. Furthermore, the use of the same term, inhibition, for what he calls *external* inhibition as well as for *internal* inhibition does not thereby guarantee that they are one and the same process. At best this is an hypothesis, at worst untrue. Certainly the notion of operational definition would lead us to be wary of applying the same name to two different procedures without further independent substantiation.

Recent Work in Respondent Conditioning

In a recent survey of the effect of Russian physiologists' psychology on American experimental psychology, Razran (1965) points out that until 1914 American psychologists were largely ignorant of Pavlovian conditioning. Watson's (1913) basic statement of behaviorism, though very much like the objective approach taken by Pavlov and Bechterev, who were his contemporaries, and by Sechenov, who made a very similar statement 50 years before, made no mention of Russian research. From 1914 to 1928, the conditioned reflex was enthusiastically accepted and skillfully incorporated into the systems of Watson and Guthrie in the United States. In the period 1929–1953, Hull and Skinner came to be considered as revisionists of Pavlov. According to Razran, the current status of Pavlov's influence is greater again (with improved communication between the U.S. and U.S.S.R.), now that there is a greater emphasis placed on actual observation of both the behavioral generalizations and the neurophysiological correlates of conditioning.

Salivary Reflex Conditioning

It is of interest to see how current experiments in salivary conditioning are performed. Ost and Lauer (1965) stress the importance of doing experiments in this country, utilizing those animals and responses which will more closely link the experiments of Pavlov and his students to American learning theory, since the latter makes use of the respondent conditioning paradigm without, perhaps, having a deep enough understanding of it. In keeping with this approach, these and other investigators study old variables, namely, the CS–US interval, as well as relatively new variables, namely, the scheduling of the US on an intermittent basis. Let us look at the last variable first. The data presented here are taken from Fitzgerald (1962), who conditioned three groups of dogs: one group (100% Group) had each CS (400 cps tone 15 secs. long) followed by the US (dilute acetic acid solution), the second group (50% Group) had the CS followed by the US on a random assignment on half of the trials, and the third group (25% Group) had the CS followed by the US on a random assignment on a fourth of the trials. After 240 trials of acquisition training, all three groups of dogs were extinguished for 240 CS–only presentations or until the dog produced no salivary response for 24 consecutive trials, whichever came first. The magnitude of the CR was defined as the number of drops secreted during the CS–US interval minus the number of drops secreted in the interval before the CS. The results of the 100% Group showed a large increase in the magnitude of response, without reaching an asymptote even after 240 trials, while the results of the 50% and 25% Groups showed only a small increase, which was substantially below the 100% Group. Inspection of the extinction data revealed that the 100% Group extinguished relatively more rapidly than the two intermittent US groups. This finding, which is even more important in operant conditioning, shows, interestingly enough, that a CR which has been produced by intermittent pairing of the CS and US shows greater resistance to extinction than a CR produced by continuous pairing.

Ost and Lauer's investigation of the effect of varying the CS–US interval utilized the following four interval lengths: 2, 5, 10, and 15 seconds. For all groups, 80% of the randomly selected CS's were followed by US's in a trace conditioning procedure. All the CS's were of the duration of 1 second. It was found that the CR occurred later and with a higher magnitude the longer the CS–US interval, with the exception of the 15-second CS–US interval, which yielded a lower CR. However, two of the dogs in the 2–, 5–, and 15–second groups, and three of the dogs in the 10–second group did not condition at all. This experiment would seem to indicate the decided need for further research.

Shapiro and Miller (1965) also presented some data on the conditioning of the salivary reflex. However, since their work is concerned primarily with the interrelationship between respondent conditioning and operant conditioning, discussion of this experiment will be deferred until after operant conditioning has been explained.

The CS–US Interval in the Respondent Conditioning of the Fish

It is of some interest to review recent work on respondent conditioning in animals quite different from the ones normally used for that purpose. Bitterman (1965) has been in the forefront of American psychologists who have urged the investigation of a larger variety of animals so as to achieve a true comparative psychology.

Bitterman's basic experimental procedure with fish consists of the following: Each fish is confined in a small dark compartment in a fish tank. The CS is a light and the US an electric shock. The CR measure consists of general activity which is picked up by a paddle attached to a rod. The rod is inserted into a phonograph cartridge, the amplified output of which then produces a signal used to monitor responding. A simultaneous conditioning procedure was used where for different fish the CS started 0, 1, 3, or 9 seconds before, and overlapping with, a .6–second shock on trials 1–9 and 11–19 of each day. During trials 10 and 20 the CS–US intervals used as tests for the conditioning effect lasted 20 seconds for all groups. A second experiment was like the first, except that the CS–US intervals were 1, 9 and 27 seconds, while the CS–US interval test for the conditioning effect was 40 seconds for all groups. All groups, except the 0 seconds CS–US interval, showed a negatively accelerated increase in magnitude of response. The maximum CR magnitude occurred approximately 5 seconds after the US was supposed to appear. Incidentally, it should be noted that the test interval here, instead of consisting of CS presentation alone, consisted of the elongation of the interval, so that the fish always had a US follow its CS. The increasingly later occurrence of the CR with the increase in CS–US interval is, of course, exactly what Pavlov found in his studies of conditioning and is, furthermore, what led him to hypothesize the process of internal inhibition in explaining why the CR did not simply occur immediately after the onset of the CS.

The Orienting Reflex

This reflex has already been mentioned within the context of the explanation of the respondent conditioning paradigm. Essentially the orienting reflex is an investigatory response to a novel, or at least significant, stimulus (significant meaning that the animal must make some response to it). Despite the fact that Pavlov himself paid very little attention either to the field of perception or specifically to the orienting reflex, recent research in Russia has shown an upsurge of interest in the problem. In his review of Russian experiments in this area, Razran (1961) listed a number of characteristics of the orienting reflex. As already mentioned, the orienting reflex occurs in response to a novel stimulus or a stimulus change of sufficiently great magnitude. Upon repeated presentation the effect of such stimuli is reduced. It is not a single reflex but consists of a centrally organized system of visceral, somatic, cognitive, and neural responses. An example of an orienting reflex in man consists of the dilatation of the blood vessels of the forehead and the constriction of the digital blood vessels. Pupillary dilations, galvanic skin responses, desynchronization of the electroencephalographic responses (brain waves), respiratory changes, and various motor changes like the oculomotor, digital, manual, and pedal responses are also under study.

There appears to be some evidence for phylogenetic and ontogenetic effects upon this reflex, i.e., the higher any animal is in the evolutionary scale, the earlier the reflex develops in its life span and the longer lasting the reflex is for the adult. Ecological factors play an important role in determining which stimuli are of specific significance to a given animal and which, in fact, elicit responses which are longer lasting than from an animal higher up in the evolutionary scale. There is some indication that, despite the fact that the orienting reflex is innate in origin, it behaves, in at least some respects, like a conditioned response undergoing extinction. Perhaps most interesting is the use of an orienting reflex in conditioning a new reflex. One example Razran gave of this was the use, with a hare, of a buzzer as the CS for an orienting reflex consisting of a change in respiration to a stimulus of a rustling sound.

If the novel stimulus eliciting an orienting response is made "significant," it need not dissipate with time. This can be accomplished by reinforcing the reflex in the manner of operant conditioning. In one experiment, fox cubs were exposed to the squeaks of mice, which evoked clear orienting reflexes. These extinguished rapidly upon repetition. When the fox cubs were permitted to make but one meal of the mice, the orienting reflex became almost impossible to extinguish thereafter.

Another exciting aspect of Russian research concerning the orienting reflex is the report that orienting reflexes can be elicited by direct electrical stimulation of the brain.

In this country, Maltzman (1967) stressed the importance of the orienting reflex with respect to its facilitation of respondent conditioning. Apparently, preliminary habituation of the orienting reflex to the CS retards subsequent conditioning.

And finally, the orienting reflex has come to be used in experiments related to language.

Interoceptive Conditioning

Perhaps the most exciting of recent developments is the phenomenon of interoceptive conditioning (Razran, 1961). Airopetyantz and Bykov (1945) first described the range of organs besides the salivary glands that could be conditioned. They cited, among other responses, the conditionability of urination, the secretion of bile, contraction of the spleen, and the heightening of oxidation processes in the muscle tissue. They also showed that a CS could be applied directly to an internal organ to produce successful respondent conditioning. Taking a rubber balloon filled with water at a low temperature and inserting it into the intestinal loop of a dog as a CS, the investigators paired this CS with an electric shock to the paw (this US elicits a raising of the paw). Using a discrimination procedure, they then inserted a balloon filled with water of a higher temperature without following it with an electric shock. After a number of combinations of these two CS's with the occurrence or nonoccurrence of the US, the dog was conditioned to raise his paw when his intestine was stimulated with cold water, but not when stimulated with warm water. The same two investigators also described an experiment in which the US was applied internally. Using a human subject who had a temporary fistula to his small intestine, they inserted a small rubber balloon into the bowels, filled in one case with cold water, and in another case with warm water. Both these thermal stimuli elicited peristaltic movements of the bowels which the subject could report. The US's were paired according to the usual conditioning procedure with two CS's. These consisted of two different colored lights each paired with a different US. After a number of conditioning trials, the light signals were effective by themselves in eliciting the CR.

On the basis of these experiments it is quite clear that the respondent conditioning paradigm provides us with an avenue connecting the internal and external environments of organisms. These experiments suggest a number of possible ways in which psychosomatic illnesses can be produced, as well as how they might possibly be eliminated.

Miscellaneous Developments

A new area of research has concerned itself with the question of interaction and overlap between respondent and operant conditioning. We will defer thorough discussion of this question until after operant conditioning has been explained. It should be mentioned here, however, that the responses which are typically conditioned by the respondent procedure are smooth and cardiac muscle movement and glandular secretions which are controlled by the autonomic nervous system, in contrast to operant responses which are emitted by the skeletal muscles and which are controlled by the somatic nervous system. Recent research has shown, however, that so-called respondent responses can also be conditioned by operant procedures, thereby implying that the terms "respondent" and "operant" should be applied to the conditioning procedures themselves rather than to the response classes.

Another important aspect of respondent conditioning which should be mentioned is an alternative way of measuring the degree of respondent conditioning, i.e., by its suppressing effect upon ongoing operant behavior. The procedure generally consists of the following: An animal is conditioned, by means of an operant procedure, to press a bar in return for food. After this behavior is stabilized, a neutral stimulus (CS) like a clicking sound is followed, after a few minutes, by an unavoidable electric shock (US). After a while the presentation of the CS results in the suppression, often complete, of the ongoing operant behavior, despite the fact that the hungry animal is, in fact, losing the opportunity to obtain food. After the US occurs, the animal returns immediately to its stable operant behavior. The CS–US interval has been said to elicit a CER (conditioned emotional response) or anxiety in the animal. This paradigm has, as we shall see later, been well used as a model for certain types of psychopathological behavior observed in neurotic individuals. Thus, respondent conditioning is of interest in abnormal psychology because it serves to elucidate both psychosomatic illnesses and neurosis.

As we shall see in later chapters, respondent conditioning is of importance also in the areas of social psychology (for the acquisition of attitudes) and of verbal behavior (for the acquisition of meaning, e.g., Mowrer, 1954, and Staats and Staats, 1963, who viewed meaning as a fractional component of the UR which becomes conditioned in language).

SUMMARY

This chapter presented both the historical background and the basic experimental paradigm for one type of learning: respondent conditioning. Respondent conditioning takes advantage of the presence of innate reflexes in the behavior repertoire of organisms by pairing these reflexes with initially neutral stimuli and thereby producing what is sometimes called a "new" reflex. This new reflex consists of an initially neutral stimulus (CS) which elicits a response (CR) that is often, but by no means always, like the response (UR) elicited by the US of the innate reflex. In describing respondent conditioning procedures the word "elicits" is used to describe the production of the UR and the CR in order to show the high degree of control these stimuli exert over the responses. The term is also used because it has the connotation of automaticity, making this kind of behavior "involuntary" in the sense that the placement of food in the mouth of an intact dog must produce salivation or the application of intense heat to the hand of a child must produce hand withdrawal. The conditioned response can be further described as a "preparatory response" where the function of the CS is to prepare the animal for the occurrence of a US. An alternative view of the CR is as a fractional component of the UR. The fractional component interpretation of the CR has been applied to the acquisition of meaning. Whatever the interpretation of the CR, it is important to remember that the CR and the UR are not the same response. The process of extinction is brought about by presentation of the CS alone. Generalization can be demonstrated by the fact that stimuli like the CS, but not identical with it, elicit the CR also, though in smaller magnitude. Discrimination is produced after a number of presentations of the CS and other similar stimuli, with only the CS and not the other stimuli being paired with the US. After some trials only the CS will elicit the CR. Simultaneous, delayed, trace, temporal, and backward conditioning procedures were discussed as different types of CS–US relations.

Having shown the pervasiveness of respondent conditioning among different animals, involving a variety of conditioned and unconditioned stimuli, and during different parts of the life span of the organism, the chapter went on to describe a typical Pavlovian experiment and its interpretation in terms of physiological concepts. Pavlov's basic physiologic concepts of excitation, inhibition, irradiation, temporary connection and the second signalling system were discussed.

A short review of recent work in respondent conditioning presented some examples of experiments. In one study, conditioning of the salivary response in the dog was studied as a function of the intermittency of the US presentation and the length of the CS–US interval. In another, the effect of the CS–US interval on the respondent conditioning of activity in the fish was investigated.

Recent work on the orienting reflex and its relation to respondent conditioning was also taken up. A description of interoceptive conditioning showed how far the respondent conditioning paradigm can go towards explaining the variables controlling behavior, since application of this paradigm demonstrates the relationship between the internal and external environments.

The areas of overlap and the interaction between respondent and operant conditioning were indicated. The extension of the respondent conditioning paradigm was illustrated by showing the effect of its superimposition upon ongoing operant behavior. It was suggested how, in this way, it could act as a model for psychopathology.

3

Basic Processes in Learning: Operant Conditioning

One need not look very carefully at the behavior of animals to notice that behavior has consequences. This fact, probably more than any other, has been the cause of much of the anthropomorphic type of description in which the layman indulges. One observes a dog barking at a door and one is tempted to say, "The dog wants to get out," or, "He is barking in order to get out." In some households that particular behavior does, in fact, have the consequence of letting the dog out. We have already noted that an ascription of purpose to a behavior puts us into the peculiar position of suggesting that a response is governed by an event which has not yet occurred. A complete and objective description of a barking dog in the situation above requires that the observer know what both the consequences and the antecedent conditions of the behavior were in the *past.* Thus the psychologist predicts behavior on the basis of the contingency which existed between a response and a consequence, since behavior is a function of its past consequences. It is by the manipulation of these consequences that operant behavior is modified. It is important to note that operant conditioning is a form of learning in which the external environment acts, not to elicit behavior, but to establish the consequences of it. Before decribing the principles of operant conditioning in detail, it might be well to review its historical background.

Historical Background of Operant Conditioning

According to Herrnstein and Boring (1966) there were three major contributors to the area of learning at the time when the field was beginning to develop. They were Ebbinghaus, Thorndike, and Pavlov. Of these three giants, Ebbinghaus was the first to study learning experimentally. Ebbinghaus's (1913) classic work was published in 1885 and was the first time the principle of association was actually transformed into a hypothesis which could be examined by means of experimentation. He arrived at a series of principles important for learning in general; students of the kind of verbal learning which make use of nonsense syllables are still examining many of the principles he proclaimed. The third great innovator in the area of learning, and the latest of the three, was Pavlov. His contribution has already been described with respect to respondent conditioning. That leaves us with E. L. Thorndike, whose first major contribution was published in 1898. He, like Ebbinghaus, made empirical use of the principle of association, but he added a number of other important principles. Of all of these, the most important was what he eventually called *the law of effect.* It states that a response which is followed by a "pleasurable or satisfying state" will tend to be repeated when next an occasion arises. Thorndike departed from the associationism of his day by adopting Darwin's theory of evolution as a basis for doing his experiments, which thereby led him into work with kittens, dogs, and chicks, as well as with human beings. He rejected the notion of an association of ideas in favor of an association of sensation and impulse, by which he meant that the animal associated the situation with a successful activity. He described the animal's behavior as being characterized by a quality of trial and error.

Thorndike's basic experiment consisted of the following: At the beginning of each trial, a hungry cat was placed in an enclosure called a puzzle box. The box had a door made of slats (enabling the cat to see the food outside) and a latch which could be operated by the cat to open the door. When the cat opened the door, it not only escaped from the enclosure (being caged is aversive), but it also obtained the food outside the box. With this procedure there were two different consequences to the cat's behavior. The experimenter measured the length of time it took the animal to open the door during each successive trial. Thorndike's data showed a gradual and somewhat erratic reduction in the time it took to escape the box. He described his animals' behavior as consisting initially of a relatively large number of different movements. He then explained the learning process by saying, "From among these movements one is selected by success." This is a very elegant way indeed of describing the process of response differentiation, that is, of narrowing down the animal's behavior repertoire to those responses most likely to be followed by a reward.

Thorndike went on to study the effect of punishment as well as reward in studies on verbal behavior and to propose *the law of exercise*. This law stated that mere repetition of a response will in and of itself strengthen responses. It was later discredited by Thorndike himself when he showed that there was no improvement in response by exercise alone. Thorndike made contributions in other areas as well, including testing, education, statistics, and language and, in general, had a profound effect upon the field of psychology. As we shall see, his most significant contribution, the law of effect, has been preserved in slightly different form to this day.

Another important part of the history of operant conditioning concerns the use of the maze as an instrument of learning. Probably the first experiment utilizing the maze was performed by Yerkes (1901) on the turtle. A description of the experiment was published in *The Popular Science Monthly*. In the same year, Small (1901) published a paper describing the use of a maze based on the Hampton Court in England. This was the beginning of the American psychologist's long and intensive interest in the rat and in the maze. The process of learning was studied by observing both the errors made, and the length of time taken to traverse the maze. At the end of the maze, in the goal box, was food for the hungry animal.

All of these early learning experiments had in common the fact that there were available objective indicators of learning. It must be noted, however, that the data which these experimental situations yielded were irregular enough to encourage the procedure of averaging the data of groups of animals in order to achieve lawfulness. In Chapter 1 we commented on the problems that such a procedure brings about and therefore need not repeat them here. Another characteristic of these studies was that all of them required the handling of animals between trials. The handling of animals itself is now known to produce artifacts. Handling can be rewarding to an animal, and it is this property of handling which can explain, at least in part, the phenomenon of latent learning, in which investigators "showed" rats around a maze and then demonstrated that learning occurred "in the absence" of a reward. But handling need not always be rewarding, and this further complicates the interpretation of experiments in which it is used. In any case, handling produces a rather drastic change in the environment just before the animal is to perform, thus introducing stimuli the exact nature of which is not fully specified. In addition, the complexity of the mazes themselves were such as to defy experimental analysis because of the many interactions of responses. As a result, there was eventually a gradual trend to simplify mazes, with today's mazes (and they are becoming ever less popular) taking the shape of the letters "T" or "Y" (consisting of a two-choice problem) or simply the form of a runway where the response is measured, not in terms of the length of time it takes the animal to traverse the entire runway, but rather in terms of how long it takes the animal to pass a point a certain distance out of the start box. In a study where such measures were taken (Graham & Gagné, 1940), a safeguard was instituted against the handling of the animal by making the start box and goal box both identical and removable, so that when the hungry rat reached the goal box and ate its food it could simply be returned to the start of the runway by interchanging start and goal boxes. The data which this instrument yielded were precise enough so that one of the earliest mathematical models of learning could actually be constructed and tested on the results.

Nonetheless, it had become clear to behavioral psychologists by this time that an experimental situation yielding still more lawful data was available, producing a change in experimental psychology whose full course is yet to be seen. This brings us to the operant conditioning enclosure constructed by B. F. Skinner, which we will describe below.

The Basic Operant Conditioning Procedure

The Classical Operant Conditioning Experiment

A rat is deprived of food for periods of 23 hours for a number of days until its eating cycle has stabilized. It is then placed inside an experimental enclosure, popularly known as a Skinner box, which is equipped with a house light, a moveable bar protruding from a wall, another light above the bar, and an opening and food tray underneath the bar. The bar, more generally termed a manipulandum, is connected to the food magazine in such a way that a certain amount of pressure on it activates the food magazine, which is attached outside the Skinner box, resulting in a pellet of food being dropped into the food tray, and the light being turned on above the bar. The experiment can be started in one of three ways: one can simply leave the rat in the box until, at some time during its explorations, it hits the bar by accident and a food pellet drops noisily into the food tray; or one can make the bar more prominent for the rat by baiting the bar with meat so as to produce an "accidental" bar press; or one can put the rat through a "shaping" procedure. The shaping procedure will be more fully explained later; suffice it to say for now that the experimenter first trains the animal to approach the food tray when the food magazine clicks, and then trains the animal to come closer and closer to the bar by making food available for successively closer and closer approximations to the response of bar pressing. When the rat presses the bar with enough force to activate the food magazine automatically, the experimenter no longer needs to observe the behavior directly. In addition to its connection with the food magazine, the bar can also be connected to a counter and a pen for indicating the occurrence of responses on a constantly moving record. Thus, the experimenter can monitor the behavior of the animal without in the least intruding upon it. The counter registers the total number of responses the animal makes and thus allows us to compare the frequency of response under different conditions. For example, one can compare the frequency of response under conditions of reinforcement to that occurring during operant level, i.e., after the animal is placed in the Skinner box, but before any shaping procedure or reinforcement for bar pressing takes place.

Let us now examine the data on the acquisition of response over time. The rate of response measure is obtained by using a cumulative recorder. It consists of the following: Paper is moved through a mechanism at a constant speed. Whenever the animal makes a response, a pen resting on the paper moves one step across the paper at right angles to the movement of the paper, without returning to the base line. Whenever the animal makes no response, the pen continues to rest upon the moving paper, drawing a line perpendicular to the direction in which the response is indicated. Thus, the slope of each curve immediately reveals the response rate. No response at all would, of course, result in a horizontal line, while the faster the animal responds, the steeper the slope becomes. Figure 3-1 shows the cumulative curves made by pigeons under different conditions of reinforcement. Differences in rates of response are clearly visible. The following discussion will show that this manner of plotting data is useful for showing many other effects in both the acquisition and the maintenance of behavior.

One might say that the animal "plots its own record" as it undergoes a variety of different conditions. In addition to the measure's timesaving characteristic, it also allows the experimenter to view the progress of his experiment as it goes on, permitting him to alter conditions as a function of the behavior of the organism being observed. Of no small moment is the fact that the Skinner box type of experimental device lends itself to automation. The fact that the animal need only be placed in an experimental enclosure, his behavior recorded, and the conditions of experimentation controlled by electronic circuits, has meant that complicated long-duration experiments could be performed, thereby revealing facts about behavior not otherwise obtainable.

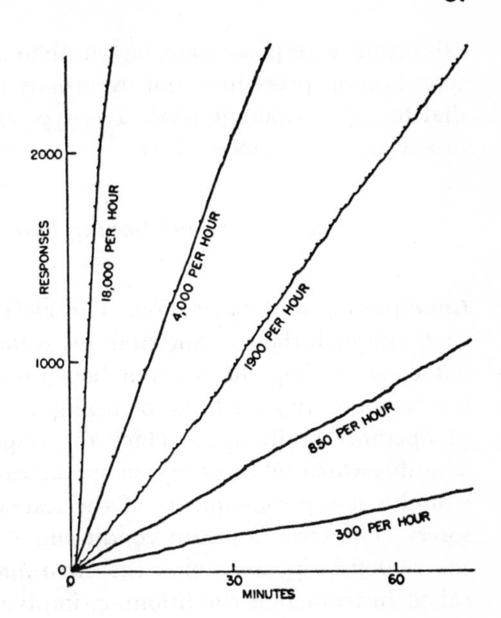

Fig. 3-1. Cumulative curves made by pigeons under various schedules of reinforcement showing relative uniform performance over a wide range of rates of responding. (Skinner, 1953 (b), Fig. 1.)

The importance of the rate of response measure and its close relation to the concept of probability of response have already been mentioned with respect to behavior theory in Chapter 1. Let us simply reiterate that a probability of response measure applied to the individual organism has the obvious advantage of being useful for describing many different types of behavior of animals up and down the phylogenetic scale, including man.

For an examination of the phenomenon of extinction of response, let us return to the experiment with the hungry rat. When the animal receives a reinforcer, such as food for pressing the bar, he may not immediately begin to respond at a high rate, but once he makes more than a handful of responses, he quickly achieves a stable rate. This is evidenced by an unchanging slope in the cumulative curve. In such an experiment, extinction is produced by simply placing the hungry rat in the experimental enclosure exactly as before, but with one critical difference—the food magazine is now empty. When the animal presses the bar, he hears the click of the food magazine, but he receives no food. After a while, the rat's response rate decreases, becoming somewhat erratic at first and often exhibiting a response rate higher than that exhibited during the conditioning procedure, but eventually assuming the same rate as that found in operant level. The typical extinction curve shows a progressively shallower slope.

The Operant Conditioning Paradigm

Conditioning and Extinction. The alert reader will have noticed that, although the eliciting stimulus is the *sine qua non* of respondent conditioning, the relation between the evoking stimulus and the response appears to be of negligible interest in the acquisition of operant conditioning. Once the response occurs, however, the stimulus which follows the response takes on some importance. That stimulus is the consequence of the response and is called the reinforcer. The term "operant conditioning" came from the idea that the response operates upon the environment. It is also sometimes called instrumental conditioning, implying that the response is instrumental in procuring the reinforcer.

The definition of the reinforcer gave psychologists trouble for some time. Thorndike tried to define a reinforcer in terms of a "satisfying state" and Clark Hull defined it in terms of the concept of need reduction. Both of those definitions invoked concepts that could not be experimentally verified. Today, we define a reinforcer in terms of its observed effect upon behavior. A reinforcer is called primary when its effect is unrelated to the conditioning history of the organism. Reinforcers such as food, water, a mate, electric shock, and loud noise are all examples of events which will act as reinforcers as a result of the biological constitution of the organism. Conditioned reinforcers are those events which become reinforcing through their association with primary reinforcers. We shall return to the genesis of the conditioned reinforcers below.

A positive reinforcer is a stimulus which increases the frequency of the response producing it and which eventually maintains that response at a stable level. A negative reinforcer is an aversive stimulus whose elimination by a response strengthens and maintains that response. Notice that the negative reinforcer is defined in what might appear to be a circumlocutious manner. In fact, both definitions are worded in such a way as to produce a measure of strength which can be observed by an increase in response rate. Since it would be most difficult to discern the effect of a negative reinforcer upon behavior whose response rate is, to begin with, quite low, the definition of the negative reinforcer given above is of more general use than a more simply worded one might be. There are two procedures in which the above definition of a negative reinforcer are employed: escape conditioning, in which the animal's response terminates the aversive stimulus, and avoidance conditioning, in which the animal's response prevents the occurrence of the aversive stimulus. The avoidance conditioning procedure is one which involves conditioned reinforcers (we will return to the discussion of avoidance later when we take up the topic of conditioned reinforcers).

A negative reinforcer can, of course, also function in the more familiar way as a punishing stimulus. As such, the punishing stimulus must be applied to behavior already existing in some strength. In other words, it must be applied to stable behavior which has been conditioned by a positive or negative reinforcer (applied in an escape or avoidance situation) so that the reduction of response rate can be reliably discerned. A recent definition given for the process of punishment (Azrin & Holz, 1966, p. 381) is: "*. . . reduction of the future probability of a specific response as a result of the immediate delivery of a stimulus for that response.*" (Authors' italics).

Associated with punishment explicitly controlled by the experimenter is the amount of effort which a given organism has to exert in order to make a response. Given the opportunity to make only one out of a number of responses, animals generally make the response involving least effort, thus acting on the basis of an avoidance contingency, i.e., avoiding making those responses which require more effort. The variable of response effort was employed in an explicit manner with human subjects. Weiner (1962) reinforced his subjects positively by giving them a number of score points for their responses. In order to simulate response effort or punishment (which is one way of viewing effort), he made use of a variable termed *response cost,* i.e., every time the subject made a response, he lost a point. This experimental technique has the interesting characteristic of having the positive and negative reinforcers measurable in the same units. It also has obvious similarities to reinforcement contingencies in real life.

Related to the problem of defining a primary reinforcer is the concept of drive. A drive consists of a set of operations preceding the conditioning experiment which will produce or enhance the reinforcing power of a stimulus. Thus, food is a reinforcing stimulus to a rat that has been deprived of food for a period of time; water is a reinforcing stimulus to an animal that has been deprived of water or fed salt. It is not surprising to find that a satiated animal will not respond when the consequence of the response is food. The concept of drive is an important one and we will return to discussion of it. Here it is important to note only that the primary reinforcers we have discussed so far have corresponding operations which must be performed on the animal to make those reinforcers effective.

One type of reinforcer that does not easily fit among the reinforcers discussed so far is the *sensory reinforcer,* e.g., onset of a light of moderate intensity. Sensory reinforcers have in common the fact that they appear to strengthen behavior which they follow, that this effect is independent of the history of the organism (in other words, they are not merely conditioned reinforcers), and that their strength as reinforcing stimuli appears to be unrelated to the usual organic drive conditions. Although the effect of sensory reinforcers is typically not as great as that of other primary reinforcers, these stimuli may well have important implications for the survival of the animal, although they do not appear to be as directly involved in survival as food and water.

An animal sensitive to changes in his environment (that is, one which responds at a higher rate when the responses are followed by changes in stimulation than when not), has a better chance of escaping a predator or coming upon prey itself. The fact that the delivery of such reinforcers results in relatively quick satiation (where the animal ceases to respond when that reinforcer is the only consequence), becoming effective again only after a passage of time, also fits well into the survival value hypothesis of the sensory reinforcer. A careful review of this area of research was recently undertaken by Kish (1966) and presents a number of different theories to explain the effectiveness of the sensory reinforcer.

It is of some interest to contemplate the relation of sensory reinforcement to the orienting reflex. Neither of these two stimuli has effects which are very strong, but both appear to have important adaptive characteristics. Thus, it may be of interest to relate the stability of the orienting reflex to a given stimulus to the reinforcing effect of that stimulus when it is produced by an operant response.

Other primary reinforcers which should be mentioned separately from the sensory reinforcers, although differing from them only in degree, are the events of exploration and manipulation for which animals work. Thus Butler (1953) and Harlow (1953) found that monkeys will acquire responses when the only consequence is the opportunity to view a complex event (e.g., a busy laboratory) or the opportunity to manipulate an object (e.g., a mechanical puzzle). Another primary reinforcer more recently uncovered by Harlow (1958) is what he calls "contact comfort." He showed that infant monkeys prefer to remain with a terry cloth surrogate-mother than with a wire surrogate-mother in the presence of aversive stimulation, even though food was obtained through the wire surrogate-mother. This finding, along with others, has led Harlow to posit contact comfort as a primary reinforcer of great importance.

The basic paradigms of operant conditioning can be diagrammed in the following way:

Positive reinforcement: $s \ldots\ldots R \rightarrow S^{+R}$

where s = some stimulus "deliberately" (e.g., by having meat smeared on the bar) or accidentally evoking an operant response, R (e.g., bar pressing). The dots make clear that R is *not* elicited.

S^{+R} = primary positively reinforcing stimulus (e.g., food).

Negative reinforcement in escape conditioning: $S^{-R} \ldots\ldots R \rightarrow \overline{S^{-R}}$

where S^{-R} = primary negatively reinforcing stimulus, the dots marking the fact that the R is *not* elicited.

R = the response (e.g., bar pressing)

$\overline{S^{-R}}$ = elimination or termination of the S^{-R}

Negative reinforcement in avoidance conditioning:

$s \ldots\ldots R \rightarrow \overline{S^{-R}}$ or $S^{-D} \ldots\ldots R \rightarrow \overline{S^{-R}}$

where s = an unidentified stimulus marking the occasion for the emission of a response which postpones the onset of the S^{-R} and is designated by $\overline{S^{-R}}$. In the absence of an exteroceptive warning stimulus, the negatively reinforcing stimulus is programmed in such a way that, if the animal makes no response, it receives a shock periodically; for every response it makes, the shock is postponed for a fixed period of time. Since this avoidance conditioning procedure was originated by Sidman (1953) it has come to be known as "Sidman avoidance." Recently, Sidman (1966) suggested the more descriptive term, "free-operant avoidance," as a name for the procedure. The term "free-operant," which is also used to characterize operant responding under the control of positive reinforcement, signifies that the animal is free to respond at any time and that, unlike puzzle box or maze situations, behavior does not take place in trials but continuously.

The second paradigm for avoidance conditioning is the same as the free-operant paradigm, except that there is an explicit discriminative (warning) stimulus, S^{-D}, under the control of the experimenter. Typically, the negatively reinforcing stimulus occurs at a fixed time after S^{-D} unless the organism responds during the interval, thereby postponing the occurrence of the S^{-R} until the next time the S^{-D} heralds the occasion of another aversive event which can be postponed by a timely response, etc.

The punishment paradigm is quite straightforward:

$$s \ldots . R \rightarrow S^{-R}$$

The production of a response is followed by a negative reinforcer. Since in most cases punishment follows a response which is also followed by a positive reinforcer, the paradigm can be represented in this way:

$$s \ldots . R \begin{array}{l} \nearrow S^{+R} \\ \searrow S^{-R} \end{array}$$

Viewed in this way, we have what Miller (1944) called an *approach-avoidance conflict,* a situation of importance with respect to abnormal psychology.

Another method of applying the reinforcement process has been called *omission training* by Kimble (1961). According to this conditioning paradigm, a positive reinforcer is delivered if the organism *fails* to make a response. Lane (1960) used this technique successfully on a vocal response in the chick, the positive reinforcer being delivered whenever a period of 2 minutes occurred without a response being emitted. Baer (1961) used withdrawal of a positive reinforcer to reduce a response in young children. The positive reinforcer consisted of an animated cartoon, with every response followed by 2 seconds of withdrawal of the cartoon. Thus, here too the positive reinforcer was delivered for failing to respond. This paradigm may be diagrammed as follows:

$$s \ldots . \overline{R} \rightarrow S^{+R}$$

where $\overline{R}$ = a time period of no response and the other symbols are as defined above.

In general, we can describe the operant conditioning paradigm to consist of the following characteristics. Responses, usually involving the skeletal muscles, are emitted, *not* elicited, i.e., they are, roughly speaking, voluntary. Rate of response is the aspect of the behavior which is measured; the typical result of the paradigm here described consists of a relative increase in rate of response, omission training being the obvious exception to that rule.

The process of extinction consists of giving the animal the opportunity to respond in the absence of reinforcing stimuli. The typical results of extinction are initially the production of relatively high rates of response which gradually alternate with increasingly longer and longer periods of no response, eventually showing a return to operant level. Extinction is also accompanied by a series of emotional responses including such behavior as gnawing at the bar, defecating, and urinating. Resistance to extinction is influenced by at least two basic variables: (1) number of reinforcers delivered during conditioning and (2) amount of effort involved in executing each response. Studies by Williams (1938) on groups of animals, and more recently by Hearst (1961) on single organisms, showed an increase in the number of extinction responses with an increase in the number of reinforcements up to a maximum of about 80 reinforcements for rats and pigeons. Experiments concerning the effect of amount of effort on rate of extinction at first suggested that resistance to extinction decreases with an increase in amount of effort. Closer analysis (cf. Deese & Hulse, 1967) of the relationship showed that it is much more complicated than that, with some experiments actually showing a reversal of the early results. It appears that there are two other important aspects of the response: one relates specifically to those topographical aspects of the response which are reinforced during conditioning and the other refers to the effect of the process of extinction upon the topography of responses in general. The fact that in some cases the emission of certain topographical aspects of interest requires such effort that the animal responds as if he were given a punishing stimulus does not mean that the topographical aspects are any less important. It appears that resistance to extinction is influenced at least as much by the similarity in conditions surrounding the conditioning and extinction situations as by the punishing aspects of the situation. Thus, as was demonstrated by Miller (1960), rats show greater accommodation to punishing stimuli (negative reinforcers) when those punishing stimuli are introduced in gradually increasing intensity, i.e., when the conditions are changed slowly, than when they are introduced in full magnitude at once. The slow introduction of variables allows for the maintenance of the current behavior by the S^D's. Rapid stimulus change destroys stimulus control and therefore breaks up the ongoing behavior. In other words, the effort variable constitutes part of the discriminative stimulus in the presence of which the animal's behavior is reinforced. We will discuss the function and importance of discriminative stimuli below.

The process of extinction has yet another effect upon the topography of responses. Antonitis (1951), in a study where rats were required to poke their noses through a horizontal 50 cm. slot at any point, showed that response topography decreased in variability during conditioning and increased in variability during extinction. More recently, Notterman (1959) presented similar results for the variable of force of bar press. These results provide evidence for the adaptive quality of the behavior of animals. Clearly, it pays for an organism, whose behavior is no longer reinforced, to vary its behavior on the chance that some of the variations in response might result in reinforcement. As for the variable of effort, this discussion should have made apparent the complications which make evaluation of this variable not quite as obvious as it might seem at first.

At this point some comments might be made about the relation between the concepts of forgetting and extinction. The term forgetting is used to denote at least 4 different processes. The first use of the word is actually simply inappropriate, but its frequency of use points up, as well, a misunderstanding of the process of learning, and therefore requires some comment. One cannot forget what has not been learned in the first place. Although this appears to be quite obvious, people, nevertheless, often say that they have forgotten someone's name, when they have never even emitted it once, or that they have forgotten how to drive to a given place to which they have never before driven (having been driven there only by someone else). In order to be learned, a response must be emitted and reinforced in the presence of those stimuli which are to control that behavior in the future.

A more sophisticated, but very similar, use of the word forgetting consists of the application of the term to experiments dealing with short-term memory. Peterson and Peterson (1959) presented data which suggested that over a period of 18 seconds forgetting occurs merely through disuse, that emission of the response (a condition necessary for extinction) is not necessary in order for a reduction of response strength to occur. A re-examination of these findings in an experiment by Keppel and Underwood (1962), however, showed that no such reduction in response strength occurred for the first in a series of nonsense syllables given to subjects to be memorized. Analysis of nonsense syllables given after the first one showed the "disuse" effect; in fact, the disuse effect became more pronounced the more nonsense syllables the subject had had to recall before. This is a well-known effect in verbal learning, known as *proactive inhibition,* and is essentially the confusing effect of material learned earlier on material to be recalled subsequently. In terms of behavior theory, the effect can be explained by the fact that the similarity of the stimulus conditions for the recall of different nonsense syllables is so great that a given stimulus is quite likely to call forth an incorrect response. Furthermore, the Peterson and Peterson procedure consisted of a single trial exposure to each nonsense syllable, resulting, of course, in very weak learning indeed. Therefore, any recall at all would most likely be attributable to still earlier learning of the letters making up the nonsense syllables to be memorized before the subject ever came into the experiment.

The third type of forgetting is extinction. When a response is emitted in the absence of reinforcement, and when this procedure is continued for a sufficiently long time, response strength is reduced. Reduction in response strength when the response is *not* emitted has no experimental basis in fact. Skinner (1953) reports the emission of a substantial number of extinction responses in pigeons as long as 6 years (approximately half their lifetime) after conditioning has taken place. In the same way, people who learn to ride a bicycle appear not to forget how to do it despite the fact that they have not ridden for many years. The explanation put forth for this maintenance of response strength is that neither the target pecking (on a vertical wall) by the pigeon, nor the bicycle riding by the human beings, constitutes a response when executed on occasions other than those called for by the experimental situation on the one hand or the bicycle on the other.

Still another process often termed forgetting can be related to the concept of interference. Essentially, interference refers to the fact that the same stimulus may mark the occasion for more than one response. Forgetting in this sense, for example, means that one may first learn to respond with the nonsense syllable "zuk" to the stimulus giw, and then, without being extinguished for the response "zuk," be reinforced for the response "fuv" to giw. A person's rate of learning, or his recall after a period of rest, of the second association can then be expected to be influenced by the interference of the earlier learning. After the subject has learned the "fuv"-to-giw association, the experimenter may ask the subject to recall the older "zuk"-to-giw association. This old association can also then be shown to be interfered with by the "fuv"-to-giw association. While the interference interpretation of forgetting is by far the most complicated, it is probably the one which is most applicable to real life. It is clear, then, that in order to gain a better understanding of such phenomena, we must understand more about the nature of stimulus control over responses.

Stimulus Generalization and Discrimination. These two processes have already been discussed with respect to respondent conditioning. In operant conditioning the process of generalization refers to the fact that responses which are reinforced in the presence of a given stimulus will be emitted in the presence of similar stimuli as well. Of course, responses must be reinforced in the presence of some stimuli and thus generalization is very much a rule of nature. The survival value of generalization is fairly obvious. Few events in nature ever completely replicate themselves, and thus learning, which is predicated on the notion of repetition of responses and stimuli, would not be possible without stimulus generalization.

An experiment by Guttman and Kalish (1956) illustrates well the phenomenon of generalization. Pigeons were positively reinforced for pecking a key when a light of a given wavelength illuminated the key. When the entire experimental cubicle was dark, the pigeons did not respond. Light and dark periods were alternated. Initially all key pecks were reinforced, but after a while only some responses were reinforced. This was done to achieve a response which was highly resistant to extinction, a necessary condition for the subsequent tests for generalization. As we shall see below, an intermittent schedule of reinforcement (where only some responses are reinforced) results in greater resistance to extinction than a continuous schedule of reinforcement (where every response is reinforced). The tests for generalization were done by presenting the pigeons with lights of wavelengths close to the wavelength used when the pigeons were conditioned. No reinforcement was given during the generalization tests. The results showed quite clearly that the pigeons responded to wavelengths other than the stimuli in the presence of which they were conditioned and that the number of responses emitted in the presence of a given wavelength decreased with the distance of that wavelength from the training stimulus. Such a pattern of responding is referred to as a generalization gradient.

According to a recent review of the areas of stimulus generalization and discrimination (Terrace, 1966) the generalization gradient is typically produced by a learning procedure in which responding is positively reinforced in the presence of one stimulus but not in the presence of others. The typical discrimination procedure consists of reinforcing a response in the presence of one stimulus, called the S^D (discriminative stimulus), and of withholding reinforcement in the presence of another stimulus, called the S^{Δ}. The development of a discrimination, as demonstrated for one rat, is shown in Figure 3-2 (Herrick, Myers, & Korotkin, 1959). Inspection of the graphs shows a gradual separation of the cumulative response curves under the S^D condition (when the animal is reinforced for responding) and the S^{Δ} condition (when the animal receives no reinforcement). Performance on Day 1 shows essentially the stimulus generalization effect. Successive S^{Δ} curves demonstrate the extinction process from one day to the next. Notice the inset in the graph showing the rate of response for lines at different slopes. This discrimination paradigm may be represented in the following way:

$$S^D \ldots . R \rightarrow S^{+R}$$

$$S^{\Delta} \ldots . R \rightarrow$$

S^D's vary along many different dimensions in experiments of this kind. An unusual dimension was utilized in a recent experiment by Herrnstein and Loveland (1964), who used the above paradigm to condition a discrimination in pigeons between pictures containing at least one human being (S^D) and pictures which contained no human being (S^{Δ}). The pictures themselves were allowed to vary dramatically in terms of the setting (city, country, etc.), tint of slide, size, number, age, sex, attire, amount of person visible, and position of the human beings. The discrimination was produced by first reinforcing the pigeons for approaching the feeding device when

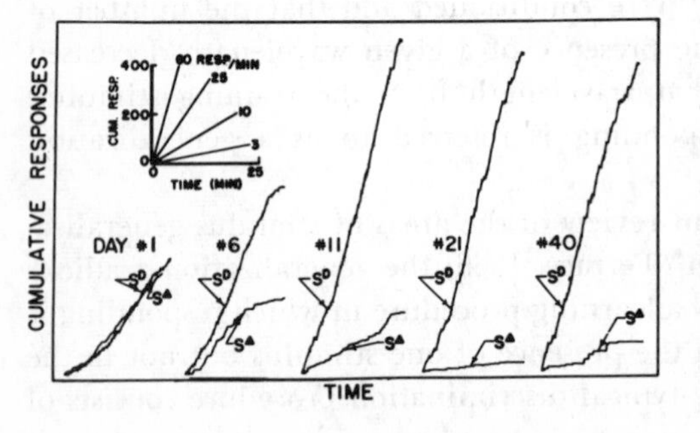

Fig. 3-2. Sample daily records of one rat during 40 days of discrimination training. The small marks on the S^D curves indicate when food pellets were delivered. The records for the higher S^D rates underestimate the number of responses by a variable amount up to about 8%. (Herrick, Myers, and Korotkin, 1959, Fig. 1.)

food was available, then for pecking at a key on the wall, then for pecking a number of times before a reinforcer became available, next for pecking only in the presence of an illuminated translucent plate, no reinforcement forthcoming in its absence, and finally for pecking only when the slide containing human beings was shown. Over 1,200 different slides were used for the experiment. Within 7 to 10 training sessions, the pigeons had begun to discriminate pictures with people from those without. They continued to improve over 70 sessions, yielding incontrovertible evidence for having acquired the complex "concept" of the human being in a two-dimensional picture.

We have already seen that the operant conditioning process is usually characterized by the gradualness of its procedures. This was shown in the shaping procedure (it will be discussed at greater length in the section on response class) and again in the Herrnstein-Loveland experiment described above. Terrace (1966) has used the technique of gradualness in training pigeons to perform a discrimination without errors. His procedure consists of two basic techniques: (1) introducing discrimination training right after the conditioned response has been acquired (instead of waiting until the response has stabilized), and (2) using as S^D and S^Δ two stimuli very different from each other initially (differing both in degree along one dimension and in number of dimensions), and then making the two stimuli progressively more similar. This procedure does, in fact, result in errorless or close to errorless discrimination learning. As a result of the fact that there is no extinction during S^Δ, no emotional responses occur in the presence of that stimulus. This point has implications for the development of negative conditioned reinforcers.

Since stimuli can acquire control over responses that have been positively reinforced in their presence, it seems only reasonable to examine how stimuli acquire control over responses under negative reinforcement contingencies. Azrin and Holz (1966), in a review of the literature on punishment, reported on some studies of discrimination in which the discrimination was produced by different punishment contingencies. Any stimulus present during the condition when punishment is given (S^P) reduces the rate of the operant response, while any stimulus associated with the no-punishment condition ($S^{\bar{P}}$) produces little or no reduction of the operant response. Nevertheless, there is a considerable amount of evidence for generalization of the response-suppression effect to the no-punishment condition early in training. Figure 3-3 shows the effect of punishing stimuli on ongoing operant behavior which has been positively reinforced by food, over a series of 15 days. The top part of the figure shows a one-hour record of responding before any punishment was introduced. The constancy of the slope indicates that the rate of response is quite stable. The record was made in such a way that the pen is automatically returned to the base level at the end of each 10 minutes. The vertical lines, therefore, indicate simply the restoration of the pen. Note that there are alternating

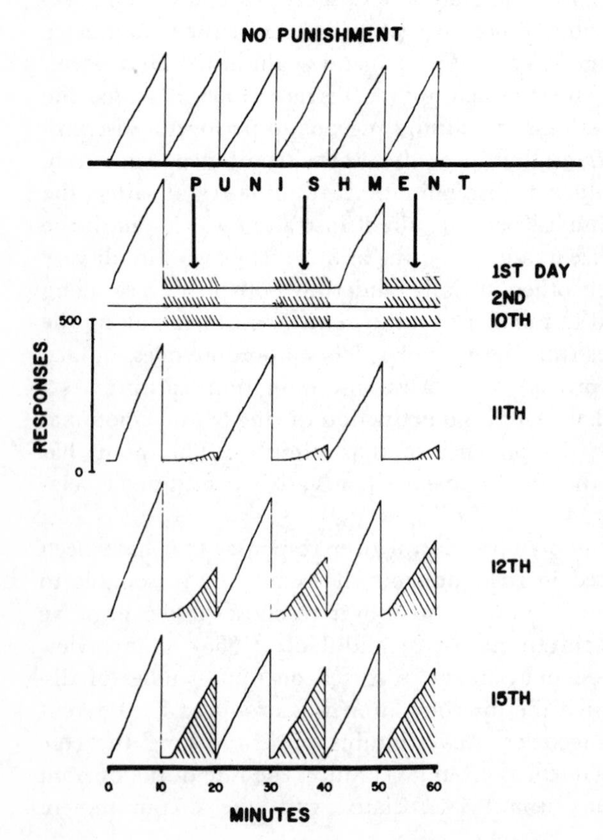

Fig. 3-3. Cumulative response records for one pigeon. The vertical line represents the moment of change-over from one stimulus color to a second stimulus color of the transilluminated response key. The responses were being reinforced on a VI schedule of food reinforcement; the food deliveries are not indicated on the record. The two stimulus lights alternated every ten minutes. The top record (no punishment) is for the condition in which no shocks were delivered. The cross-hatched marks designate the stimulus condition in which each response was punished by a brief (100 msec.) shock of 60 volts. (Azrin and Holz, 1966, Fig. 12.)

periods of punishment and no-punishment. The S^P and $S^{\bar{P}}$ periods are associated with two different stimulus lights. During the first day of punishment there was immediate generalization from the S^P to the $S^{\bar{P}}$, the effect being so large that for the next 9 days it suppressed all responding. On the eleventh day responding during the $S^{\bar{P}}$ periods returned, with some recovery of response during the S^P periods. In addition to this evidence for generalization of punishment early in the procedure, the figure also shows that the effect of punishment is not permanent except at very high intensities.

It has been traditional to view punishing stimuli in terms of their suppressive effects alone. Punishing stimuli can, like neutral stimuli, or for that matter, like positive reinforcers, act as discriminative stimuli (S^D) as well. Thus, the S^{-R} may act as a discriminative stimulus for other punishing stimuli or for their absence, or for the presence of positive reinforcement or for its absence. The S^{-R} acquires its discriminative properties simply by having its presence associated with the other conditions listed above. This means that any consideration of the effects of punishment independent of its discriminative effect will reveal only part of its mechanism. These interacting effects will be discussed again in the chapter on abnormal psychology.

Stimulus generalization in an avoidance situation was studied by Sidman (1961). Monkeys were trained to press a lever in a free operant shock-avoidance procedure. The S^{-D} was an auditory click of 2 per second; the $S^{-\Delta}$ was an auditory click of 6 per second. After the monkeys had been well trained on this discrimination they were given generalization tests for the intermediate click values. Figure 3-4 presents the generalization data in terms of the proportion of responses made for the S^{-D} clicking rate, indicated in the figure by a "+," for the $S^{-\Delta}$ clicking rate, indicated in the figure by a "−", and for the generalization stimuli of 3, 4, and 5 clicks per second. The different lines provide data for different "RS" (response-shock) intervals, i.e., for different intervals of shock postponement for each response. All the generalization tests were conducted under extinction conditions, i.e., no shocks were given during any session. Comparisons of the stimulus generalization of avoidance conditioning with generalization of appetitive conditioning (where S^R is food) yields the interesting fact that there is a steeper gradient for the food-reinforced than for the shock-avoidance generalization (Sidman, 1966; Hoffman, 1966). The greater degree of generalization exhibited by avoidance responses may well have important implications for abnormal psychology since much abnormal behavior can be aptly described as having this characteristic.

In comparing respondent conditioning with operant conditioning, we have stressed the fact that in the former the stimulus (CS or US) elicits the response, while in the latter the manner of response evocation is not as important as the nature of the strengthening process, namely the fact that operant responses generally have conse-

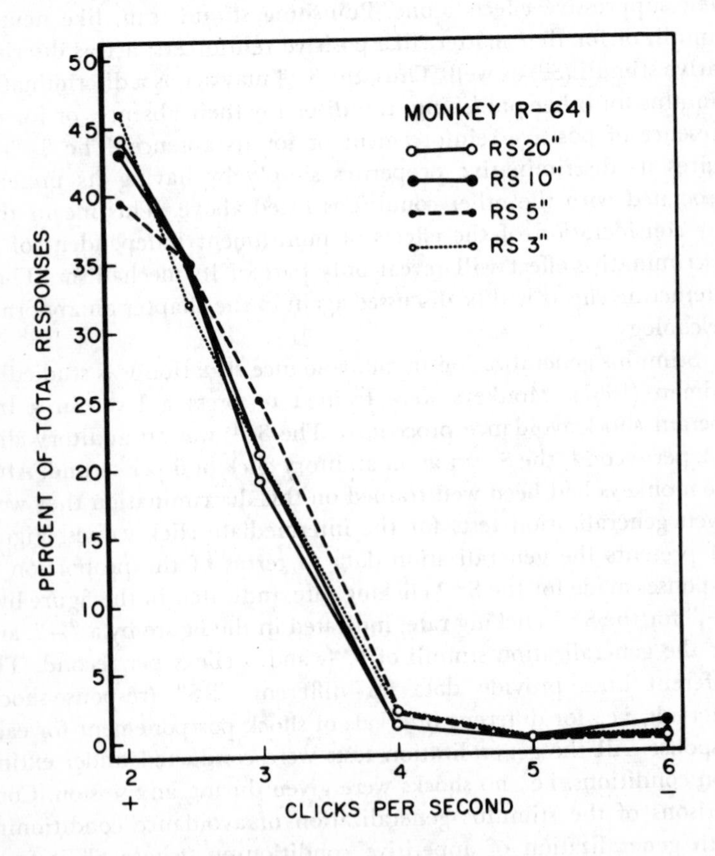

Fig. 3-4. Median relative generalization gradients. (Sidman, 1961, Fig. 7.)

quences. It should be clear to the reader, however, that while stimuli might not control the emission of operant responses initially, they can acquire control over responses which in many ways are as compelling and specific as the stimulus control exerted in respondent conditioning. The control of responses by stimuli in conjunction with schedules of reinforcement is, in fact, quite dramatic indeed.

Conditioned Reinforcement. We have already had occasion to speak of two different types of primary reinforcers. Some further thought about behavior, and about human behavior in particular, makes it quite clear that many consequences of behavior are of significance, not in and of themselves, but because of their association with significant stimuli, i.e., with primary reinforcing stimuli. In respondent conditioning, the CS is, of course, typically a stimulus which acquires its eliciting effect through its association with a stimulus that elicits a response without any special learning process taking place, namely, the unconditioned stimulus.

The definition of a conditioned reinforcer (sometimes called a secondary reinforcer) as "a stimulus whose reinforcing properties are established by conditioning" (Kelleher, 1966), does not allow us to choose from among a number of conflicting theories which attempt to explain precisely the kind of conditioning that is necessary for such establishment to take place. This area was recently reviewed by Kelleher (1966) and by Wike (1966). Two major theories are of interest here. One states that a stimulus must be an S^D before it becomes a conditioned reinforcer, S^r. The other states that an S^r becomes established as a conditioned reinforcer by means of a respondent conditioning paradigm. When we examine the typical experiment used to establish a conditioned reinforcer, it becomes clear why both of these theories can be used to describe the same data. For example, such a typical experiment would be carried out as follows: A rat is placed in a Skinner box and magazine training proceeds through presentation of a click immediately followed by a food pellet. A bar is then inserted into the box and each bar-press is followed by a click. The rate of bar-pressing is then compared in rats who have had the pairing of the click and the food with rats who did not experience the pairing. The general result is that rats who have been given the pairing condition respond in a way which indicates that the click has become a conditioned reinforcer, since these rats emit more responses when the click follows.

Now, how does the pairing of a click with food leave itself open to two interpretations? Since the click is followed by the animal's approach to the food magazine, it may be viewed as an S^D for approaching the food tray and thus as evidence for the hypothesis which states that a stimulus must be an S^D before it can be an S^r. On the other hand, the click-food sequence conforms perfectly to the respondent conditioning paradigm, suggesting that the click simply becomes a CS eliciting a reaction similar to that of the US, food, and thus acquires similar reinforcing properties. The experimental evidence for and against these interpretations is as plentiful as it is complicated. The interested reader should see Kelleher (1966) and Wike (1966) for a detailed exploration of the issues. In general, we can say that today the evidence leans in the direction of the respondent conditioning hypothesis.

Experiments in avoidance conditioning (described in the preceding section) provide the paradigm for producing an S^{-r} (negative conditioned reinforcer). The experiments show that the animals actually make responses for escaping from S^{-r}'s in the same way as they make responses for escaping from S^{-R}'s (Schoenfeld, 1950). In the typical discrimination experiment two effects occur: The S^D becomes a conditioned positive reinforcer and the S^Δ becomes a conditioned negative reinforcer. Terrace's (1966) errorless discrimination procedure leads to an S^Δ without the typical negative reinforcer characteristics, since the animal makes no responses during S^Δ. Azrin, according to Terrace (1966), showed that an S^Δ like the S^{-R} elicited aggressive behavior toward another organism. More evidence for the similarity of effect of an S^{-r} and S^{-R} is provided by an experiment performed by Brown and Wagner (1964) who showed that the delivery of punishment and S^Δ periods were, to a limited extent, interchangeable as preparation for each other. S^Δ periods made contingent on responses served to attenuate the suppression effects produced by making punishment contingent upon the responses later. Punishment made contingent on responses, in a similar way, served to attenuate the subsequent effect of S^Δ periods.

The conditioned reinforcing stimulus is obviously of great importance in behavior theory. Such a stimulus can be made even more powerful by associating it with a number of different primary reinforcers. Skinner (1953a) has named this the generalized reinforcer and has pointed out its significance, particularly with reference to human subjects. The superiority of the generalized reinforcer over the conditioned reinforcer which has become so established by being associated with only one type of reinforcer has been demonstrated for rats (Wike & Barrientos, 1958; Wunderlich, 1961) as well as for human subjects (Kanfer & Matarazzo, 1959). Among human beings the generalized reinforcer often takes the shape of attention expressed in verbal form. We shall have occasion to speak of it again with respect to verbal behavior and social psychology.

Schedules of Reinforcement. One of Skinner's great contributions towards widening the scope of behavior theory was his development of the idea of intermittent reinforcement. We know only too well that, although behavior produces consequences, it does not *always* produce them. Although we can, in the laboratory, reinforce behavior on a regular basis, i.e., by continuous reinforcement, we do not thereby generate behavior which is either most interesting or most likely to be found in nature. On the other hand, the behavior generated by means of intermittent reinforcement is *more* stable than that generated by continuous reinforcement. It is also more efficient in generating stable behavior when that behavior is under the control of complex stimulus patterns or when that behavior itself is complexly patterned in time. A great deal of research has been done in the area of intermittent reinforcement. We will be able to review only the most salient of the issues and procedures. Excellent reviews of the procedures in the area are available in Ferster and Skinner (1957) and in Morse (1966) and should be consulted for further information.

The success of intermittent reinforcement can be partly explained by the fact that during the experimental procedure of extinction there is, initially, an *increase* in rate of response. If the reinforcer is delivered while the animal is responding at this higher rate, it becomes contingent on continuation of the higher rate of response.

The concept of reinforcement contingency can be defined as the program which specifies the occurrence of discriminative and reinforcing stimuli in time and in relation to the animal's responses. This contingency has come to overshadow many of the old learning theory concepts. Thus, while it has been customary to explain large differences in response rate in terms of differences in motivation, we now know that large differences can often be ascribed to variations in scheduling. Different schedules of reinforcement can as easily result in low as in high rates of response. Furthermore, the motivational variable is more critical in the acquisition of behavior than in its maintenance. What schedules do is to explain the tenacity of behavior as we find it in nature in the face of the many adverse conditions which might well appear to prevent any consistent reinforcement of behavior.

In point of fact, all of us are well acquainted with schedules of reinforcement. The generalized reinforcer, money, is delivered essentially in terms of two contingencies: People work on a time basis, by which is meant that periodically, say every Friday, they receive their salary, or they work on a "piece" basis, i.e., their salary depends on the number of items they worked on. Both of these reinforcement contingencies are fixed: So much time and work, or so much work irrespective of time produces a certain amount of money. There are other cases, however, where the reinforcement contingency is expressed by variable lengths of time or variable amounts of work. This can perhaps be illustrated by the work of a salesman. With some of his customers, the more often he calls on them the more likely he is to make a sale which results in a commission for him (the reinforcer); with other customers, the salesman's ability to make a sale depends on a combination of the passage of time (i.e., until the customer runs out of the item the salesman is selling) and his calling on the customer. Of additional interest is the fact that a good salesman's selling behavior varies as a function of the kind of schedule of reinforcement his particular customer places him on, i.e., his behavior is stimulus controlled. There are, of course, innumerable examples of man's behavior on reinforcement schedules, but rather than listing any more of them it would be helpful at this point to specify in more precise terms at least some of the schedules in use and some of their effects upon behavior.

In order to gain a better understanding of the different schedules we must define a number of terms. Broadly speaking, there are two types of schedules: *ratio* schedules in which a response is reinforced after the emission of a given number of responses following the last reinforced response or sometimes some other event, and *interval* schedules in which an emitted response is reinforced after a given period of time since some event (either an arbitrary point in time or more usually the last reinforcement). The ratio and the interval may be either fixed or variable, giving rise to the terms fixed ratio (FR), variable ratio (VR), fixed interval (FI), and variable interval (VI). Notice that in all cases the animal must emit a response for a reinforcer to be forthcoming. In ratio schedules the rate of reinforcement is controlled by the animal's response rate. In interval schedules, on the other hand, the minimal requirement is only one response after the interval is up. This leaves unspecified (by the schedule) what the animal does in the interval before reinforcement is forthcoming.

Before proceeding to discuss more complicated schedules, it might be well to detail some of the effects of the above schedules. First it should be noted that the final schedule is approximated gradually, i.e., first an animal is reinforced on a continuous basis and then the intermittency is gradually extended by going, for example, from a FR of 1:1 (one reinforcement per response) to a FR of 2:1, FR 3:1, FR 8:1, and so on. Actual ratios successfully conditioned have been quite high. As early as 1938 Skinner was able to get rats to respond on a FR 192:1. In a more recent paper, Skinner (1953b) showed that pigeons will "continue indefinitely to respond when reinforcements are spaced as much as 45 minutes apart." More recent experiments have shown behavior to be maintained by FI's several hours long. What is the general effect of intermittent reinforcement? Responses subject to such contingencies are far more resistant to extinction than the same responses under continuous (crf) reinforcement contingencies. Thus, it becomes clear why nature's choice of reinforcement contingency would be an intermittent one.

Different schedules of reinforcement give rise to characteristic responding over time. Inspection of Figure 3-5 shows the development of a fixed interval of one minute (FI-1) for a pigeon. The cumulative curves represent the first five 15-minute periods of FI responding in a pigeon. Curve E represents the stable behavior

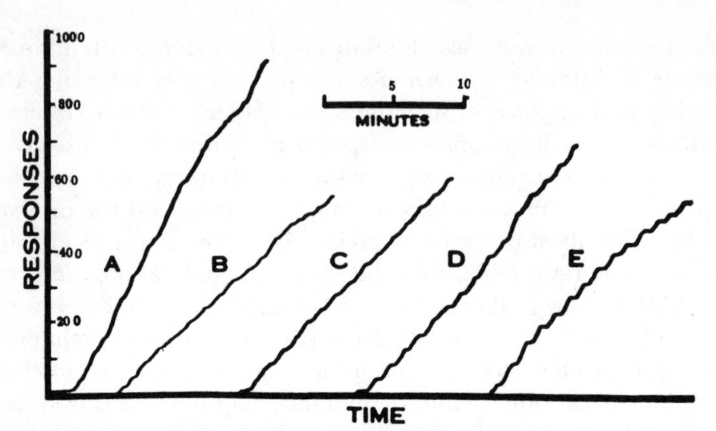

Fig. 3-5. The development of fixed interval behavior. (Skinner, 1950, Fig. 6.)

usually found under an FI contingency where the response rate towards the end of each interval is high, and immediately after the end of the interval, following the reinforcer, becomes very low (often 0). The low rate following reinforcement reflects the fact that the animal never receives a reinforcer immediately after another. Here then is a case where the positive reinforcer acts as an S^{Δ} for immediate responding. The high rate towards the end of the interval is maintained, since in the past the animal's reinforcement occurred when it was responding rapidly. Thus, here the stimulus conditions surrounding the time of reinforcement (the S^{D}) are provided by the animal's own behavior. A VI schedule results in stable behavior which is marked by its steady moderate rate, i.e., the cumulative curves exhibit slopes which are typically not too high but constant. Since the interval between potential reinforcers varies, no temporal discrimination can develop.

Figure 3-6 presents fixed ratio performance of a pigeon under FR 210:1 on the left and under FR 900:1 at the right. As can be seen, FR schedules produce typically steady behavior at high rates with short pauses immediately after receipt of the reinforcer. Unlike the relatively long pause after reinforcement which characterizes FI behavior, the brevity of the pause characterizing FR behavior reflects the fact that a pause in this instance postpones the next reinforcer, since it leaves less time for emission of the requisite number of responses for the next reinforcer to be forthcoming.

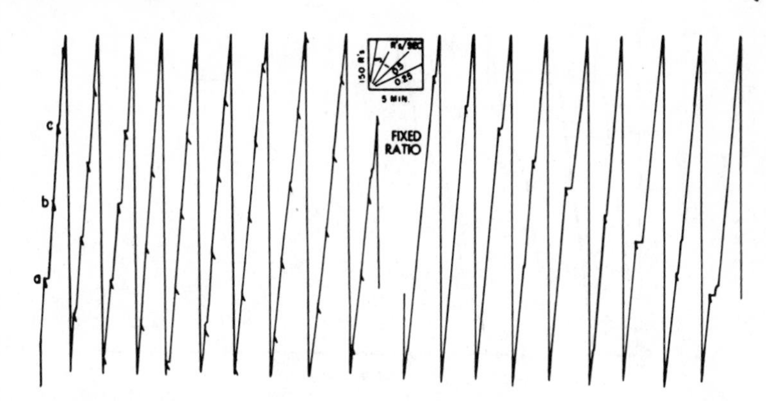

Fig. 3-6. Typical performance by a pigeon under fixed-ratio reinforcement. At the left every 210th response is reinforced; at the right every 900th response. (Skinner, 1957 (a), Fig. 4.)

Variable ratio schedules of reinforcement eliminate post-reinforcement pauses almost completely and generate very high response rates. Figure 3-7 presents some extinction data taken from an animal reinforced on a VR 110:1, meaning that, on the average, 110 responses had to be emitted before a reinforcer was administered; the range of the actual number of responses between successive reinforcers varied in this case from 0 to 500. The high steady rate despite the long periods of no reinforcement is characteristic of this schedule.

Still another schedule of importance is called DRL (differential reinforcement of low rates). For this schedule, the reinforcement contingency consists of the emission of a response only after a fixed time has elapsed after the immediately preceding response. If the animal responds before the interval is up, timing of the interval begins again. This schedule produces quite low, but steady, response rates.

A recent development which has made excellent use of the single organism has been the establishment of procedures for producing entirely different response repertoires within a single organism. *Multiple* schedules consist of subschedules (components) which can be brought to bear on the behavior of the organism by changing from one discriminative stimulus to another. The basic procedure is the same as the one employed in the discrimination procedure.

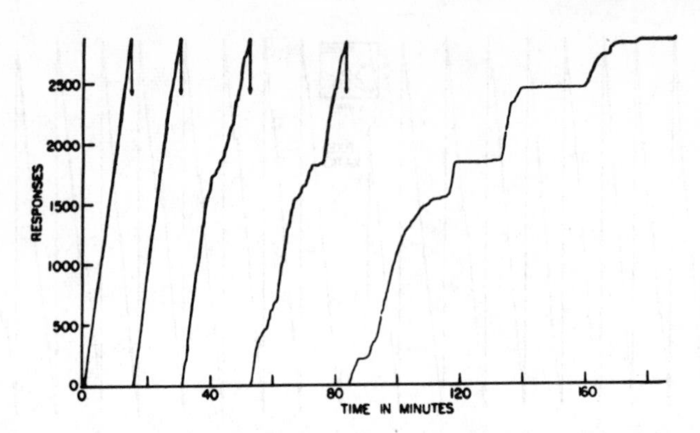

Fig. 3-7. Extinction after variable-ratio reinforcement. The mean ratio was 110 responses per reinforcement. The record has been broken into segments. (Skinner, 1953 (b), Fig. 10.)

Instead of merely reinforcing in the presence of one stimulus and not another, the multiple schedule consists of components where the reinforcement contingencies differ from one another as in FI, VR, DRL, or where FR's of different values make up the various components, etc. Combinations of schedules have been useful in the study of the process of conditioned reinforcement. A *tandem* schedule, for example, consists of a particular sequence of component schedules in which, with the exception of the last component, the consequences of successive components are none other than the response rate (which acts as the response-produced conditioned reinforcement) controlled by the next component of the schedule. In a *chained* schedule, the same reinforcement contingency holds as in the tandem schedule, except that the changeover from one component to the next is signalled by a stimulus (which becomes a conditioned reinforcer) associated with that schedule. These schedules are of particular importance with respect to understanding human behavior (as well as animal behavior) because it is quite clear that people behave differently depending upon the particular circumstances in which they find themselves. The tandem and chained schedules, which involve a particular sequence of different components, are of significance with regard to such typically human behavior as language. The fact that complicated schedules of sequential behavior can be produced, together with the fact that such behavior is more stable under conditions of intermittent than continuous reinforcement, makes behavior theory an eminently successful system for the explanation of the behavior of organisms in nature. Thus here, as in our previous discussions, the two important factors which stand out are the discriminative stimulus and the reinforcement contingency. By switching the color of the light from blue to yellow, the experimenter can change the pigeon's behavior from typical VR behavior to typical FI behavior; by switching from yellow to red he can get the animal to stop responding altogether, and so forth.

In his review of the area of chaining and conditioned reinforcement, Kelleher (1966) interpreted Ferster's (1958) greater success in reducing the error rate of a chimpanzee performing a complex task when he reinforced it on a FR 33 schedule (achieving 98 per cent correct responses) than when he reinforced it on a crf schedule (achieving 80 per cent correct responses), by appealing to a finding by Herrnstein (1961) that intermittency introduces greater stereotypy. This greater stereotypy might well produce the sort of consistency necessary for the execution of a complex response.

Another type of schedule, concurrent operants, has recently been the subject of some experimental examination. Concurrent operants consist of two or more operant responses which can be emitted, either simultaneously or in rapid alternation, without interfering with each other. Typically, this means that two separate manipulanda (response devices) are made available to the animal. The possibility of changing from one response to another allows one to deal with the changeover as a separate response, if the experimenter so desires. In a review of research on concurrent operants, Catania (1966) concluded that, with appropriate programming, one could make the rates of concurrent responses independent of each other. On the other hand, it is possible to demonstrate that the consequences of one response can influence the rate of response of other responses. We shall have occasion later to see how reinforcement of one response may be used indirectly to control the frequency of occurrence of other responses in a behavior therapy situation.

Mention should be made of the fact that, generally speaking, the scheduling of intermittent conditioned reinforcement has an effect similar to the scheduling of intermittent primary reinforcement, namely, greater resistance to extinction.

Much more work has been done on schedules of reinforcement than can be profitably discussed here. However, this brief discussion should make clear the complexity of behavior and the exquisiteness of control over behavior which it has been found possible to engender by scheduling.

Response Class and Response Variability. So far we have spoken about individual responses. A more exact usage would have required the term "response class" to be substituted for the term "response" in many cases. In an early paper, Skinner (1935) referred to the generic nature of stimulus and response. An operant response class may be defined as a number of responses which have in common the fact that they all produce the same consequence or are controlled by the same reinforcement contingency. Thus, a response class may consist of responses which differ from each other in many respects, sometimes quite radically. As Skinner pointed out, such a concept of responses differs quite a bit from the typical physiological reflex or even the typical respondent where responses are very much alike. A definition of responses in terms of a response class means that an organism's reactions are measured on the basis of functional rather than topographical properties. Taking the example of the response class of bar pressing, we can demonstrate how two responses which are very similar topographically do not belong to the same response class, while two other responses which are very different, are members of the same response class. Applying the above definition of response class to bar pressing, it becomes apparent that the one property which all response members must share is the ability to activate the food magazine. If the rat presses the bar with its right front paw, but not with enough force to activate the food magazine, he will not get any food, his response not qualifying for membership in the same class as other responses which did activate the food magazine. If the rat executes the same response with enough force to activate the food magazine, then food will be forthcoming. Other responses, consisting of gnawing at the bar, pressing with the left hind paw, or even swatting the bar with the tail, would all belong to the same response class provided they all activated the food magazine. Only the functional similarity of the consequence of responses is critical for response class definition. It should be noted that, being defined on this basis, response classes may differ from one organism to another and from one time to another. Certainly the variety of overlapping and changing response classes is greatest in the verbal behavior of human beings.

Interesting as the concept of response class is, it seems to have stimulated little research, probably because the primary work in behavior theory has been devoted to finding lawful variation of behavior as a function of a number of independent variables. The dependent variable of response rate, which in fact is based on the concept of counting instances of occurrence of a response class, gave rise to so much lawful data with so little effort that only a very few investigators went beyond the counting of responses. Certain problems have remained unsolved on the basis of these data, however, namely, a scientific description of the process of shaping responses (response differentiation), an account of response generalization, and an account of the changes in response topography which accompany the changes occurring in rate due to the application of different schedules of reinforcement.

The first of a series of extensive studies, and one which we have described before, on the exact nature of the responses making up a response class was undertaken by Antonitis (1951). In a later study, Notterman (1959) measured the amount of force exerted by each response and found, as did Antonitis, a decrease in response variability with conditioning, and an increase with extinction. His data (Figure 3-8) show, in addition, that during conditioning (crf) there is stabilization of response force at a time when response rate is still increasing. Herrnstein (1961) used pigeons to study the variability of location of a pecking response as a function of intermittent reinforcement (VI 3 min.). He found a marked reduction in variability of the response from the continuous reinforcement to the intermittent reinforcement schedule. Still another study was carried out by Hefferline and Keenan (1961), who conditioned a thumb contraction too small for the subject to detect. The response class was specified in terms of a 2-microvolt wide electromyographic signal. Figure 3-9 demonstrates the progress of the reinforced response class, as well as related classes, through the conditions of operant level (a period of

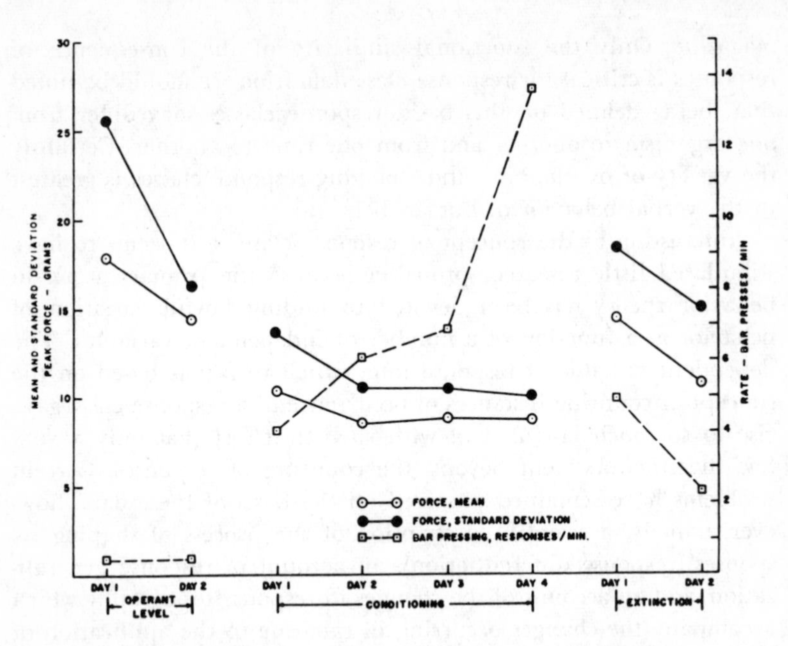

Fig. 3-8. Comparison of force (mean and SD) and rate of bar pressing. (Notterman, 1959, Fig. 6.)

time in which rate of response was measured but not yet reinforced), two short periods of conditioning, a period of extinction, and another period of operant level. Inspection of the figure reveals response generalization (also sometimes called induction) taking place at the beginning of conditioning (Conditioning 1). It is shown by the progressively greater response rate as the response class becomes more and more similar to the reinforced response class. (The response pattern of the 1 microvolt response class is to be ignored because it is influenced by artifacts.) During Conditioning 2 there is evidence for response differentiation during the course of which response classes other than the reinforced one become much less involved. In extinction there is a new increase in occurrence of non–reinforced response classes. This can be taken as evidence that an increase in response variability occurs from conditioning to extinction. The variability found in extinction is quite different from that found in operant level. From an adaptive point of view this difference is easily explained, since only in extinction would there be reason for sustained "search" for the response class that might be followed by the reinforcer that had been forthcoming during conditioning. Another study concerning response differentiation was carried out by Notterman and Mintz (1962). They

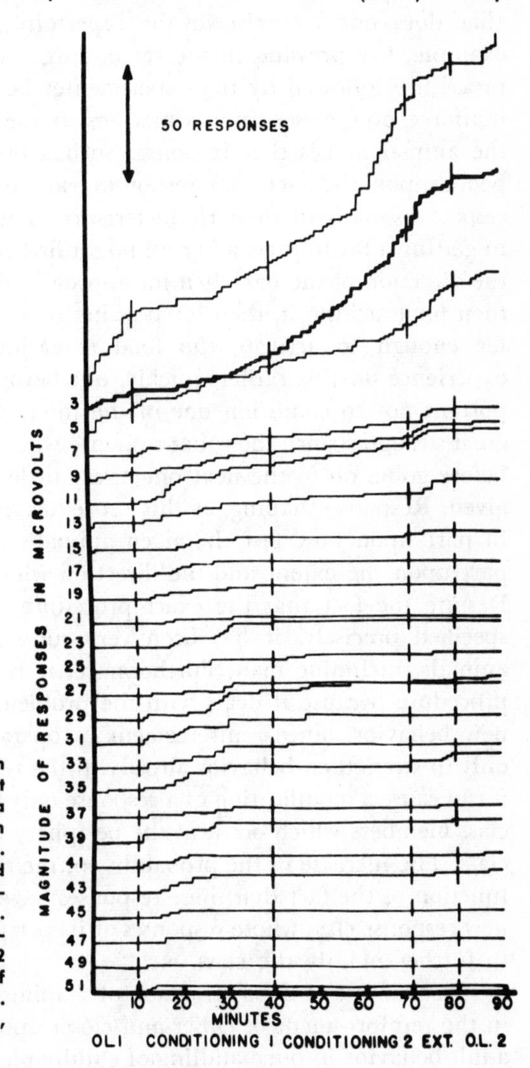

Fig. 3-9. Amplitude-induction gradient of a small operant (thumb contraction) for a single human subject in an escape-avoidance situation. OL 1 and OL 2 are initial and final operant-level determinations, and EXT is extinction. Values on the ordinate represent midpoints of steps 2 microvolts wide in size of electromyographic signal. (Hefferline and Keenan, 1961, Fig. 1.)

successfully demonstrated that rats could be trained to emit responses of two different ranges of force under the control of "light-on" and "light-off" stimuli.

All of these studies give us some insight into the process of response differentiation. When it is necessary to produce a response that does not yet exist in the repertoire of the animal, as for example, bar pressing in the rat or target striking in the fish, the procedure followed by the experimenter becomes an art. He must reinforce ever closer approximations to the desired response until the animal makes that response. Such a procedure, of course, depends upon the fact that responses vary from time to time with respect to many of their characteristics. Thus, if we are interested in getting a rat to press a bar we might first reinforce it for facing in the direction of the bar, then for approaching it, then for sniffing it, then for touching it, then for pressing it, and finally for pressing it far enough to activate the food magazine. Experimenters with experience do this rather quickly, but beyond saying that it is important not to condition one of the intermediate responses in too great strength (since then that response will have to be extinguished before going on to the next one), very little concrete advice can be given. Response shaping, as this procedure is termed, must depend in part upon how fast the given animal's response varies, and in part upon the extent and the direction which that variation takes. Despite the fact that the exact procedure cannot at this time be specified precisely, it has been very successful for a great many animals, including man. Furthermore, it is also a very important procedure because it deals with the problem of the instatement of new behavior. Since reinforcement in operant conditioning serves only to strengthen behavior already in the repertoire of the animal, it can cause a modification of a response only by reinforcing response class members which occur at the periphery of the current response class. The increase in the probability of the reinforced responses is a function of the fact that these responses have become members of a new response class whose responses at its periphery can be reinforced to further modify the class, etc.

An example of the application of shaping procedures can be seen in the reinforcement of closer and closer approximations to desired adult behavior in our handling of children as they grow up, i.e., the responses which adults expect of children are allowed to change slowly. Reinforcers are administered throughout the process. When the adult withholds reinforcement, waiting for a response to occur which is closer to the adult response than the child can then emit, extinction sets in. The problem which then arises is not different from the one which the experimenter encounters when he halts his reinforcement to wait for a response which cannot yet occur. In both cases reinforcement must be administered to responses which have a high enough probability of occurrence so that extinction does not occur before the opportunity for reinforcement presents itself.

Lest it be assumed that response differentiation is the only method available for the production of new responses, it must be pointed out that the conditioning of imitation is another. Miller and Dollard (1941) studied imitative learning at a time when it was necessary to lay to rest the concept of imitation as an instinct. Relatively little work was done after that until the last decade (cf. Bandura & Walters, 1963), when imitation was studied in relation to social, child, and abnormal psychology. Imitation is best considered as a response class characterized by the special property of matching the response of the imitator to the response of the organism being imitated. There is no question but that in the life of most animals (including man) imitation is reinforced (e.g., seeking food, avoiding a predator in animals, looking at something of general interest, or avoiding some potential misfortune), as is evidenced in the collection and movement of crowds.

Baer and Sherman (1964) demonstrated the acquisition of a response class of imitation in young children. A puppet performed all the acts that were to be imitated. The children were then reinforced for imitating head nodding, opening and closing the mouth, and making nonsense statements—but they were never reinforced for bar pressing. The response measured throughout the experiment was the rate of bar pressing. The results showed that when imitation of all the responses except the bar presses were reinforced, the children imitated the bar pressing as well, even though it had never been specifically reinforced. Furthermore, when the puppet stopped reinforcing non-bar pressing responses, the imitative bar presses decreased. This experiment ingeniously presents evidence for the existence of a response class of imitation, a class whose membership is defined only by the fact that reinforcement is forthcoming for making responses which match another organism's responses.

Motivation. The term motivation is generally used to cover a multitude of phenomena. It is a term which psychologists have come to realize is imbued with what might be called surplus meaning. It is the state most often blamed for behavioral deficits, as when we say that a bright child who is not learning in school is not motivated. It is also a term sometimes confused with the term reinforcement, as when we say that a teacher does not motivate her class, meaning by that that the teacher does not set up appropriate reinforcement contingencies. The concept of motivation is also closely associated with psychoanalytic theory where we are told that behavior, or the lack of it, is always motivated and where, if we cannot locate the motive, it is said to be unconscious. Among some learning theorists the apparent usefulness of the concept of drive has given rise to the concept of secondary, or conditioned, drives to coordinate with secondary, or conditioned, reinforcers.

Thus, the term motivation is sometimes used as a label in place of an analysis of the cause of a behavioral deficit, as with a child who does not learn. It is sometimes confused with the more easily specified activity of the reinforcing behavior (or lack of same) of the teacher. It is sometimes not demonstrable, but must be inferred, as in psychoanalytic theory. Finally, it is sometimes posited simply to round out a theory which, initially making the observation that the effectiveness of primary reinforcers can be modified by primary drives, further states that there must be a parallel phenomenon of secondary drives exerting the same effect upon secondary reinforcers.

Having listed the instances in which the term motivation is incorrectly used, it is necessary to explain how part of this concept can fruitfully be retained in the systematic analysis of behavior. Again making use of operational definitions, we can specify a set of operations, describable by the term *drive,* which influences the reinforcing value of a reinforcer. Thus, it is possible, by means of deprivation, i.e., by depriving the animal of food for a given period of time, to make food a more powerful reinforcer. On the other hand, it is also possible to reduce the power of a reinforcer by *satiation,* i.e., feeding the animal before the experiment begins. Food and water deprivation are probably the most common in use. Other drives are also utilized, however, each of them having its own set of operations. Thus, the introduction of aversive stimuli like electric shock, loud noise, a bright light, and low temperatures are all operations which make the termination or avoidance of these aversive stimuli reinforcing.

Early studies on the effect of drive on operant behavior seemed straightforward enough. Up to a certain level, in studies using food as the reinforcer, an increase in drive (stipulated in terms of hours of food deprivation or percentage reduction in body weight) caused an increase in general activity and therefore an increase in response rate. Both the drive concept and the operant response have turned out to be more complicated, however. For example, the application of the drive concept to different animals varies. While rats and mice appear to show definite temporal perferences for feeding times, fish appear to distribute their feeding behavior fairly evenly over time (Teitelbaum, 1966). On the other side of the drive-response rate relation is the complication introduced by the important variable of the schedule of reinforcement. We have already indicated that, by the judicious use of discriminative stimuli in conjunction with schedules of reinforcement, we can produce differences in behavior as large as those which were formerly attributed to differences in drive level. But perhaps more important, the effect of drive level varies in a complex way with the schedule of reinforcement employed. Clark (1958) was able to show a lawful relation between number of hours of food deprivation and rate of response on rats reinforced on three different VI schedules (Figure 3-10). Notice the negatively accelerated increase in response rate as a function of number of hours of deprivation. On the other hand, the relation between deprivation and FR performance appears to be quite different. Sidman and Stebbins (1954) observed FR in the cat, monkey, and rat. Figure 3-11 presents the stabilized performance of these three animals over extended periods of time so that the animals either reached, or came close to, satiation. The data represented in the figure are notable for the fact that as the animals become satiated there is not a general reduction of response rate but rather a specific increase in length and number of post-reinforce-

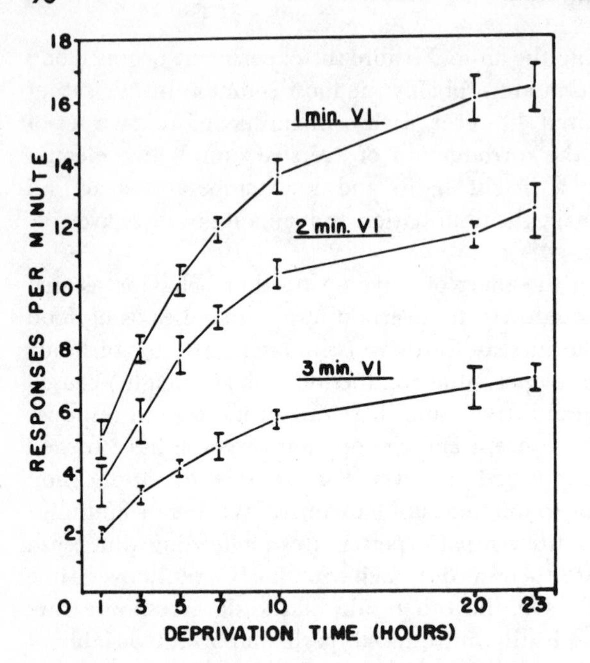

Fig. 3-10. Average rate of responding as a function of deprivation time for each schedule. (Clark, 1958, Fig. 1.)

ment pauses. In order to test this effect more carefully the monkey and the rat were fed before they were placed in the experimental chamber. Figure 3-12 shows again an alternation of maximum response rate and post-reinforcement pause. The response rate in between the post-reinforcement pauses is the same whether they are pre-fed or not. This effect is best explained by the fact that a FR schedule has the characteristic that reinforcement occurs when response rate is high. This in turn further increases response rate by means of the fact that, once a run of responses begins, the increasing number by itself becomes an important S^D for the occurrence of S^R. Under these circumstances the run is completed to the point of receiving the S^R. The effect of drive must therefore be looked for, not only in the rate, but also in the pattern of response. Morse (1966, p. 79) summarizes the state of this area of research: ". . . an orderly relation between rate of responding and deprivation is not obtained in many experiments involving intermittent reinforcment (Ferster & Skinner, 1957). Deprivation is most important during the early stages of conditioning when strong conditioned

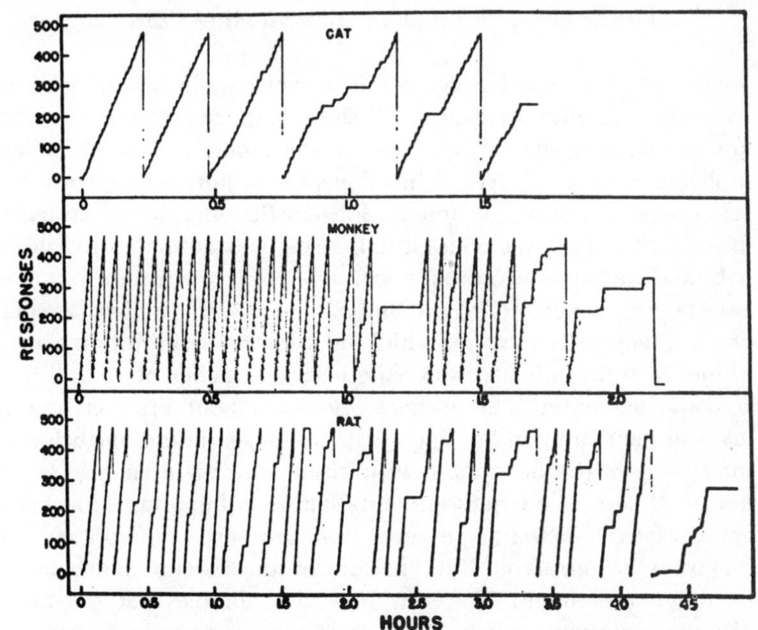

Fig. 3-11. Sample cumulative response records under fixed-ratio schedules of reinforcement. Ratio of responses to reinforcements is 25:1 for the rat and monkey, and 20:1 for the cat. The short diagonal strokes indicate reinforcements. (Sidman and Stebbins, 1954, Fig. 1.)

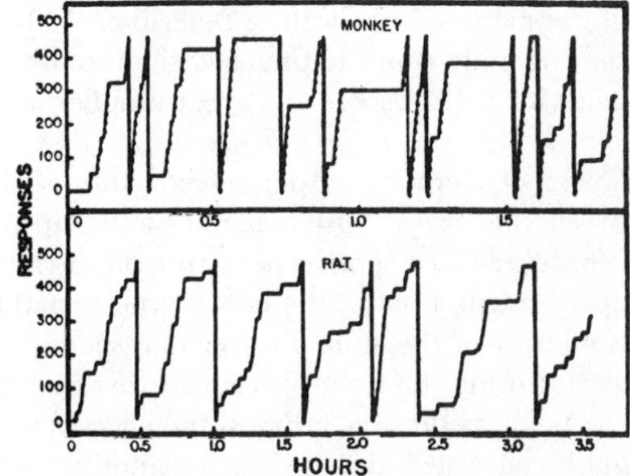

Fig. 3-12. Sample records following prefeeding. Animals and schedules are the same as those in Fig. 3-11. (Sidman and Stebbins, 1954, Fig. 2.)

behavior is not yet developed." He also points out that the actual scheduling of food and water intake may be as important in determining the effectiveness of reinforcers as their quality.

The Scope of the Operant Conditioning Procedure

Types of Animals. Inspection of recent psychological journals covering animal experiments will show that, despite some favorite animals such as the rat, the pigeon, the monkey, and the college sophomore, the range has included elephants, horses, cats, fruit flies, grasshoppers, worms, octopuses, fish, turtles, dolphins, parakeets, mice, chicks, dogs, raccoons, sheep, goats, and adults and children with and without various pathologies, physical or mental. In a most entertaining paper by Breland and Breland (1961), we find a report of a commercial enterprise which used operant conditioning techniques to train animals to execute a large number of complicated response sequences. The authors complain about the fact that in many of their animals they find instinctive or species-specific behavior interfering with the smooth acquisition and maintenance of behavior. There is no question but that it is important to choose appropriate responses as one goes from one species to another and that one take into account the "natural" responses emitted or released by different animals. However, it is also notable that the range of types of animals which can be conditioned is extremely large as evidenced by the fact that the Brelands were able to condition 38 species including some 6,000 individual organisms. Among the few failures of operant conditioning is its application to the behavior of the paramecium (Katz & Deterline, 1958). Nevertheless, it is clear that operant conditioning has significance for the modification of behavior with respect to a great number of animals.

Types of Responses. Sometimes a line of distinction is drawn between the terms "instrumental" and "operant." The former term is restricted to responses occurring on discrete trials, as when a rat is put through a maze; the latter term, sometimes called free operant, is used when the animal is free to respond at any time. In this book, we are using the term operant to cover both meanings.

As far as the generality of the effectiveness of operant conditioning is concerned, despite the Brelands' warning to the contrary with respect to species-specific behavior, there appears to be an increase in the types of responses which have shown themselves amenable to operant conditioning. At this point, research has been extended, at least in man, from motor responses, through observing responses, to verbal behavior. Perhaps even more significant has been the extension of the operant conditioning paradigm to responses formerly considered to be respondent. Thus, vocalizations of animals once viewed only as respondents, i.e., as emotional responses, have since shown themselves to be amenable to operant conditioning. Salzinger and Waller (1962), who successfully conditioned barking by using the operant paradigm, suggested: "The terms operant and respondent probably should be restricted to conditioned rather than unconditioned behavior, since the *a priori* classification of behavior into types lacks experimental validity and contributes little to behavioral analysis" (Salzinger & Waller, 1962, p. 389). On the basis of current research, one is tempted to go a step further and suggest that the restrictions brought about by the application of the two terms to behavior, prior to experimental work with both conditioning procedures, have prevented the kind of interesting research which is finally being carried out now (cf. Prokasy, 1965; Kimmel, 1967; Rescorla & Solomon, 1967). Recent research has shown that heart rate, the vasomotor reflex, salivation, intestinal contractions, and the galvanic skin response (GSR), all until recently viewed as typically respondent, are conditionable within the framework of the operant paradigm. The early restriction of operant conditioning to skeletal responses under the control of the somatic nervous system appears to have been lifted. The only difference left between operant and respondent conditioning appears to be that the critical stimulus (sometimes called the reinforcing stimulus), i.e., the US, must precede the response in respondent conditioning, while in operant conditioning the critical stimulus, i.e., S^R, must follow the response. In purely operational terms, for respondent conditioning the experimenter must present the US after the CS in accordance with an experimental program and independent of the behavior of the subject, whereas the scheduling of the S^R in operant conditioning, must be related to the behavior. The fact that only a procedural distinction remains has led to renewed interest in varying types and degrees of operant-respondent overlap.

Operant-Respondent Overlap and Interaction

We have already mentioned one area of articulation between the types of learning and that is the area of the establishment of conditioned reinforcers. That discussion, as you recall, led to the tentative conclusion that conditioned reinforcers, used in operant conditioning, are most likely established through the respondent conditioning paradigm.

In the above discussion it was pointed out that the same response class can be conditioned according to both conditioning paradigms. We have already cited examples of autonomic responses which can be conditioned operantly. On the other hand, eyelid conditioning (Prokasy, 1965) is a good example of a skeletal response which can be conditioned by the respondent paradigm. All of these experiments, nevertheless, leave unresolved the possibility that one of the types of response actually mediates the conditioning process of the other. Thus, the respondent conditioning process which established the conditioned reinforcer in operant conditioning furnishes one example. In a similar way, investigators have suggested that some form of operant mediation occurs to explain the supposed operant conditioning of autonomic responses. In order to be certain that the autonomic response is not *indirectly* influenced through the conditioning of an operant, curare agents have been utilized to immobilize the skeletal musculature of the organism. Operant conditioning of autonomic responses under these conditions has been found to be successful (Miller & DiCara, 1967). Nevertheless, the hypothesized interaction of operants and respondents has provoked investigators to carry out a number of systematic studies of the phenomenon.

The most obvious approach to the problem of interaction of operant and respondent conditioning is to measure both in the same experiment. Thus, in the typical operant conditioning situation where, for example, the rat's response is followed by food and where typically only the bar press response is measured, it is nevertheless the case that the animal is also simultaneously subjected to the respondent conditioning paradigm. Review of such experiments (Rescorla & Solomon, 1967) has suggested that the operant response may well act as the CS for conditioned salivation under some experimental conditions; under other conditions conditioned salivation has been found to precede the operant response. Clearly, experiments can be done to study both types of response classes but the exact interaction is not yet clear.

Another interaction of some interest is the effect of a conditioned respondent on an ongoing stabilized operant. Estes and Skinner (1941) called one such conditioned respondent "anxiety." Later, when Hunt and Brady (1951) embarked upon a series of studies on this phenomenon, they called it a conditioned emotional response (CER). More recent nomenclature refers to the phenomenon as conditioned suppression, a term more descriptive of the actual behavior. Inspection of Figure 3-13 shows the typical effect of the sequence of stimuli CS (tone)–US (electric shock) when this sequence is superimposed on ongoing behavior. First the rats were reinforced on a FI 4-minute schedule of reinforcement. When the resulting behavior had stabilized, the sequence of tone-shock (first of 3 minutes and then of 5 minutes duration) was superimposed on the operant behavior. Despite the fact that there is no response contingency involved in the conditioned suppression paradigm, the rats stopped responding during the CS–US interval with continued exposure to the sequence. Note that the slope during the period marked T (tone–CS)...... S (shock–UCS) becomes progressively

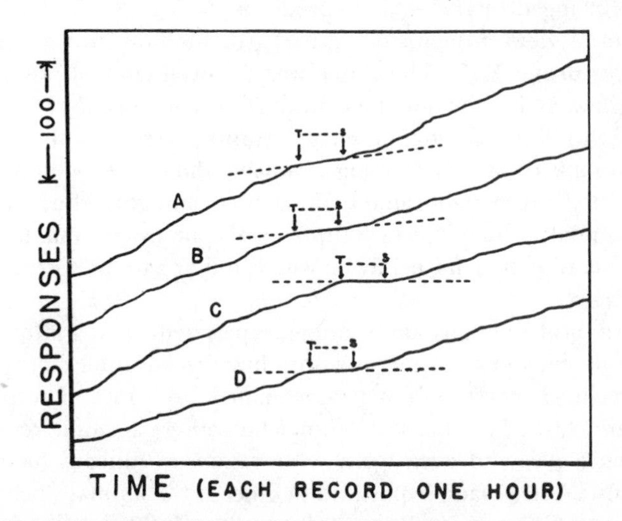

Fig. 3-13. Reduction in rate of responding during successive periods of anxiety. Averaged curves for six rats on four consecutive days. By the third or fourth day responding practically ceases during the presentation of the tone. (Estes and Skinner, 1941, Fig. 2.)

shallower until it is parallel to the abscissa, indicating that the animal has stopped responding altogether. The conditioned suppression paradigm consists, therefore, of a respondent conditioning procedure, the effect of which is measured by its influence in depressing ongoing operant behavior.

An analagous sequence was reported in a very interesting experiment by Herrnstein and Morse (1957) who showed that the superimposition of a CS–US respondent sequence, where the US was free food, on an ongoing operant maintained on a DRL schedule of 5 minutes, caused an increase (conditioned elation) in rate at the onset of the CS. One must conclude that the effect of the superimposition of a non-contingent CS–US sequence on ongoing operant behavior is such as to greatly influence that operant behavior.

SUMMARY

This chapter dealt with the operant conditioning paradigm. According to it, behavior is modified by its consequences. Operant behavior typically acts upon its environment and subsequently becomes changed by the effect it produces.

A short review of the historical background of operant conditioning disclosed that E. L. Thorndike was the originator of the law of effect, a law which, in modified form, is still in use. Early experiments with the puzzle box, maze, and runway were described and a listing of some of the disadvantages of using those types of apparatus were pointed out. Notable among these disadvantages is the handling of the animals which the techniques make necessary and the discontinuous trial by trial behavior which the apparatus forces upon the animals.

The typical operant conditioning experiment which allows the continuous emission of free operants has the advantage of giving rise to a direct measure of behavior, namely, the rate of response. Furthermore, the fact that the Skinner box allows a simple response to be made over and over again without any extraneous handling of the animal has made it possible to observe the animal's behavior under many different conditions for great lengths of time by the use of the latest electronic devices for programming and recording. The recording devices include the cumulative recorder which allows the experimenter to monitor the animal's behavior as it is emitted.

A primary reinforcer was distinguished from a conditioned reinforcer in terms of the former's independence of, and the latter's dependence on, the history of the organism. A positive reinforcer was distinguished from a negative one in that the former strengthens responses (by increasing their rate) which produce it, while the latter strengthens responses which postpone or terminate it. A negative reinforcer applied to behavior (usually under a positive reinforcement contingency) directly acts as a punishing stimulus by reducing the probability of responses it follows. In addition to the primary reinforcers whose effectiveness can be increased or reduced by drive operations such as deprivation and satiation, there are sensory reinforcers which act as positive reinforcers simply by virtue of exerting moderate changes in the sensory environment. Additional primary reinforcers appear to be complex events, such as the opportunity to view a busy laboratory, to manipulate a mechanical puzzle, or to receive "contact comfort."

Different operant conditioning paradigms were reviewed and diagrammed, including that for positive reinforcement ($s \ldots R \rightarrow S^{+R}$) and that for negative reinforcement (escape— $S^{-R} \ldots R \rightarrow S^{-\bar{R}}$; avoidance–free–operant $s \ldots R \rightarrow \overline{S^{-R}}$ or discriminated $S^{-D} \ldots R \rightarrow \overline{S^{-R}}$). The punishment paradigm was shown as $s \ldots R \begin{smallmatrix} \nearrow S^{+R} \\ \searrow S^{-R} \end{smallmatrix}$

The final paradigm discussed, i.e., omission training, was diagrammed as $s \ldots \bar{R} \rightarrow S^{+R}$.

The process of extinction was described simply as being the same as the conditioning paradigm without the reinforcing stimuli. Resistance to extinction was shown to vary as a function of number of reinforcements; its relation to response effort appeared to be more complicated. Other effects of extinction on response topography were briefly discussed. Finally, discussion of the relation of extinction to forgetting showed that what is generally meant by forgetting occurs either when the responses in question or similar responses are emitted in the absence of reinforcement, or when new incompatible responses are conditioned to the old stimuli, thus reducing the probability of occurrence of the old responses because of their incompatibility with the new ones.

Evidence for stimulus generalization and discrimination was presented. Very complicated discriminations can be conditioned and, by the application of the principle of gradualness, discrimination behavior can be set up in such a way that the animals never respond during S^{Δ}.

Investigations of generalization of punishment showed that immediate generalization of the suppression effect takes place at first, with eventual recovery occurring both in the periods when punishment is given and when it is not. The effect of punishing stimuli was explored, not only in terms of their suppressive effects, but also in terms of their discriminative effects, thus pointing out the complicated aspects of punishment.

Comparison of the generalization gradients for appetitive conditioning and avoidance conditioning showed the former to result in a steeper gradient.

Conditioned reinforcers acquire their reinforcing value through association with primary reinforcers. Although there still appears to be some controversy about it, present consensus suggests that it is the respondent conditioning paradigm which produces the conditioned reinforcer. Conditioned reinforcers, like the primary ones, can be either positive or negative. The generalized reinforcer is a conditioned reinforcer which has been associated with a number of different primary reinforcers. The superiority of its power over other conditioned reinforcers and its obvious ubiquity in human society makes it a very important variable indeed for our subsequent discussions.

Schedules of reinforcement were discussed next, along with a consideration of their implications for exerting increased control over behavior. Intermittent scheduling, which is the way reinforcers are presented under natural conditions, results in greater resistance to extinction than reinforcers delivered on a continuous basis. Furthermore, the use of schedules under the control of discriminative stimuli gives rise to differences in behavior at least as large as those which resulted from different conditions of motivation. The schedules described consisted of those where the delivery of reinforcers is contingent on the number of responses—fixed ratio, variable ratio, DRL (reinforcement in this case is given whenever a response is emitted a minimal time period after the last response) and those where delivery is contingent on the emission of a response a given time period after the last reinforcement—fixed interval and variable interval. These different schedules produce characteristic patterns and rates of response. Recent research has combined different schedules of reinforcement in the form of multiple schedules, the components of which can be put into effect by presenting the discriminative stimulus associated with each of them. Other combinations of schedules (tandem and chained) have been made by arranging the components in a set sequence, thus simulating the kind of complex sequences found in much of human behavior.

The discussion of the concept of response class stressed the importance of the factor of response variability in the shaping of new response classes. In addition to response differentiation, reinforcement of imitation was cited as a method of instating new behavior.

The concept of motivation was examined in terms of its common usages. The advantages of stripping it of surplus meanings were explicated. The concept of motivation was pared down to the set of operations used to describe the term drive. As such, the concept is used to designate that set of operations which influences the reinforcing value of a reinforcer by increasing or reducing its effectiveness. It was pointed out that the influence of drive on behavior is more evident in the process of acquisition of behavior than in its maintenance. The effect of drive on behavior maintained under intermittent reinforcement schedules appears to be considerably more complex.

Examination of the scope of operant conditioning has shown that it is applicable to a very large range of organisms. Furthermore, response classes which were thought to be conditionable only by the respondent paradigm have shown themselves to be conditionable by the operant paradigm as well.

The general problem of operant-respondent overlap and interaction was explored. Experiments measuring both response types in the same situation revealed complex interactions. Finally, the effect of the superimposition of a respondent on ongoing operant behavior was described.

4

Ethology

The variables which control behavior are clearly not all of one kind While we do not pretend to familiarize the reader with all the relevant variables, it is important that he gain an appreciation of at least some of the variables determining behavior other than those typically studied by psychologists. Ethology, to which we have already referred in Chapter 1, consists of the study of some of these variables. In an attempt to facilitate communication between the fields of psychology and ethology, Verplanck (1957) compiled a glossary of terms for use by workers in both areas. Being a part of biology, ethology is concerned with behavior that is controlled by variables related to the structure and function of the animal's body. For the same reason, it is also concerned with the comparative study of behavior, i.e., with behavior which is significant with respect to the survival of the individual and the species. One can find an interesting parallel between Darwin's theory of evolution and the process of response differentiation in operant conditioning. An analogy can be drawn between Thorndike's felicitous phrase that the reinforced response "is selected by success" and the selection of animals for survival. The difference lies in the following: The reinforcement mechanism both modifies *and* selects the responses which are to survive, whereas in the mechanism for the survival of animals, selection takes place through the environmental mechanism while the modification is caused by a genetic change.

Basic Ethological Concepts

We have already noted the relation between the ethological study of behavior and the theory of evolution. Because of the consequent interest in classifying animals phylogenetically on the basis of behavior, ethologists have stressed the study of behavior which is species-specific and therefore relatively invariant. This means that the ethologist's major interest has been in innate behavior as it is released by the natural environment in which the animal lives. The system of classification of body parts by structure and function which is used in comparative anatomy has been adopted for use in the study of comparative behavior. The tracing of similarities has been accomplished in terms of the two broad classes of homologues and analogues. A homologue in behavior results from a similarity in structure and is supposed to be due to a common ancestor. Thus, the imprinting responses of following in a duckling and a chick (examples are from Gray, 1966) are examples of homologues. These related animals manifest the behavior of following the first large moving object in their visual field after they are hatched. An example of an analogue is the behavior of following in the birds already mentioned and the human infant's smiling response towards its mother. The two responses are obviously quite different structurally but they can be described as similar in that they both consist of orientations and social acts. In other words, the similarity in the analogue is based upon considerations of function.

Two other concepts of importance with respect to the relation of behavior to the theory of evolution are the genetic basis of behavior and the adaptive basis of behavior.

Behavior and Genetics

In psychology, the argument of nature vs. nurture, or genetic endowment vs. environment, has been waged many times. To this day the argument still goes on concerning the influence of the two factors on such presumed classes of behavior as, for example, intelligence, despite the fact that it is generally accepted that environment and genetic effects interact in a multiplicative manner to give rise to the behavior. This means that either the absence of the appropriate gene (essentially the blueprint, or the program for the occurrence of the behavior directly or through sensory control) or the absence of the appropriate environment (essentially the external conditions that promote the occurrence of the behavior directly or through the development of the sensory apparatus) would make it impossible for the behavior to occur, since if either of two values of a multiplicative relationship is zero, the product must be zero.

One of the complications in the study of inheritance of behavior is the fact that it is more difficult to demonstrate the genetic relationship for complex behaviors than for simple behaviors. Thus, while evidence has been collected for the heritability of intelligence, schizophrenia (a form of psychosis), learning ability, and emotionality, the complexity of these behaviors has been such as to elicit different operational definitions from different investigators, with resultant disagreement on conclusion. The heritability of innate behavior, because of its relative invariance over time, and from one member of a species to another, and because of the certainty with which it occurs under a given circumscribed set of conditions, is more easily measured.

Let us look at an experiment by Hirsch and Boudreau (1958), who investigated the heritability of a taxis (an innate response orienting the organism toward or away from something). The experiment dealt with phototaxis, i.e., the tendency to move toward light. Successive generations of fruit flies were run repeatedly through Y-mazes with one arm of the maze being lit and the other not. The 3,424 fruit flies which constituted the sample were selected from successive generations for inbreeding. Flies with a low tendency to respond toward light were mated only to other flies of a similar low tendency, whereas flies of a high tendency to approach light were mated only to other flies of a similar high tendency. The inbreeding was continued over 29 generations with the results as pictured in Figure 4-1. Notice how the two inbred groups of flies separate over successive generations. During generations 10, 11, 12 and 13, mass mating (rather than selective inbreeding) within each group was allowed, and no behavior tests were made. The influence of heredity on the behavior of the flies was demonstrated by the fact that successive generations produced more of a discrepancy in the behavioral tendency, as can be seen in the increased separation of the curves.

Other research in the area of behavioral genetics has demonstrated the importance of the genetic variable in a large variety of animals. In addition, well-known general genetic techniques have been brought to bear on behavior so that some information on the mode of gene action has been collected. Among these general genetic concepts which are beginning to be applied to the analysis of behavior are the estimates of the heritability of the behavior. In the study cited above (Hirsch & Boudreau, 1958), a conservative estimate of the heritability of phototaxis (the proportion of the variance of the

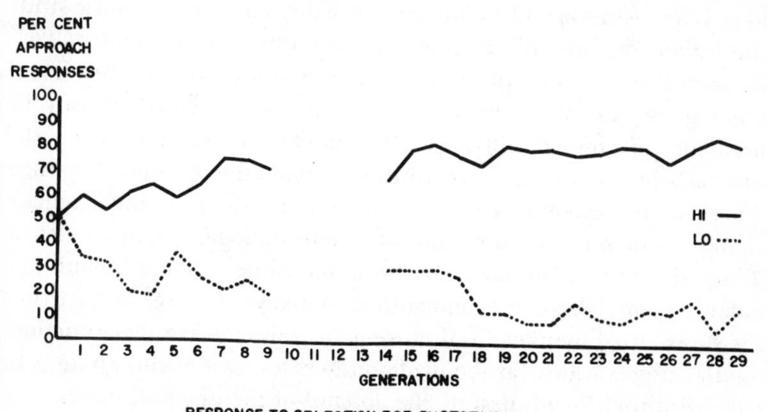

Fig. 4-1. Percentage of trials on which light was approached per generation. (Hirsch and Boudreau, 1958, Fig. 2.)

selected to that of the foundation population) was 57 per cent, meaning that at least 57 per cent of the variation in the phototaxis can be attributed to the genetic variable.

In summary, it can be said that this area has seen an important increase in interest and sophistication in research. The idea that evolutionary pressures exert themselves on behavior has become almost as credible as are their influence on other more physical traits. The interested reader should look at Fuller and Thompson (1960) for additional studies.

Types of Instinctive Behavior

Breland and Breland ascribe some of their problems in conditioning animals to interference by innate behavior patterns: "Thus, learning is not one of nature's most prevalent ways of guaranteeing the preservation and reproduction of the individual or the species. Learning is an advanced 'improvement patent'. . . nature does not bet very heavily on the learning process. . . . There are behaviors, sequences of events, muscular or otherwise, that will fire off in a particular sequence and in a particular sequence only, and they will do so in the presence of very clearly, already predetermined aspects of the environment" (Breland & Breland, 1966). Thus, although, as one moves up the phylogenetic scale the importance of learning looms larger, nevertheless, for a great many animals, we must study the innate patterns of response and stimulus control. Hess (1962) has reviewed the area of ethology for psychologists. The history of ethology begins with the discovery that innate behavior can be used for purposes of phylogenetic comparison. In some cases the innate behavior can be used to differentiate closely related species. These innate responses are apparently more resistant to phylogenetic change than some of the associated morphological characteristics. Thus, short-tailed monkeys perform the same tail movements for balancing on a branch as long-tailed monkeys, despite the fact that the short-tailed monkeys' tail movements cannot have that function. Similar observations can be made on hornless cattle who attempt to fight with their heads despite the absence of the essential horns.

The general division of behavior into types comes from the early ethologists Lorenz and Craig and is still used today: (1) The appetitive and aversive behaviors and (2) the consummatory act. Appetitive or aversive behavior consists of a motor component and an orientation component to specific stimuli—a kinesis or taxis. The consummatory act is a response pattern known for its invariance; it is species specific and is also called the fixed action pattern (FAP). Of interest here with respect to the relation of these behaviors to learned responses is the fact that the appetitive and aversive response classes constitute the operant responses generally conditioned.

There are two types of orienting responses—taxes and kineses (Ratner & Denny, 1964). A kinesis is typically found in invertebrates and is usually defined to consist of undirected motor reactions which are associated with increases in stimulus intensity. An undirected response having to do with the speed of movement is called an *ortho-kinetic* response; one involving frequency of turning is called a *klino-kinetic* response. Although these responses involve undirected movement, this movement does at least make alteration of the animal's situation more probable so that the "sought after" substance is more likely to come within its reach. Thus, the woodlouse, which survives well in an environment of high humidity, remains motionless when in that environment but moves when in an environment of low humidity. In an experiment by Gunn (Gunn, 1937, cited in Ratner and Denny, 1964), it was demonstrated that the woodlouse will, in fact, simply by means of its general increased movement, situate itself in an environment of higher humidity.

Taxes, the other class of orienting response, consist of movements of the animal directly toward, or away from, a particular source of stimulation. There are three different kinds of taxes. The *klino-taxis* involves bending or twisting motions as part of the orientation movement. The second type of taxis is called *tropo-taxis.* This response is found in invertebrates which have pairs of sensory receptors. The sensory receptors guide the movement in such a way that it takes place in that direction which equalizes stimulation on both receptors. Once the animal has turned in the appropriate direction, either towards or away from the stimulation, it keeps going straight in that direction. The third type of taxis is called *telo-taxis.* Telo-taxis depends on a more sophisticated type of invertebrate receptor mechanism, as is found in the compound eye of the bee. In this case, the animal must adjust its response to both the intensity and direction of stimulation.

The kineses and taxes described above are orienting responses unrestrained by the internal conditions of the animal. In that sense they differ from consummatory acts (fixed action patterns) which do depend on the internal conditions (e.g., hormonal balance) of the animal. Furthermore, a taxis is found to precede a consummatory act.

The fixed action pattern consists of a sequence of coordinated movements performed without any learning. It is an invariant pattern, is not equivalent to or composed of reflexes, occurs in animals isolated from other members of their species, is species specific, and is determined by genetic and physiological factors (Hess, 1962).

The Function of the Stimulus in Innate Behavior

We have found in our discussions of both operant and respondent behavior that responses either begin by being under stimulus control (respondent) or can eventually be brought under stimulus control (operant). Instinctive behavior is very much under stimulus control. Both the appetitive and the consummatory responses are controlled by events variously known as *sign stimuli* or *releasers*. Responses to releasers are quite circumscribed and the releasers themselves are typically only a small part (e.g., red color patch) of the natural stimulus (another animal). Although the releaser may impinge on a number of receptors of the animal, only one of these may be that which controls the occurrence of the instinctive response. Some examples of releasers are highly distinctive characteristics like a patch of red color on the breast of a bird, an odor, or a movement of another animal.

Ethologists posit a special mechanism for the reception of the releasers, namely the innate releasing mechanism (I.R.M.). They also postulate an inhibitory block which the I.R.M. removes upon appropriate stimulation by the releaser. The presence of an inhibitory mechanism is postulated as the device necessary to prevent the release of the response with a consequent dissipation of internally produced energy. Because of its selective function upon incoming stimuli, the I.R.M. is responsive to evolutionary pressure. Thus, if the releasers which evoke the behavior do not contribute to the organism's survival, or interfere with it in some way, then the I.R.M. adapts to the new conditions, i.e., changes over generations. In addition, the I.R.M. changes its selectivity for releasers during the life of the individual organism. Hess (1962) discusses two types of increased selectivity of the I.R.M. One type results in a narrowing of the range of stimuli which may act as releasers by the elimination of certain kinds of stimuli. Thus, a toad will initially snap at all small objects. After one trial of snapping at a bee, however, it will exclude that stimulus forever after. A second type of change in the I.R.M. consists of the well-known phenomenon of imprinting. This phenomenon, as we have described it before, consists of the fact that a precocial bird, exposed to a large moving object shortly after hatching, will follow that moving object around afterward to the exclusion of other things or animals. Under normal circumstances this large moving object is, of course, the bird's mother and thus the response has survival value in that the young keep close to the mother for protection and food. When the bird reaches maturity, it has a tendency to mate with objects which manifest characteristics like those of the original imprinted object, the response thus again having survival value for the species.

A Classificatory System of Adaptive Behavior

As already indicated, biologists have used an approach to behavior based upon Darwin's principle of adaptation. By studying representatives of the different classes of adaptive behavior they are in an excellent position to compare different species. Furthermore, they avoid the mistake which they attribute to psychologists, namely, studying only one class of appetitive behavior, that of ingestive behavior. At this time it is difficult to know to what extent psychological studies of the conditionability of ingestive behavior may be generalized to studies of the conditionability of contactual and other behavior. In fact, since only the consummatory act of instinctive behavior is fixed, species specific, etc., and the appetitive component is not, it would seem possible to simply couple different consummatory acts to the same appetitive component, or different appetitive components to the same consummatory act. Nevertheless,

Breland and Breland (1961) have shown that it is exactly in this area where difficulty arises. They found, for example, that a pig conditioned to transport coins (the appetitive component supposed to be linked to the consummatory act of eating) to a "piggy bank," despite being under a high hunger drive, dilly-dallied with the coins, alternately tossing them up into the air and rooting them. The presence of the rooting behavior was explained in terms of its importance in the usual food getting repertoire (part of the consummatory act?). Only further research will give us information as to the extent of such interactions between behavior types (operants and instincts) and how high up they are found in the phylogenetic scale. In the meantime, it is important for us to examine a classificatory scheme of behavior which makes available a tool for analyses of experiments similar to those described above.

Scott (1956) provided a classification scheme of general behavior patterns which he used for the analysis of the social organization of animals. His classification is sufficiently general, however, to yield a method for the comparative study of animals. The first category is that of *contactual behavior*. As already mentioned, Harlow's (1958) thorough experiment demonstrated the importance of "contact comfort" as a primary reinforcer for infant monkeys. Although the adaptive significance of this class of behavior varies widely, the phenomenon can be found in paramecia as well as in mammals.

The second category is one to which we have already had occasion to refer, namely, *ingestive behavior*. This simply consists of the intake of solid and/or liquid foods. This class of behavior is involved in the acquisition of social behavior for those animals that feed their young.

The third category is that of *eliminative behavior* which is quite straightforward in aquatic animals. With terrestrial animals more highly developed patterns of behavior are observed. In some animals this class of behavior acquires special significance.

Sexual behavior includes courtship as well as copulation behavior. It occurs very widely in the animal kingdom and constitutes an obvious example of social behavior. In some animals such behavior is simple, whereas in others the courtship patterns are very elaborate indeed.

The next category of behavior is *epimeletic behavior.* Scott defines it as "giving of care or attention." He points out that this class of behavior is sometimes referred to as maternal behavior. Since the behavior involved is sometimes practiced by the father, and sometimes even by adults on each other (as in grooming of adult primates), Scott's term is preferred.

Et-epimeletic behavior constitutes the next category. It consists of the act of calling for care and is particularly frequent in animals that care for their young. In most infant mammals this response is vocal. It is also found in adult animals.

Agonistic behavior is the term applied to that class of behavior which is involved in conflict between animals. The term refers to fighting but is not limited to that behavior. Since both escape and passivity are often involved when fighting takes place, it was decided to include both types of behavior in the general class of agonistic behavior.

Allelomimetic behavior consists of behavior in which animals act the same way under at least some degree of mutual stimulation. The resulting coordination can be observed in the behavior of schools of fishes and flocks of birds.

Investigative behavior is essentially the sensory inspection which one finds when placing an animal in a new environment. Behavior of this kind has been dealt with by psychologists under the term exploratory behavior and has figured particularly in the study of the rat.

Another class of behavior of some importance is that of *territoriality.* It is characteristic of both individual animals as well as groups. It refers generally to the staking out of optimal environmental conditions and of general territorial boundaries which will be defended by the owner.

Some Experiments

Having explained the general approach taken by ethologists, it remains for us to present some experiments illustrating the methods of observation and the results that are obtained by this approach.

An Experiment on Releasing Stimuli

Free (1961) investigated the characteristics of stimuli which released the stinging response of the bee. The method of recording the stinging response consisted of suspending, and then jerking, a cotton wool ball approximately one inch in diameter and wrapped in muslin, in front of beehive entrances. All the balls were handled and so all had some human odor. In addition, the stimulus characteristics were varied along a number of dimensions. To test the effect of color, muslin coverings were white, black, blue, or yellow. Two differently colored sets of 8 balls each were suspended at a time. Five tests were made with each color. Since the bees left their stings in the balls, counting the responses was quite simple. In general, the dark-colored balls were stung more frequently than the light ones. The effect of previous stings in the balls was to increase the number of additional stings. Smoke, however, reduced the effect of previous stings. Other variables found to increase bee-stinging behavior were: animal scent, human sweat, and rapid movement. Since many mammals are natural enemies of the honeybee, it should not be surprising that such characteristics release the protective and, most probably, adaptive stinging behavior. On the other hand, it is not clear why the honeybees attacked balls scented with their own colony odor more often than balls scented with that of another colony.

While this experiment was not done under completely natural conditions, the reader should note that only part of the independent variable was controlled experimentally. In any case, the bees were allowed to remain in their natural environment and to respond in a manner requiring no special training or even preparation.

An Experiment Illustrating Et-epimeletic Behavior

The use of models in the study of releasers is well illustrated in a study done by Hailman (1962). The animal studied was the Laughing Gull chick, whose et-epimeletic behavior consists of pecking at the parent's bill. The pecking then releases the epimeletic behavior of the parents, which results in the transfer of semidigested food to the chick. The models consisted of flat cardboard painted with watercolor. Chicks were presented with a series of models which were arranged in random order to control for any sequential effects. Each model was placed in front of the chick and was moved slightly for a period of one minute. The number of pecks made at the model constituted the dependent variable. In response to one series of models, in which the head was presented alone without the bill, the smallest number of pecks was evoked (1.1). When the bill was presented without a head, more responses were evoked (7.1), and when a "normal" diagrammatic Laughing Gull was presented, it evoked the largest number of pecks (19.2). This study presented a number of other interesting results. Perhaps most important of these was a comparison of the Laughing Gull model with the models of other gull species. Inspection of Figure 4-2 shows the models of the various gulls presented to the chicks along with the mean number of pecks given each of them. Notice that the top picture consists of a slightly more detailed head than the next lower head (the standard). The more lifelike head evoked the largest number of pecks. The third and fourth heads are pictures of other gull species. These show a significantly smaller number of pecks than the number given to a member of the chick's own species and thus illustrate the species-specific characteristic of this behavior,

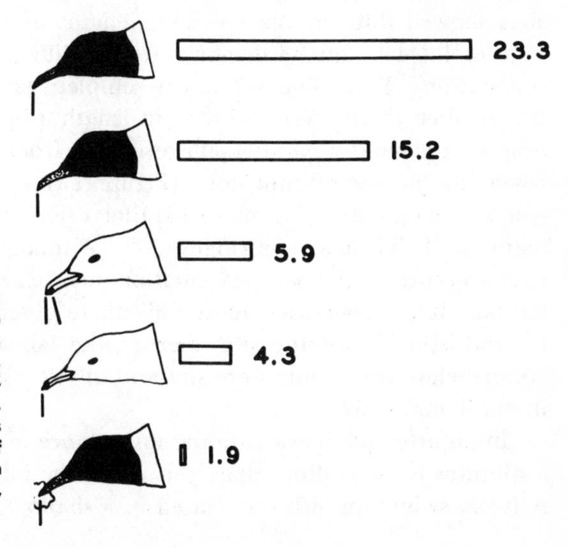

Fig. 4-2. Models used in the third series (from the top): Laughing Gull, standard, Herring Gull, Ring-billed Gull, Laughing Gull with food. The numbers and bars refer to the number of pecks evoked by each model. (Hailman, 1962, Fig. 3.)

though the discrimination between "own" vs. "other" species is in fact not very great. The pecking rate for the lowest picture, which differs from the more lifelike own-species head only in that it has food in its beak, is not so easily explainable. The author suggests that possibly the white color of the projecting food is of some importance. Observation of the chicks in response to the Laughing Gull with food indicates that the model actually frightened the chick. It appears, therefore, that while models as investigatory tools are quite useful, they too raise some problems which require special study.

An Experiment Illustrating Allelomimetic Behavior

The experiment to be described here traces the development of the instinctive behavior both in the laboratory and in the natural environment of the organism. Shaw (1960) studied the phenomenon of schooling in fry. She observed some 1,000 fry in the laboratory and some 10,000 in the field. The fry observed in the laboratory were hatched there. The periods of daily observation consisted of 3 half-hour periods (morning, afternoon, and evening) until the fry were 4 weeks old. The size of the fry increased from about 4.5 mm. to 16 mm. during this time period. Observations of the fry at different sizes showed different degrees and lengths of time of orientation. Figures 4-3, 4-4, and 4-5 demonstrate the different stages of parallel orientation. These figures show a complete lack of parallel orientation when the fry were 5-7 mm. in length (Figure 4-3), the beginning of a generally parallel course lasting from one to two seconds when the fry are 8-9 mm. long (Figure 4-4), and by the time they reach a length of 11-12 mm., parallel orientation is found in as many as 10 fry at a time (Figure 4-5). Although disruption in the school occurred, the same orientation was re-formed within a few seconds. It was somewhat more difficult to observe a population of fry consisting of all the sizes seen in the laboratory, in the field. Nevertheless, the results were substantially the same as those found in the laboratory.

In an attempt to evaluate the importance of visual attraction as a stimulus for schooling, Shaw performed the following experiment. A freely swimming fish was placed in a shallow container; the con-

Fig. 4-3.

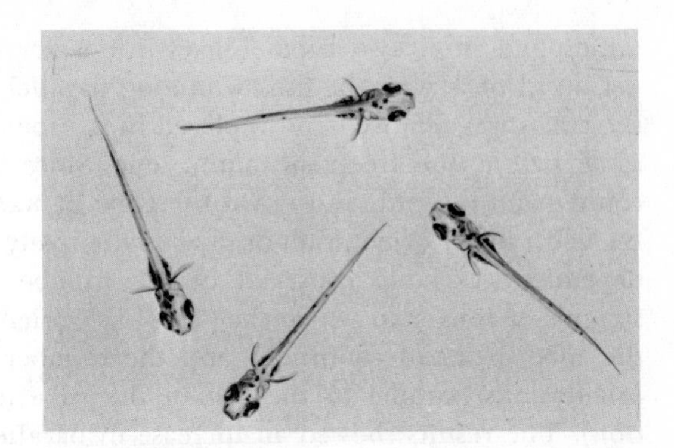

Fig. 4-4.

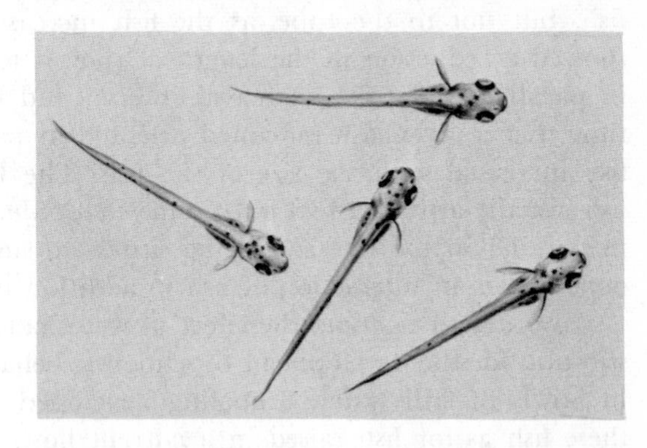

Fig. 4-5.

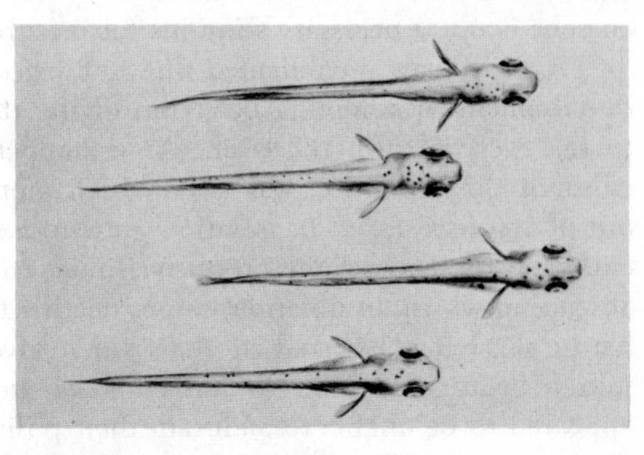

Fig. 4-3. Fry 5-7 mm. in length. Parallel orientation is not seen.
Fig. 4-4. Fry 8-9 mm. in length. The first indications of parallel orientation and incipient schooling are seen.
Fig. 4-5. Fry 11-12 mm. in length. Fry are oriented parallel and schooling is established. (Shaw, 1960, Figs. 1, 2, 3.)

tainer had in it two tubes filled with water. After a five-minute period of observing the fish swimming parallel to the tubes, one of the tubes was removed and replaced by a tube containing a fish the same size as the freely swimming one. Since the fish in the tube could swim only up and down the tube, it was possible to observe the effect of his orientation on that of the freely swimming fish. The dependent variable consisted of the number of periods of five seconds or longer in which the "free" fish oriented the same way as the tube (control condition) and the number of such periods of orientations parallel to the fish in the tube (experimental condition). The results showed an increase in parallel orientation to the fish, but not to the tube, as the fish increased in size; they also showed a reduction in the length of time it took the fry to orient in parallel as the fish increased in size; and finally the length of time that a given fish remained oriented in parallel with the tube fish increased with the size of the fish. The further fact that the fish visually attracted had to be somewhat older than those oriented in parallel in the free swimming situation, suggests that schooling depends on an interaction of fish in addition to visual stimulation.

In order to evaluate the effect of water current orientation as a stimulus for the development of schooling behavior, fish were raised in bowls of still water. Schooling developed at the same age for these fish as for fish raised in a current flow, thus indicating that current is not a necessary stimulus for orientation in a school.

Finally, Shaw investigated the influence of isolation on the development of schooling behavior, giving the fish no opportunity to see even its own reflection. As it happens the most dramatic effect of this condition was a very high mortality rate. Only four out of 400 fish reared in isolation grew to a size of 15 mm. Apparently the presence of the group facilitates eating, the reduction or absence of which, in isolation, causes death. The results on the four hardy surviving fish showed that, when given an opportunity to join a group, they did so immediately. In the beginning, they appeared to be unable to maintain their position in the school, but after a period of only four hours they were indistinguishable from the fish reared in groups. This result suggests that the fish require some experience in orientation before they can do it well, albeit this experience need not be extensive.

This study illustrates the uses of natural observation and experiment as well as the uses of qualitative (relative orientation) and quantitative (length of time of orientation, latency to first orientation, etc.) data in ethological work. The reader should also notice the importance of the topography of response in this experiment in contrast with the importance of functional definitions in operant conditioning studies. Nevertheless, the point must be made that the topographical description of the response class of interest goes hand-in-hand with its functional importance. Schooling behavior is functional in that it has adaptive importance, i.e., survival value for the species and the individual.

Imprinting

As already mentioned, the I.R.M. has been shown to be adaptable, not only to evolutionary pressures, but also to important events occurring in the lifetime of the organism. In other words, innate behavior shows some evidence of flexibility in that the stimulus which gains control over it can be any one of a class of events as long as it occurs during the so-called critical period. Ramsay and Hess (1954) demonstrated in a controlled experiment that Mallard ducklings have a critical period for imprinting. The ducklings were hatched in an incubator. Then, a predetermined number of hours after hatching they were exposed to a papier-mâché Mallard duck decoy. Different decoys were used. One such decoy even had a heating element implanted in it and was equipped with a speaker making a series of calls. The ducklings were placed in the imprinting situation (exposed to the decoy) for a given period of time (10 minutes in one case, 30 in another). Each subgroup of ducklings was exposed a different number of hours after hatching. The ducklings, of course, had had *no* other opportunity to see any other large moving object before seeing the decoy. Five to 70 hours after imprinting the ducklings were given a test for following. Figure 4-6 presents the percentage of animals that made "perfect" imprinting responses following a varying number of hours after hatching. It is quite clear that exposure to a large moving object 13 to 16 hours after hatching results in the greatest amount of imprinting.

As is usual in any experimental field, once the existence of a phenomenon has been established, attempts are made to modify it (e.g., to extend the critical period) in an effort to gain a better understanding of it. Moltz and Stettner (1961) studied the effect of two different conditions of light stimulation prior to the imprinting experience of Peking ducks. One randomly selected group of ducks had hoods placed over their heads immediately after hatching, so that they were stimulated by differences in brightness but were unable to discriminate visual forms. The other group (control) was fitted with hoods having holes which allowed the retinas to be stimulated by regular patterned light. Both groups were further divided into subgroups in accordance with the number of hours between hatching and imprinting. The "following" scores resulting from the imprinting experience are diagrammed in Figure 4-7. The experimental group which was not permitted to experience patterned vision shows statistically significantly higher following scores over the control birds when imprinting (exposure age) takes place 24 and 48 hours after hatching and a tendency (which can be attributed to chance alone) in the same direction for the 12- and 72-hour exposure ages. The authors interpreted their study to mean that maturational changes alone could not explain the critical period, since deprivation of form perception apparently extends the

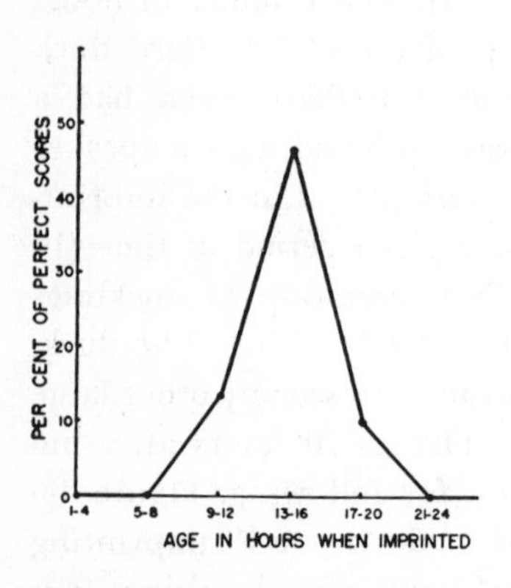

Fig. 4-6. Percentage of "perfect" scores for Mallards imprinted in various age groups. (Ramsay and Hess, 1954, Fig. 2.)

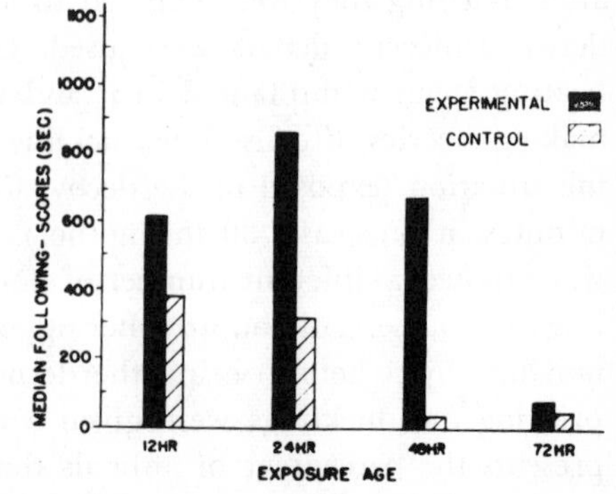

Fig. 4-7. Median following-scores obtained by experimental and control Ss after different exposure ages. (Moltz and Stettner, 1961, Fig. 1.)

time period during which the imprinting procedure induces following. This is evidenced by the fact that there is no diminution in the following response in the experimental ducklings through 48 hours.

Operant Conditioning and Innate Behavior

We have already pointed out that the appetitive and aversive component of instinctive behavior is the flexible, conditionable part. This constitutes, then, an important bridge between conditioning and ethology. There are other bridges as well and we will discuss two experiments relevant to them here.

Murphay (1967) conditioned the fruit fly in a simple T maze. The operation used to produce a reinforcer is particularly interesting. It consisted essentially of genetic selection for a negative geotaxis. Negative geotaxis means that the fruit flies have a tendency to move away from the pull of gravity. It also means that being allowed to move in a direction opposite to that of gravity is reinforcing. Thus the reinforcer used was simply "being allowed to move up a vertical tube." The response consisted of making a right or a left turn. The positive reinforcer was used in a variety of different conditions demonstrating both acquisition and extinction.

An experiment done by Thompson (1964) compared three reinforcers, one of which made use of the visual image of one rooster as a reinforcer for the operant behavior of another. What is of special interest here is the fact that this type of stimulus is often viewed as the releaser for agonistic behavior although it is here used as a reinforcer. As in the preceding chapters on respondent and operant conditioning, we find it necessary to view stimuli from a functional point of view in order to account for their effect on behavior. The fighting cocks used in this experiment were run on a rather complicated schedule—a so-called three-choice nonreversible option situation. The enclosure in which the animal was housed contained three illuminated keys which could be pecked. Pecking of one key was reinforced by water, pecking of another by food, and pecking of a third key by viewing a mirror image of itself in one experiment and viewing a different rooster in another experiment. The animal could switch from one key to another, but only after completion of the response requirement. The response requirement consisted of a fixed ratio which was gradually increased to a FR 75. After the ratio remained at the value of 75 for a few sessions, it was found that the response rate dropped to zero and the FR had to be decreased to 25 to elevate the response rate again. After the response rate had returned to its former level, the mirror was removed to determine whether the rooster would work merely for a stimulus change. When the mirror was removed the rooster's response rate on that key quickly dropped to zero. Inspection of Figure 4-8 shows a plot of 61 successive 24-hour sessions against number of responses emitted per session on the 3 keys. Changes in the FR and mirror removal are indicated on the graph. Note that the stabilized behavior shows a constant relationship between the three different response classes: the response class reinforced by food yields approximately 10,000 responses per day; the class reinforced by water, approximately 700 responses; and the class reinforced by mirror image or a view of another rooster, approximately 500 responses. This study again suggests the rather intricate relations that exist between instincts and operant behavior. Experiments such as the ones we have cited are recent and understanding of their full implications will have to await further research.

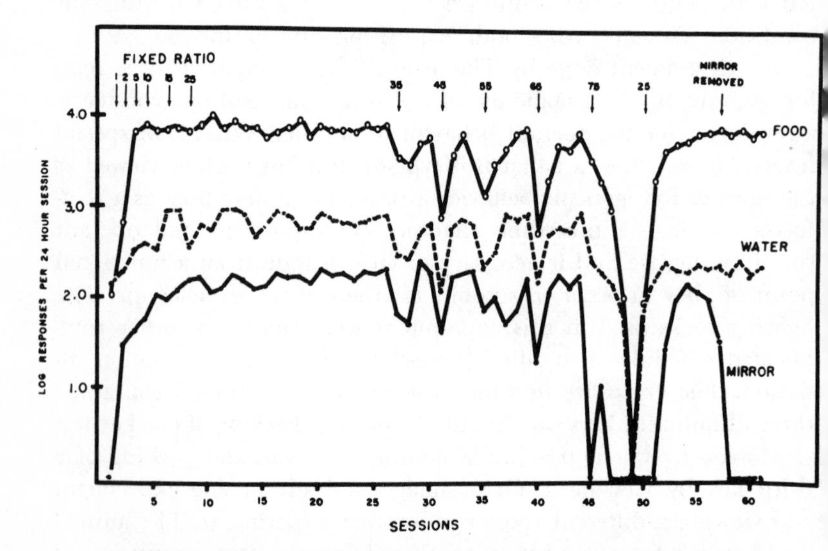

Fig. 4-8. The logarithms of the numbers of responses for food, water, and social reinforcement during the first 61 days of the study. The ratio size is indicated by the numbers along the top of the figure. (Thompson, 1964, Fig. 1.)

The Importance of Innate Behavior

The analysis of innate behavior must be included in the study of behavior by any serious student of the subject, if only for the purpose of obtaining a complete picture of the field. Animals low on the phylogenetic scale give evidence that a relatively large part of their behavior is under the control of innate, unlearned variables. Furthermore, species-specific behavior is not quite so inflexible as might appear at first. Imprinting can be likened to a very rapid type of conditioning process which occurs at specific times in the life of an organism and constitutes an example of the modifiability of innate behavior. The complexity of the relationships between innate and learned behavior is only now beginning to become uncovered. Finally, the importance of studying innate behavior stems from the fact that there is evidence that such behavior occurs among human beings, e.g., an "imprinting" response in human infants' smiling responses. All of these are reasons for the inclusion of an area of investigation in which psychologists are just beginning to become involved.

SUMMARY

The compartmentalization of science resulting from the typical academic disciplines does not furnish us with reasonable lines of division for subject matter such as behavior. While treatment of behavior from the point of view of ethology in a psychology book must needs be short, some review of this approach is definitely called for.

The ethological approach, as it was explained in this chapter, is related to a biological view which, in turn, is largely influenced by Darwin's theory of evolution. Ethology makes use of the constructs of homologue (a similarity of behavior in animals having a common ancestor) and analogue (a similarity based upon considerations of commonality of function rather than structure).

The relationship between behavior and genetics was then described, presenting evidence for the heritability of the phototaxis in fruit flies. It also considered the advantages of dealing with innate behavior from the point of view of evolution.

Classification of behavior into two components, an appetitive or aversive one, followed by the consummatory act (fixed action pattern), indicates that the former part is conditionable while the latter is relatively inflexible, and therefore useful for phylogenetic classification. Two types of orienting responses were discussed—kinesis (innate undirected movement resulting from changes in stimulus intensity) and a taxis (innate movement directed towards or away from a particular source of stimulation).

The function of the releaser or sign stimulus in releasing behavior was discussed. The I.R.M., the innate releasing mechanism, which restricts effective stimulation under certain conditions, was also described. It was shown to be responsive to evolutionary pressure as well as to a special kind of behavior change taking place during the organism's life time. The latter is called imprinting.

A gross classification system of adaptive behavior was presented, yielding the following categories of behavior: contactual, ingestive, eliminative, sexual, epimeletic, et-epimeletic, agonistic, allelomimetic, investigative, and territorial.

A number of experiments were presented in detail illustrating the various concepts discussed. One experiment dealt with methods of discovering the releasing stimuli for the stinging response in the honey-bee. Another illustrated et-epimeletic behavior in the Laughing Gull chick, making use of a model as a standard stimulus. A third experiment illustrated allelomimetic behavior in schooling behavior of the fish, tracing its development both by naturalistic and experimental methods. The fourth and fith experiments dealt with imprinting in Mallard ducklings and in Peking ducks, demonstrating the general phenomenon and showing the importance of sensory experience in determining the time of the critical period. The next two experiments showed some points of articulation between innate behavior and operant conditioning, suggesting more of an interaction between these different response types than is probably now being taken into consideration.

Finally, the general importance of innate behavior was emphasized as a requisite for the serious study of behavior.

5

Psychology and Physiology

SOME THEORETICAL ISSUES

The espousal of the behavioral approach to psychology has for many years meant the exclusion of physiology. It is important to note, however, that the physiology which was excluded in the past is not the same physiology which behaviorists today unashamedly study in their experiments. Even the physiology used by Pavlov in explaining respondent conditioning was, in the main, only theoretical. His descriptions of the activity of the higher nervous system were simply a translation of the relations Pavlov observed between the stimuli he presented to his dogs and the responses which were elicited by them. The objections raised by behaviorists to such "explanations" of behavior were twofold: (1) The statements made about the physiological "bases" of behavior were not explanations at all but simply a rewording of the more precise descriptions of what actually could be observed of the behavior. (2) A more fundamental objection against physiological explanations of behavior, however—one which cannot be dismissed by the independent measurement of physiological activity—is to the characterization of physiological events as a substrate of behavior, as the essence of the explanation of behavior, and therefore as somehow prerequisite for the study of behavior. The behavioral approach to psychology rejects this conception of the relation of psychology and physiology. This conception was listed by Skinner (1961) as one of the unfortunate flights, the flight to the inner man, which some disillusioned pyschologists have taken from the laboratory.

In this chapter we will take the view that the assumption of priority of behavior over physiological events, or vice versa, is to be made, not on the basis of some theoretical preconception, but rather on the basis of which of these domains gives rise to the independent variable and which to the dependent variable in any particular experiment. Physiology relevant to behavior has come a long way since Pavlov's time. Current sophistication in the measurement of physiological events is such that such events can be utilized as variables in experiments. The view of psychology and physiology as equal partners may be surprising to some readers, but it is shared by one of the most prominent physiological psychologists. Hebb (1966) says in his introductory psychology book (p. 319): "Psychology cannot become a branch of physiology. We cannot escape the need for large-scale units of analysis, nor the need for the special methods of behavioral study on which such analysis is based. Some of the most important aspects of brain function, that is, can only be known and studied by psychological methods."

The last sentence is particularly interesting since it calls to our attention the fact that behavioral data can be used to supply us with hypothetical inferences concerning the physiology of the organism. To take but one example, the fact that there are two different light receptors in the retina is evidenced by the behavioral data obtained from dark adaptation experiments. Thus, an organism, say, a pigeon or man, placed in a dark room will show a reduction in the threshold value (amount of light necessary for the organism to detect its presence) as a function of time in the dark (dark adaptation) before onset of the light. If the organism is preadapted to a light before dark adaptation, the threshold values show first one reduction of threshold value which shortly, with increasing time in the dark, reaches an asymptote, followed by a longer reduction which reaches a new asymptote. The break in the curve (the abrupt change from the first to the second plateau) provides evidence for the action of two processes, which upon anatomical and physiological examination were shown to be the photochemical processes identified with cones and rods (two types of visual receptors). Inspection of Figure 5-1 shows this psychophysical curve for the pigeon.

The reasons for the combined study of physiological and psychological variables with respect to behavior lie in the fact that the study of each potentially sheds light on the other. Experiments in behavioral genetics demonstrate a happy confluence of these two approaches since both the biochemical action of the genes as well as the behavior under observation are given equal study. Another reason for a fruitful collaboration of the two areas is the recent application of the respondent conditioning paradigm to the different organs of the body (cf. Chapter 2). The possibility of conditioning internal organs by means of external and internal stimuli in the same way as behavior, which is characterized by more obvious external manifestations, has eliminated the skin as a boundary between what was supposed to belong to the physiological and what to the behavioral domain. At the border between psychology and physiology there lies an area into which investigators from either subject may venture.

Behavioral Influences upon Physiological Events

Intero-ceptive conditioning, which has been so well established in Russia (Razran, 1961), provides us with a very important gateway for the influence of external events on internal organs. The mechanism of respondent conditioning has been mentioned in this regard already (cf. Chapter 2). In addition, we have also described (cf.

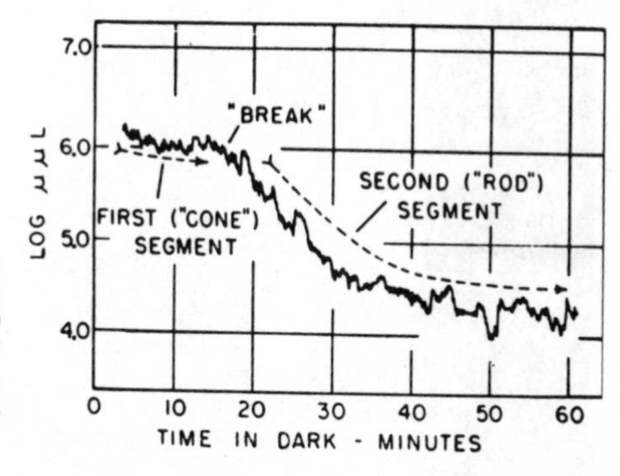

Fig. 5-1. Sample dark-adaptation curve secured from a bird in a single hour. Pre-exposure was 10 min. at 22 mL. The luminance of the stimulus patch, in log micro-microlamberts, is on the ordinate. (Blough, 1956, Fig. 2.)

Chapter 3) the operant conditioning of muscle movements so small that the subject himself cannot describe or control them by means of his verbal responses (Hefferline & Keenan, 1961). Thus, we may conclude that control over those parts of the body which used to be exclusively attributed to physiology has been shifted to behavioral control.

A by now classical experiment demonstrating the effect of one response class upon neurophysiological functioning to a new stimulus was reported by Hernández-Peón, Scherrer, and Jouvet (1956). Having observed that organisms attending to a given stimulus would quite frequently ignore other new stimuli, these investigators hypothesized that concentration upon one class of sensory information would preclude the influx of information from new sources. This hypothetical inhibition was tested for in cats by implanting electrodes in the second or third order neurons of the auditory pathway. Thus, if attention to a given visual stimulus (e.g. mice) inhibits the registration of an unrelated sound, then the auditory responses in the cochlear nucleus of an unanaesthetized cat should be diminished in the presence of such an attention-getting stimulus. Figure 5-2 presents pictures of the behavior of the cat as well as a record of its auditory response to a short click before mice were placed in front of it, while they were placed in front of it, and after they had been removed. Notice the presence of the response in the

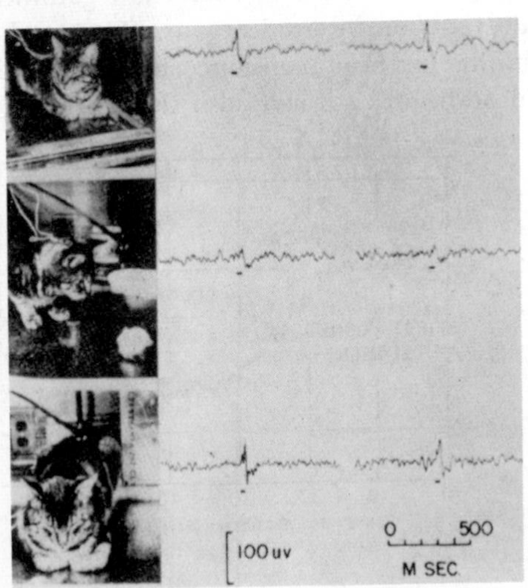

Fig. 5-2. Direct recording of click responses in the cochlear nucleus during three periods; the photographs were taken simultaneously. (Top and bottom) Cat is relaxed; the click responses are large. (Middle) While the cat is visually attentive to the mice in the jar, the click responses are diminished in amplitude. (Hernández-Peón, Scherrer, and Jouvet, 1956, Fig. 1.)

cochlear nucleus when the cat is alone, but its absence when the mice are present. The experimenters demonstrated similar incoming stimulus suppression of the click when the attention getting stimulus was either fish odor or an electric shock delivered to the forepaw.

The importance of the stimulation which surrounds an organism can be critical with respect to its behavior on later occasions. The experiment by Moltz and Stettner (1961) described in Chapter 4 showed that if the bird was precluded from stimulation by patterned light, then his critical period for imprinting could be postponed for as long as 48 hours. Another experiment took a similar approach to the problem of stimulation surrounding man. Heron (1957) deprived adult human subjects of all patterned stimulation—visual, auditory, and tactual—for as long as they were willing to remain under such conditions. The behavior of the subjects was monitored in a number of ways. In tests of their functioning on a variety of conceptual and perceptual tasks, the subjects typically showed decrements in performance, both during and immediately after their isolation. Even more dramatic, subjects reported "seeing things" and being unable to rid themselves of these scenes, thus evincing hallucinatory behavior as well as perceptual and conceptual decrements in performance at various tasks. Concomitantly with those marked changes in behavior, there occurred significant changes in neurophysiological events which were recorded by the electroencephalogram (EEG) and which consisted, after a period of isolation, of the appearance of slow waves during wakefulness which resembled the brain waves typically obtained from subjects during sleep. The interpretation of these results has been based on the functioning of a neurophysiological structure in the midbrain known as the reticular formation. This structure alerts the brain by emitting a stream of stimuli. The reticular formation itself requires sensory stimulation to activate it. Apparently the isolation condition, which admits only an even steady rate of stimulation into the reticular formation, is not sufficient to trigger the diffuse arousal pattern. It is this kind of relationship, between the impaired functioning of the cortex (evidenced by changes in the EEG) and specific behavioral abnormalities, which shows how behavioral findings may be used to shed light on the neurophysiology of the subject.

One of the significant effects of advances in knowledge and technology in operant conditioning has been the availability of continuous objective response measures for more precise correlational studies with neurophysiological measures. In a recent review of this area, Brady (1966) distinguished three different physiological effects of various operant conditioning procedures: transient physiological changes, durable physiological alterations, and somatic pathology.

Among the transient physiological changes, both respiratory and cardiovascular changes have been reported. Eldridge (1954) found an increase in respiration rate during conditioning and a decrease during extinction of an avoidance response to a bright light. Brady (1966) commented on this experiment by pointing out that it was not clear whether the differences in respiration rate were due to the avoidance procedure or whether they were unconditioned responses to the bright light. In an experiment free of this criticism, Wenzel (1961) conditioned cats to make two responses each under the control of a different auditory S^D. One response was reinforced by food and the other was under the control of a shock avoidance contingency. Responding under the food contingency was associated with an acceleration of heart rate, whereas responding under the avoidance contingency was associated with a deceleration of heart rate. These changes were temporary only, the experimenter being unable to show a change in heart rate due to the stimuli associated with food or shock when these discriminative stimuli were presented outside the conditioning apparatus.

Brain wave activity, already mentioned above in a slightly different context, is another transient physiological change found to be associated with operant conditioning. No simple relationships were found between the EEG patterns and different schedules of reinforcement which were imposed on the operant behavior. In general, one can only say that the EEG appears to show general so-called "alerting" patterns in response to different schedules.

The durable physiological effects were described by Brady (1966) almost exclusively in terms of neuroendocrinological effects which were studied in large part in Brady's own laboratory. It should be pointed out that the endocrine glands which secrete their chemical substances (hormones) directly into the blood stream have, like the nervous system, an important integrating function in the organism.

The endocrine system interacts with the nervous system and, what is most important in this context, the organism's response to the hormones is slow and relatively long lasting. In order to study these longer lasting physiological effects, it was decided to study pituitary-adrenocortical activity. The pituitary gland secretes a hormone known as ACTH (adrenocorticotropic hormone) into the blood stream, which in addition to its other effects, stimulates release of corticoids from another endocrine gland, the adrenal gland. The resultant adrenocortical activity was found to relate to a variety of psychopathological conditions including "anxiety." With that as a background, 17-hydroxy-corticosteroid (17-OH-CS) levels were used as an index of ACTH secretion and related to operant behavior maintained under positive and negative reinforcement control. The results of these experiments showed no change in 17-OH-CS levels when under the positive reinforcement contingency—either under crf, FR, or even when the FR was abruptly increased from low to high requirements.

When the conditioned suppression paradigm (cf. Chapter 3) was superimposed on a VI schedule under a food reinforcement contingency, a marked increase in 17-OH-CS levels was found in all five monkeys tested in this manner. In addition, it should be noted that the increase in 17-OH-CS could not be attributed to the electric shock used in the conditioned suppression paradigm because no shock was ever delivered when hormone measurements were made.

The other behavioral procedure which caused a change in 17-OH-CS levels also involved a negative reinforcer and consisted of a free-operant avoidance schedule. Again it should be noted that the increase in 17-OH-CS levels could not be attributed to electric shock, since it rose to the same extent even when the monkeys successfully avoided all of the shocks.

These basic studies have since been extended along behavioral lines, by employing multiple schedules of reinforcement having as components conditioned suppression, free-operant avoidance, discriminated punishment, VI food reinforcement alone, and S^{Δ} components, as well as along physiological lines, by measuring patterns of endocrine secretions (thyroid, gonadal, and adrenal hormones) both in the intact organism and in the animal which has had neurological controlling mechanisms removed. These studies are too complex to go into in this book, but they do reveal the possibility of defining such relatively vague concepts as "emotion" by means of a series of converging operations based upon specification of behavioral contingencies and hormonal levels in the blood stream.

The last, and certainly the most dramatic, physiological effect of a behavioral procedure is the one which Brady (1966) calls somatic pathology. He reported on some studies in which rats developed gastric ulcers in experimental conflict situations but showed that variables other than conflict were involved in the production of the ulcer. Other experiments showed an increased susceptibility to infection by a virus as a result of being subjected to an avoidance conditioning procedure but left unanswered the question of the contribution of physical trauma to the resulting illness. A more controlled experiment, the origin of which was, in fact, fortuitous, was performed by Brady, Porter, Conrad and Mason (1958). They discovered a very high incidence of gastrointestinal disease in a group of monkeys who were subjected to a variety of conditioning procedures involving negative reinforcers and long conditioning sessions. They therefore embarked upon the following experiment. Eight monkeys were paired in a "yoked-chair" arrangement. The two monkeys of each pair were placed side by side and both had a lever available to them. Lever pressing by one of them postponed the electric shock for both animals. Shocks were otherwise programmed to occur every 20 seconds. Responding by the other monkey had no effect on the occurrence of the shocks. In other words, one monkey (sometimes called the "executive monkey") was in a free-operant avoidance schedule while the other constituted a yoked control. The procedure was in effect for alternating periods of 6 hours. A discriminative stimulus consisting of a red light, and visible to both animals, was associated with the avoidance procedure. Thus the yoked control animal received shocks whenever the executive monkey did and under the same stimulus conditions, namely when the red light was on. The experiment was carried out on a continuous basis for a period of six to seven weeks. Figure 5-3 is a picture of the two monkeys in the yoked-chair arrangement. The monkey on the left is the "executive," the other the control.

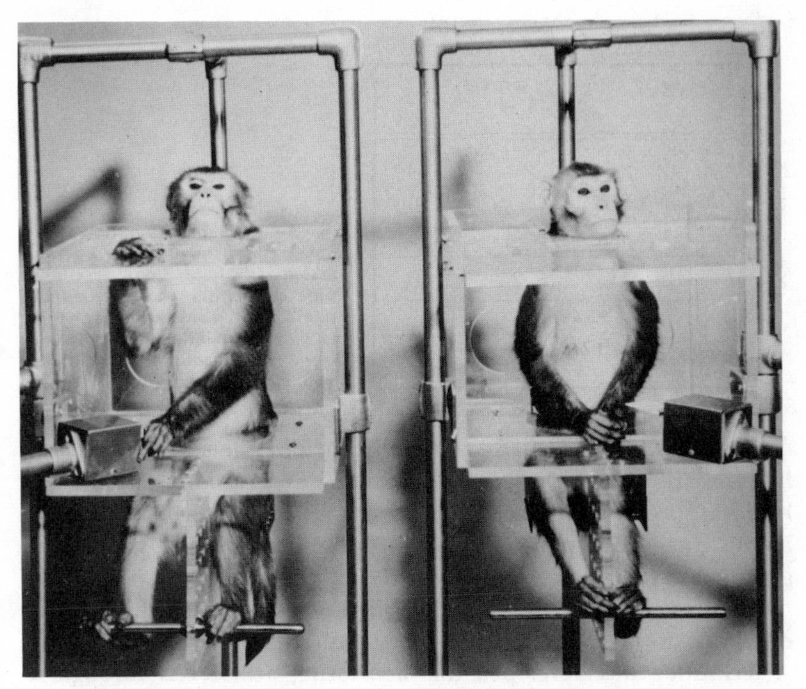

Fig. 5-3. An experimental monkey and a control monkey, gently restrained in primate chairs, illustrate the "yoked-chair" avoidance procedure. The lever available to each animal is shown within easy reach, although only the experimental "avoidance" monkey on the left is observed to press the lever. (Brady, 1966, Fig. 2.)

The stable performance developed for the executive monkey is depicted in Figure 5-4 for the alternating avoidance, non-avoidance conditions. Notice that the number of shocks actually received by the two monkeys (indicated in the curve by oblique pips) was small indeed, typically coming at the rate of less than one per hour. The dramatic result of this procedure was the development of gastrointestinal lesions in all of the executive monkeys and in none of the control animals. Executive monkeys that did not die of the lesions, and all of the control monkeys, were sacrificed for complete post-mortem examinations, thus confirming the result. Follow-up of these results, a clear illustration of experimentally induced psychosomatic illness, showed that a number of variations on the basic behavioral paradigm, even using situations which might be considered to pro-

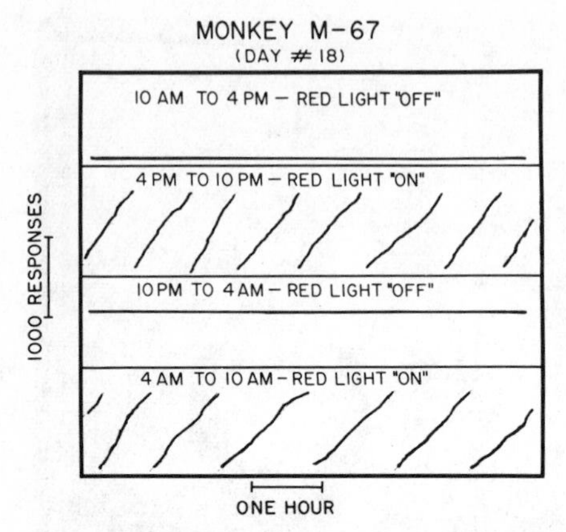

Fig. 5-4. Sample cumulative response curve showing one 24-hour session (six-hour "on," six-hour "off" cycles) for an experimental "avoidance" monkey on day 18 of the experiment. The oblique pips on the record indicate shocks. (Brady, 1966, Fig. 3.)

duce greater stress, actually resulted in a lower incidence of ulcers by comparison to the original procedure. The variations in the behavioral procedure which apparently reduced the incidence of lesions included the introduction of an added punishment contingency and different work-rest cycles.

Subsequent work on the physiological aspects was directed at questions of the time during which the ulcers were actually formed. A technique was developed for monitoring acid levels through a cannula in the stomach wall (shades of Pavlov!) in association with the occurrence of behavior under the control of an avoidance schedule. It was during the rest periods, rather than during the avoidance periods, that the investigators found dramatic secretions in gastric acid. It is clear that these very suggestive results in turn require further experimental analysis, particularly since their implications are both theoretical and practical. This is what makes science exciting.

Physiological Influences upon Behavior

Investigations in which the physiological event constitutes the independent variable are much more common than studies of the reverse relationship.

Perhaps the most obvious study of this variable consists of examination of the "wiring" and the elements in the circuits, i.e., an examination of the connections of the nervous system and the functions of its various parts. Such examination is done with the aid of the microscope, since many important neural structures cannot otherwise be viewed. Connections between different structures can be traced by making very thin cross sections at different locations. Thus, in examining the spinal cord, which together with the brain constitutes the central nervous system and which is essentially the line of communication between the sensory influx of stimuli and the motor outflow of neural impulses to the muscles, we can trace neurons from the coccyx all the way up through the cord and into the brain. By making cross sections of the cord at different levels, it is possible, by following the natural colors of different parts of neurons from one section to another, or stained parts of the neurons (since different parts of each nerve cell absorb dyes to a different degree), to learn where particular fibers go and how they connect.

Unfortunately, the above method of evaluating the different parts of the nervous system does not take function into account. This is accomplished by the so-called extirpation or ablation method. The concept behind this technique is frighteningly simple. If you want to find out the function of a part of the nervous system, remove that part and observe what happens to the behavior that results after removal. The technique has the obvious disadvantage of being irreversible. Furthermore, the cutting out of particular structures of the nervous system must be checked later by *post mortem* examination to make certain that only the intended part of the nervous system was affected. Finally, the excised part of the nervous system may not have a unitary function.

A recently developed and unique surgical procedure, known as the split brain preparation, has given rise to some fascinating experiments. An excellent summary is presented in Sperry (1964). Despite the fact that the human brain generally acts as a unitary organ, it consists, in fact, of two separate halves called hemispheres. The innervation patterns are such that the right hemisphere is generally associated with the left side of the body and the left hemisphere with the right side. Nevertheless, when one hemisphere is damaged the corresponding section of the other hemisphere can often take over that function. The experiments using the split brain preparation were done to determine more precisely the effect of making the hemispheres independent of each other.

Anatomical investigation suggests that there are special "bridges" connecting the two parts of the brain. The largest among these is the corpus collosum, a bundle of neurons connecting the two halves of the cerebrum (the upper part of the brain). The corpus callosum also contains most of the neurons connecting the two sides of the cerebral cortex, which is the highest integrating part of the brain.

Early operations on the corpus callosum were performed in epileptic patients to mitigate the severity of their seizures. Subsequent examination of these patients revealed no discernible loss of function under normal conditions. It took special testing to make manifest the function of the corpus callosum. When both the corpus callosum and the optic chiasm are cut, the two cerebral hemispheres are separated from one another and visual stimuli impinge separately on each eye. The optic chiasm is the point along the visual pathway where the optic tract from each eye separates into two sections, one going to one hemisphere, the other going to the second. If one wants to make sure that visual stimulus information goes to one cerebral hemisphere only, the optic chiasm must be severed. The first experiment using such a preparation consisted of training an animal to discriminate between a square and a circle. The S^D presented to one eye (with the other eye blindfolded) might be a square, the S^Δ the circle. After discrimination was achieved using the first eye, it was blindfolded and the second eye was exposed to the same S^D and S^Δ. The remarkable result consisted in the fact that the animals reacted to the stimuli as if they had never before been presented to it, i.e., there was no evidence at all for any transfer of training from one eye to the other. Furthermore, when the stimulus which functioned as an S^D for one eye was used as an S^Δ for the other eye, the animal showed no conflict in learning both discriminations.

In an experiment on tactual and thermal discrimination, Ebner and Myers (1962) worked with young monkeys, half of whom had their corpus callosum and anterior commissure (another neural bridge between the two hemispheres) transected and the other half of whom were left intact. The monkeys were then placed in an apparatus which made it possible to train one limb at a time. The general procedure consisted of presenting the monkey with two different bars at a time and training him to press one of them using as S^D and S^Δ differences of shape for one experiment and temperature for another. The procedure was first carried out with one hand (left in some and right in other monkeys) and then with the other. The animals were all food deprived and were given a small banana for bar pressing on a crf schedule. Then the discrimination task was presented on a trial-by-trial basis until the monkey moved the correct lever 85 out of a 100 times, plus 5 more additional days of 100 trials each for stabilization. Whenever the animal moved an incorrect lever, a bright oversize light was flashed and a time-out of 15 seconds was initiated (for that period of time the monkey had no way at all of receiving reinforcement). Inspection of Figure 5-5 shows the positive transfer from one hand to another in intact animals. Notice that in all three animals performance begins at chance level, i.e., 50 per cent of the responses are correct. Then, with more trials, performance levels of 85 correct out of 100 are achieved. The solid line shows learning with the first hand; the dashed line indi-

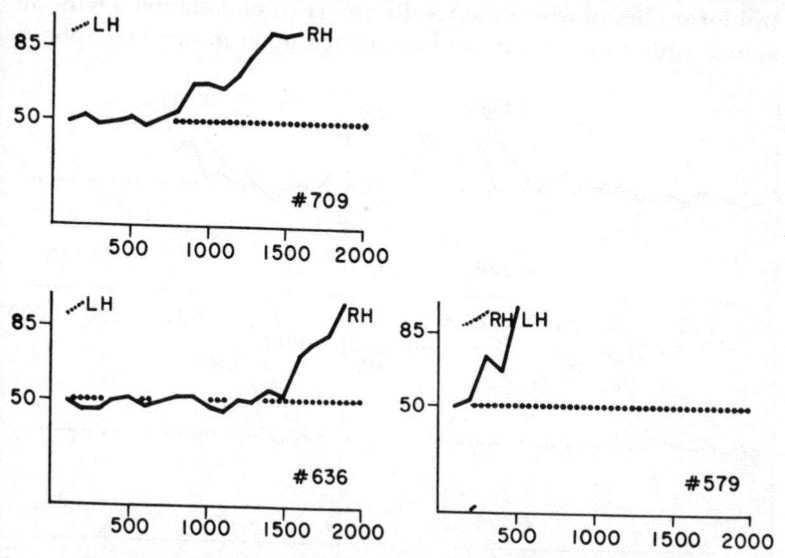

Fig. 5-5. Serial learning curves achieved through the two hands of three normal monkeys on the groove-smooth problem. Learning through the first hand is represented by the solid line; through the second hand by the dashed line. The second hand benefited greatly from the previous experiences through the first hand. (Ebner and Myers, 1962, Fig. 3.)

cates learning with the second hand. The contrast of these intact animals with 4 corpus callosum sectioned monkeys shows a dramatic difference. Figure 5-6 shows that both hands take approximately the same number of trials to achieve the learning criterion, i.e., as indicated in the visual discrimination experiment, the animals with a cut corpus callosum react to the old discrimination (touch in this case) as if it were new. Similar results were obtained when the transfer was tried out between feet on the same tactual task. Furthermore, the warm-cold discrimination task also led to similar results.

This particular operation has confirmed what we know about the dominance of one (usually the left) hemisphere for language. Thus when a person whose corpus callosum has been cut is presented with an object in the left half of his visual field only (these visual fibers go only to the right hemisphere which does not have the language function represented), he may react to it appropriately but be unable to name or describe it. Finally, we should mention the fact that this operation makes available a literally built-in control for studies in which the results are based on ablation. Thus an animal with a split brain can be operated upon in one hemisphere,

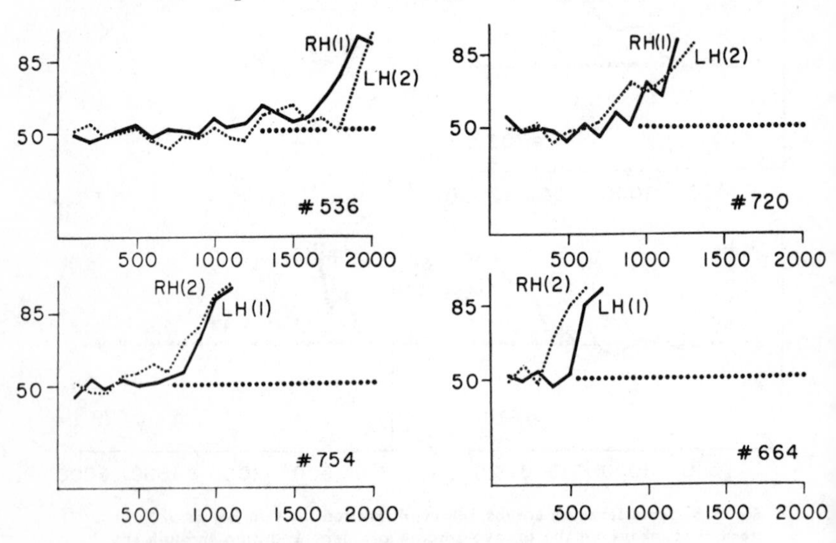

Fig. 5-6. First and second hand learning curves on groove-smooth problem in four corpus callosum sectioned monkeys. Similarity of learning through the two hands is striking. (Ebner and Myers, 1962 Fig. 4.)

with the other left intact. Since we have evidence for the lack of transfer from one hemisphere to the other, the animal's ability to learn or maintain behavior under the control of different stimuli can then be compared, with one lobe functioning as the experimental condition and the other as the control condition.

Another type of "ablation" technique should be mentioned. It is called "spreading cortical depression" and consists essentially of the application of a piece of filter paper that is soaked with potassium chloride directly to the cortex (the outermost part of the cerebral hemispheres) of an animal. This treatment makes the cortex of the treated hemisphere nonfunctional for a number of hours, after which time it recovers. This, therefore, is one type of "ablation" which appears to be reversible. What is more, because it can be applied to one hemisphere at a time, it allows for the study of functional split brain preparations with the possibility of recovering the connected brain when the effect has worn off. A recent paper by Schneider (1967) discusses the phenomenon of spreading cortical depression in terms of two different theoretical interpretations.

The discovery of electrical currents on the surface of the brain, which gave rise to the study of the EEG, has already been mentioned. We should point out that such recordings are essentially a composite picture of the overall electrical activity of the entire cortex. Nevertheless, the EEG records during different activities are discriminably different. There is, for example, a waking and a sleeping pattern. Furthermore, the analysis of EEG patterns has proved to be useful in the medical diagnosis of pathology of the brain. The recording of brain waves in response to specific stimuli has given rise to the term "evoked potential." It has been found to vary not only with physical aspects of the stimulus but more recently with what Sutton, Braren, Zubin, and John (1965) have called stimulus uncertainty (the probability with which a given stimulus follows another in the preceding trials).

Having shown that electrical activity can be discerned in the brain, it was only natural for investigators eventually to try to reverse the procedure, i.e., to stimulate the brain electrically. Wilder Penfield, the neurosurgeon, was able, in the course of the brain operations he performed on his epileptic patients, to map out various areas of the cortex. Thus, stimulation of what is now called visual cortex produced, according to the reports of the patient (who is subjected only to local anaesthesia since there are no pain receptors in the brain), "colors, lights, and shadows that move and take on crude outlines" (Penfield, 1959). Application of a small current to the auditory cortex produced ringing or other sounds. Motor responses could be elicited by electrical stimulation of the motor cortex. In addition, it was possible to evoke memories of past events from that area which Penfield called the "interpretive cortex."

Having shown that electrical stimulation of the surface of the brain yields interesting results about the function of corresponding parts of the nervous system, investigators turned to deeper structures. These experiments showed that electrical stimulation carried by very small electrodes which were implanted in the deeper parts of the brain could in some areas act as positive reinforcers and in other areas as negative reinforcers. The experiments that confirmed this utilized reinforcement contingencies in such a way that the depression of the bar in a Skinner box in some cases produced the electrical stimulation and in others prevented it from occurring. Under such circumstances very high rates of response were generated simply by the possibility of self-stimulation (Olds, 1956).

In an ingenious experiment, Delgado (1963) made use of the effects of electrical stimulation of the lower parts of the brain in a relatively complicated social environment. Electrical stimulation of some structures in the brain (e.g., the caudate nucleus) causes inhibition of behavior, whereas stimulation of other structures (e.g. the posteroventral nucleus of the thalamus) causes aggressiveness. By placing a bar in a cage which housed a colony of four monkeys and connecting the bar by radio to the boss monkey's electrodes, a monkey low (third out of 4) in the social hierarchy learned to control the aggressive behavior of that boss monkey. Inspection of Figure 5-7 pictures Elsa (low rank monkey) pressing the lever to inhibit the aggressive behavior of Ali (boss monkey). Note that Elsa is looking directly at the boss monkey as she presses the bar. This is unusual, since lower-ranking monkeys do not normally look straight at a higher ranking monkey because this evokes aggressive behavior. When the connection between the lever and the electrodes in the boss monkey was broken, the bar pressing was

Fig. 5-7. Elsa, pressing the lever, stimulates by radio the caudate nucleus of Ali (on right side of cage), producing behavioral inhibition. Elsa's attitude is significant because her attention is directed not to the lever but to Ali. It is unusual for lower-ranking monkeys to look straight at the boss of the colony because this evokes retaliation. (Delgado, 1963, Fig. 2.)

discontinued. When the lever pressing stimulated the electrode eliciting aggressive behavior in the boss monkey, it was pressed no more than 7 times during 3 days.

Some Comments on the Concept of Emotion

The concept of emotion is often associated with physiological measures. In part, this is certainly the scientist's legacy from our writers. "Have a heart," "heartfelt thanks," "this makes my blood boil," "it broke my heart," etc., are all examples of how the layman views emotion. The psychologist too has contributed to this concept of emotion by using the rat's elimination processes as an index of that animal's emotion, or by defining emotion in human beings as a change in rate of breathing, sweating, or heart rate. The difficulty in arriving at reliable behavioral judgments of emotion has driven many psychologists to the measurement of physiological events.

What is forgotten in these cases, however, is the fact that emotion, recognized behaviorally, has certain behavioral stimulus properties. Thus, when we are interested in how one animal responds to the "emotional responses" of another animal, measurement of the emotional animal's physiological events is largely irrelevant. Delgado (1963), in the experiment described above, reveals one very interesting method for making behavioral descriptions of emotions objective, i.e., let the observing animal's responses be contingent on the other animal's behavior. The conditioned suppression paradigm provides the psychologist with another situation in which to observe an emotion; this one is often referred to as "anxiety." Ethologists have for a long time described emotions in terms of behavioral criteria. No one less than Charles Darwin (1872) himself presented pictures of emotion in animals which many of us recognize. Finally, Brady's (1966) studies, cited above, present some excellent examples of how physiological and behavioral measures taken concurrently can supply us with the converging operations to define emotion in an objective fashion. Certainly such a definition is called for in the field of psychopathology where the term "emotion" is very much in use.

Before leaving discussion of this term we must consider the possibility that much of the argument about it concerns verbal behavior only. The verbal responses which the patient makes to his psychotherapist about his "feelings" may be determined by a different set of variables than the "feelings" ascribed to the subject by an outside observer of his respondent behavior, the breakdown of his nonverbal operant responses, or his endocrine secretions. We shall have occasion to return to this topic under the heading of private events when we discuss verbal behavior and psychopathology.

SUMMARY

Beginning with the important point that neither behavior nor physiological events are to be viewed as more basic, this chapter reviewed a number of relevant experiments.

Behavioral influences upon physiological events were demonstrated by experiments in which attending behavior prevented the influx of stimuli from a new source, deprivation of stimulation (extreme isolation) caused changes in EEG patterns, and conditioning and extinction procedures produced temporary short-term changes in respiration, heart rate, and EEG patterns. Changes in the functioning of endocrine glands as a result of different conditioning procedures were found to produce longer lasting effects. Finally, consideration was given to experiments which showed the production of gastrointestinal lesions particularly by means of free-operant avoidance schedules.

Physiological influences upon behavior were discussed, by listing the general techniques used to evaluate and modify physiological events. The first method listed for evaluating physiological events consisted simply of tracing the intact nervous system. The second method consisted essentially of destroying a part of the nervous system and observing the effects upon behavior. A technique derived from this is the split brain preparation in which an animal is used as his own control by ablating part of one hemisphere and then testing the animal separately, stimulating first one hemisphere and then the other. The technique of spreading cortical depression was taken up next. This procedure causes a temporary "ablation" involving one hemisphere at a time, which, because of its reversibility, appears to be applicable to many of the problems formerly dealt with by the split brain preparation. Electrical stimulation of the cortex was shown to be useful in mapping out the functions of the different parts of the cortex. When electrical stimulation was applied to deeper structures in the brain, it was found to have the properties of positive and negative reinforcers, depending upon the precise place of stimulation.

Emotion was discussed as one example of a concept for which physiological events were thought by some to be most important. Some discussion made it clear, however, that the manner of study had to depend on a number of issues and that in some cases a behavioral approach is called for, in others a physiological one, and in still others a combination. The importance of verbal behavior in the analysis of what is meant by emotion was briefly mentioned.

6

Sensation and Perception

THEORETICAL ISSUES

The study of sensation was, of course, psychology's first love. Knowledge of the basic sensations was to be the cornerstone of the science of psychology. The method of introspectionism was to reveal those basic elements, the sensations, and to synthesize perception and thus all experience. As already indicated, the method of introspection was inadequate, but the importance of the area is undeniable, for it deals with the stimulus, the input to the organism.

Sensation and Perception Compared

We will consider this area from the point of view of the importance of the physical properties of the stimulus in determining the response. The use of two terms, sensation and perception, means that there are two processes, but the fact that these terms are typically found together correctly suggests that the line of demarcation is difficult to draw. In general, sensation refers to a stimulus effect in which responses are determined almost exclusively by the physical properties of the stimulus and the physiological properties of the receptor mechanism, including the neural pathways up to the brain. Perception, which had formerly been defined as a combination of elements of sensation, has come to be viewed as a stimulus effect in which the responses are determined by factors other than, or in addition to, the ones controlling responses in sensation. These factors consist of interactions of stimuli and the conditioning history of the organism. Stimuli involved in the process of perception are also generally more complex and therefore often involve intermediary observing responses. These observing responses are discontinuous discrete responses, sometimes referred to as attention, which function so as to enable the subject to expose himself to a series of stimuli, thus causing fluctuation in his responses from time to time and variability among the responses of different subjects. This fact has sometimes been interpreted as a property of the stimulus and, as such, is seen as giving rise to "different perceptions"; looked at from the point of view of observing responses, these different perceptions can be tested for by means of direct experimental intervention. An example of the fluctuation of responses to a complex stimulus is to be found in Figures 6-1 and 6-2. Figure 6-1 shows a cube. Sometimes it appears to be seen from above and sometimes from below. Figure 6-2 shows a more complicated fluctuating figure. Sometimes the observing responses compel one to "see" a young woman, and sometimes an old woman. An interpretation of fluctuating figures in terms of interactions between cell assemblies (hypothetical physiological units) is presented in Hebb (1966).

Two Psychophysical Laws

The concern which the early psychologists had with the scientific study of sensation, of course, immediately led them to attempts at quantitative description.

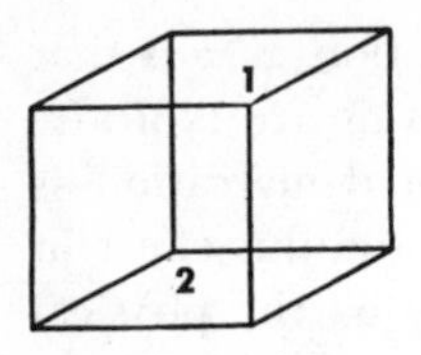

Fig. 6-1. The Necker Cube. When you fixate 1, you are looking down on the cube; when you fixate 2, you are looking up at the cube.

Fig. 6-2. An Ambiguous Figure. (Boring, 1930.)

In 1834, Ernst H. Weber made the trenchant observation that the greater the magnitude of a given stimulus, the greater the increment in the magnitude of another stimulus must be for a subject to be able to tell them apart. As Weber himself put it (Herrnstein & Boring, 1966, p. 64): "In observing the disparity between things that are compared, we perceive not the difference between the things, but the ratio of this difference to the magnitude of the things compared." Weber made this same observation in enough different sensory modalities to convince himself that each modality gave rise to a different constant ratio between detectable increment (I) and magnitude of stimulus considered (M), i.e., $\frac{I}{M} = K$.

In 1860, Gustav T. Fechner published an extension of Weber's generalization for the purpose of measuring sensation, a problem which fascinated him. Fechner derived his formulation of the measurement of sensation in order to fight the spectre of materialism of his day. As Miller (1962) pointed out, Fechner was so successful in the "measurement" of sensation that the subjective concept of sensation which Fechner had wanted to preserve could be entirely eliminated. Fechner's law, or the Weber-Fechner law, as it is called to give both men credit, states that the magnitude of sensation (S) is proportional to the logarithm of the magnitude (M) of the physical stimulus: $S = \log_e M$. The reader should note, of course, that both the Weber constant and the Weber-Fechner law enable one to describe subjective factors in terms of objective physical units. The experimental operations which one must perform to obtain data which can be fitted by the above equations consist of comparison judgments (discriminative behavior) which give rise to data describing the magnitude of the difference between two stimuli that a subject can just detect. Fechner assumed that the physical difference between any two stimuli regardless of their magnitude, which is "just noticeable," gives rise to a psychological difference which is equal in magnitude to any other "just noticeable" difference. In this way, Fechner reasoned, the scale of sensation could be established simply by adding up the just noticeable differences (jnd). This gave rise to the now well known *jnd* scale.

The second psychophysical law ("law" here referring to a description of the relationship between sensation, derived from the subject's discriminative behavior and the physical magnitude of the stimulus) is known as the power law. In a publication in 1872, Joseph A. F. Plateau first formulated the power law, which has more recently been revived and extended by S. S. Stevens to apply to a large number of sensory modalities (see for example, Stevens & Galanter, 1957). According to this formulation, sensation (S) is proportional to the physical magnitude (M) of the stimulus raised to a power (P): $S = KM^P$. The value of the power has been shown to vary with the sensory modality. Stevens has made use of methods of data collection which are different from those used to validate Fechner's law. We shall discuss these methods below. For the present it suffices merely to point out the difference between Fechner's and Steven's basic assumptions. Fechner's assumption is one of equality of differences (jnd's) and therefore requires subjects to make judgments about psychological differences. Stevens's assumption is one of equality of psychological ratios and therefore requires subjects to estimate whether one stimulus is half or twice the magnitude of another stimulus. Method and theory go hand in hand.

The Behavioral Approach to Sensation and Perception

While it is the author's contention that learning theory is well able to deal with the problems of sensation and perception, the reader must realize that psychophysics and learning have developed along parallel lines and now require translation from one area to another, a translation which involves not only nomenclature, but central problems and methods of investigation. Since psychophysics has concentrated on the stimulus, it has generally ignored the reinforcement conditions under which the responses were emitted, as well as the characteristics of the responses and the scales from which they come. Recent research shows these to be critical variables. On the other hand, learning theory has not, until fairly recently, been applied to "sensory" problems and is therefore only now working out the relevant methodology. Furthermore, the area of psychophysics has become concerned with tracing the movement of the stimulus through the organism in order to shed some light on the physiological transducers of the physical inputs before they appear as responses.

This chapter will afford us the opportunity to review the mutually beneficial effects of the relationship between learning and psychophysics. However, the question still remains: In what way does a behavioral approach to sensation and perception distinguish itself from other approaches? The answer is relatively straightforward. It is distinguished, first of all, in that the same concern is devoted to specification of the responses as to the stimuli. Furthermore, it deals explicitly with the problems raised in connection with the use of subjects to generate responses upon which are later performed the operations of measurement in order to determine the functional stimulus-response relations. In using a subject as an informant, the psychologist lets the subject do the measuring (using criteria which remain unknown to the experimenter). The behavioral approach ensures that the variables which influence the subject in making his circumscribed response (s) are subjected to further investigation. We know, for example, that certain responses have, in general, a higher probability of occurrence than others, that this difference in probability of occurrence varies with the responses previously emitted by the subject, and that it also varies with the response scale of which the response is currently a member.

The behavioral approach views sensation and perception as involving a discriminative response, and proceeds to identify, as suggested by Garner, Hake and Ericksen (1956), and Graham (1958), in a systematic fashion, the S^D's and the S^R's and S^r's (positive and negative) which contribute to the response, to estimate the contribution of the state variables (drugs, health, physiological apparatus, social factors, etc.) to the response, to define the role the particular response scale in use plays, and to determine what effect the particular instructions have on the resulting functional stimulus-response relations obtained.

Sensation

Psychophysical Methods and the Threshold Concept

Many of the psychophysical methods currently in use in the area of sensation and perception came from the time and work of Weber, Fechner, Wundt, and Plateau. A good deal of research is still directed at many of the same problems of measurement. The concept of *threshold* is still with us and the argument about its reality is, if anything, greater than ever. A threshold, defined most generally, is the physical value of stimulus or difference between two stimuli which is just detectable by the subject. In practice this value turns out to be a statistical concept rather than a single value. Let us take as an example an experiment designed to discover the absolute threshold for light, i.e., that stimulus value which is just detectable. In such an experiment the experimenter might well make use of the method of constant stimuli, a method that consists essentially of presenting in random order literally hundreds of light stimuli, varying in magnitude, and covering, in particularly great density, values around the suspected threshold value, with a warning signal preceding each stimulus. Each of the stimuli is then presented many (e.g., 100) times, thus affording the experimenter a sample of responses to each of the stimulus values. Instructions are given to the subject, usually buttressed by some training, to make certain he knows what to do and makes consistent responses. They might, for example, direct the subject to rest his chin on a chin rest, to maintain his gaze at a fixation point, and to restrict his responses to two, either verbal ("I see it" or "I don't") or manual (pressing one key for seeing, one for failing to see it). Ordinarily, the experimenter gives the subject no feedback after his responses so that he never knows when he was right or when he was wrong in his judgment. The data yielded by such an experiment are generally plotted with stimulus intensity on the abscissa and proportion of "I see it" responses on the ordinate. Typically, this gives rise to a smooth curve signifying a slow change in the proportion. Figure 6-3 shows a typical stimulus response plot. Notice that at very low intensities practically none of the responses are "I see it," while at high intensities all are. The point which is usually taken as the absolute threshold is that stimulus value which corresponds to the proportion of seeing 50 per cent of the time. The threshold is indicated by the line marked "limen," which is another term for threshold. The rationale behind this concept of the threshold is that there are many events that can and do interfere with the sensing of a particular stimulus, particularly at low intensities of stimulation. The subject may blink at the time the stimulus goes on, he may not be looking at the fixation point, an internal disturbance such as a pain may divert his attention from the visual stimulus, and so on. It is because of this multiplicity of small events that the threshold is viewed as a statistical concept. The point at which the probability of seeing is equal to the probability of not seeing is the point of greatest uncertainty and therefore, by definition, the threshold value.

This statistical concept of the threshold ought to make clearer the concept of *subliminal,* which means below threshold. A report that a given stimulus has subliminal effects should no longer seem contradictory when you consider that a subliminal stimulus simply means that the proportion of "seeing" responses is less than one half (see Figure 6-3). Such a stimulus, even though below threshold, can influence behavior. On the other hand, it need not be feared that stimuli which are below threshold are as influential as they were pictured to be when reports of subliminal advertising were current, since inspection of Figure 6-3 makes clear that the proportion of "seeing" responses is lower for subliminal stimuli.

Let us return to the threshold value obtained in Figure 6-3. This threshold value yields one point on a dark adaptation curve. In other words, the threshold value depicted in Figure 6-3 might be

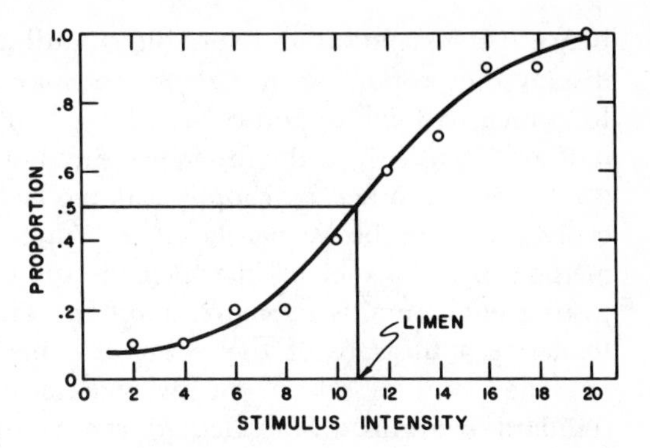

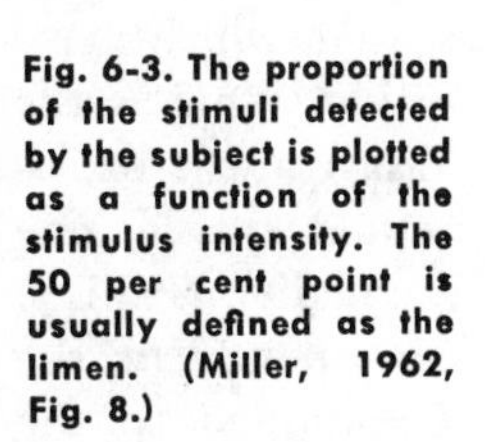
Fig. 6-3. The proportion of the stimuli detected by the subject is plotted as a function of the stimulus intensity. The 50 per cent point is usually defined as the limen. (Miller, 1962, Fig. 8.)

that one which would be obtained after 10 minutes of dark adaptation. To plot the entire dark adaptation curve, a threshold value must be obtained at a number of different time periods of dark adaptation. Turning back to look at Figure 5-1, you will notice that the graph plots two physical values against each other. This kind of plot is typical for psychophysical functions. The subject's response enters the picture in the following way: The physical values usually plotted on the ordinate are those to which the subject makes a characteristic response, namely, sensing it half the time, which is, of course, the threshold value.

The method of constant stimuli can also be applied to the problem of the difference threshold. The experiment would be performed in much the same way as detailed above. Instead of presenting a single stimulus on any one trial, however, the subject would be presented with two, either next to one another or in temporal sequence. One stimulus, the standard, would be presented first (or on one side) half the time and the second (or on the other side) the other half of the time. These pairs of stimuli, consisting of the standard and a variable stimulus, would then be presented in random order so that the subject would derive no information from the order in which the stimuli are presented as to the amount or direction of difference. The subject's task, as specified by instructions to him, would consist of judgments of whether the second stimulus is of greater or smaller magnitude than the first stimulus. The resulting plot of the data would resemble that found in Figure 6-3, except that the abscissa would display the differences between the standard and variable stimuli and the ordinate would display the proportion of "larger" responses. The difference value for which half the responses are "larger" (and therefore the other half are "smaller") is the difference threshold.

There are other psychophysical methods as well which have evolved out of the Weber–Fechner–Wundt tradition. One is the method of average error in which the subject's task consists of adjusting one stimulus to match another. This method enables one to derive a measure of the point of subjective equality (P.S.E.), i.e., the point at which the average setting corresponds to the standard stimulus. The method can readily be applied to the measurement of illusions. Let us look, for example, at the Mueller-Lyer illusion. In viewing the two lines (Figure 6-4), the line on the bottom appears to be longer than the one on the top. Upon measuring the two lines, however, it is clear that they are equal in length. Still another purpose is served by the method of

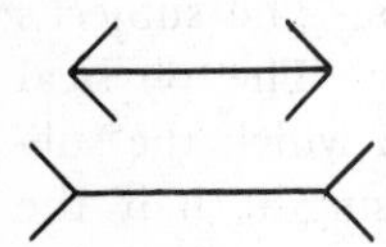

Fig. 6-4. The Müller-Lyer illusion. Although the two horizontal lines are of equal size, the line on the bottom appears to be longer.

average error in that it enables the experimenter to evaluate the magnitude of the constant error (C.E.) by using the difference between the standard line and the P.S.E. This involves presenting each subject on a number of trials with different lines of standard length to which he must match another line. A related method is the method of limits in which the experimenter exposes both the standard stimuli and the variable stimuli. In the presence of the standard stimulus the experimenter changes the value of the variable stimulus in discrete steps, requiring the subject at each step to say "longer" or "shorter." On each trial, the initial value of the variable stimulus is greater or smaller than the standard stimulus. Whether the initial value is greater or smaller, the magnitude of that value on each trial is determined randomly. The point of interest occurs when the subject changes his response from the one to the other. The point between the two different responses is then a one-trial estimate of the P.S.E. The final P.S.E. is computed by averaging over a number of trials of response changes.

A fourth psychophysical method is called the method of absolute judgment or single stimuli. It is similar to the method of constant stimuli in that each stimulus is presented alone. It differs in that the subject is allowed to make more than two responses. It is the method applied to experiments in color vision where a stimulus of a given wavelength is presented to a subject and the subject's task is to name the color. For each wavelength, it is then possible to plot a distribution of the different responses made by the subject. This method has also been employed in the judgment of heaviness of weights and in the problem of shift in judgment. Helson (1964) successfully applied the notion of adaptation level, the reference point with respect to which the subjects make their judgments, to many stimulus continua, including social stimuli. A subject is given a series of weights to judge and told to apply the responses "very light," "light," "medium," "heavy," or "very heavy" to them. Once the subject has lifted all of the weights, he will generally emit his responses consistently, applying them to the various stimuli. In other words, the subject is said to have established a scale of judgment. The shift phenomenon occurs when the experimenter introduces a new anchor stimulus; in the case of weights, a stimulus much heavier or much lighter than those in the series. The effect causes a shift in judgment such that when the anchor weight is extra heavy, the weight which used to be called "very heavy" comes to be called, "heavy," the one which used to be called "heavy" is now called "medium," and so on down the line. It is of interest that the *relativity* of such judgments (the unfortunate name, "method of absolute judgment," notwithstanding) can be shown to apply to complicated stimulus dimensions such as the social desirability of professions. In other words, what one deems appropriate or desirable behavior varies with the kinds of behaviors to which that person is exposed.

As already suggested, application of the power law requires different psychophysical methods. One of these methods is magnitude estimation. The subject in such an experiment is first presented with a stimulus and told to assign to it a numerical value of 100. Then the experimenter presents him with other stimuli along the same dimension, and asks the subject to assign other numbers to the new stimuli *in proportion* to the psychological effect of the first stimulus. Thus, if a sound appears twice as loud as the first stimulus (assigned the value of 100) then the subject is told to say 200. If it feels only about half as loud, then the subject is told to say 50 and so on. Generally, in order to avoid the problems of the subject's responses being determined by the series of stimuli to which he is exposed, each subject is given only a few stimuli to judge. As a result, unlike the methods described above, the values computed have to be based upon averaging the results of a number of subjects. Some objection can also be raised to the procedure of averaging verbal responses, since the estimates are obviously not based upon physical measurement operations. These objections have led Stevens to use other psychophysical methods which do not require the averaging of verbal responses. It should be noted, however, that there are methods of quantifying verbal responses which do not require the assumption that verbal responses have the same properties as numbers derived from physical operations (Salzinger, 1956).

The technique which Stevens has used to circumvent the problem of averaging over verbal number responses is the method of crossmodality matching. In this technique, the subject is required to match the magnitude of a stimulus in one modality to the magnitude of a stimulus in another modality. A subject may be required to draw a line "as long as a sound is loud." It should be obvious to the reader than an understanding of those instructions is rather important. In point of fact, an experimental analysis of the effect of instructions on the results yielded by psychophysical experiments is still very much needed. Interestingly enough, the analysis of the effects of instructions is coming to us, at least in part, from experiments with animals, because specifications of any task with an animal, unlike with a human subject, must be made wholly explicit. How do we get an animal to tell us when he sees a light and when he does not? The answer comes from a conditioning procedure.

The Operant Conditioning Approach to Sensation

Sensory processes in animals form an important part of the area of sensation and perception because the animal's sensory apparatus, innervation patterns, and biochemical processes underlying the sensory processes can be studied with procedures which are unacceptable for work with human subjects.

One of the most interesting psychophysical methods recently applied to animals was used to obtain data on dark adaptation in the pigeon. The procedure was based on von Bekesy's (1947) audiometer, which is basically derived from the method of constant stimuli. The subject's task with respect to the audiometer is to press a key as long as a sound is audible. When the subject keeps the key depressed the sound slowly diminishes in intensity, until he no longer hears the tone and releases the key. Then the audiometer automatically increases the intensity of the tone until it is again audible to the subject and he presses the key, etc. Blough (1958, 1966) modified the above procedure for use with the pigeon. The experimental situation consists basically of two responses. The presence of light on the stimulus patch was the S^D for pecking Key A, the absence of light on the stimulus patch was the S^D for pecking Key B. This is, of course, the basic method of constant stimuli. To change it to a tracking procedure, the following modifications were made. Each peck on Key A reduced the intensity of the light and each peck on Key B increased the intensity of the light. At first the pigeon was reinforced for pecking the two keys at random. Then the procedure was changed so that when Key A was pecked in the presence of light, the light turned completely out and a peck at Key B was followed by a food reinforcer in the form of access to grain for a period of 5 seconds. This means that the experimenter can reinforce one response when the light is on (by the S^{+r} of "light out") and the other when it is out (by the S^{+R} of food). This modified procedure can be viewed as establishing a response chain where pecks on Key A are followed by S^{+r}, the S^D (darkness), marking the occasion for responses on Key B, which, when made, are followed by primary reinforcement. But now the problem which remains is how the experimenter reinforces responses made to stimuli whose visibility he is trying to determine. Clearly the pigeon could respond as if he were being reinforced on an intermittent schedule and not respond to the light at all. It is critical therefore that the animal attend the stimulus. This is assured by the simple imposition of a short pause between responses on Keys A and B. If the animal simply responds back and forth from one key to the other, then no reinforcement is given. The general experimental set-up is depicted in Figure 6-5, showing how the pigeon inserts his head through an opening, and when pausing, is stimulated by the light patch. This still does not tell us when the experimenter should reinforce a response on Key B. The solution is quite simple (after you have thought of it). Responses on Key A and on Key B are first put on an intermittent reinforcement basis, so that the pigeon has to make a number of responses before it is reinforced with a conditioned reinforcer for A and a primary reinforcer for B. Then a shutter system is used. The shutter is closed on an intermittent basis after pecks on Key A. Key pecks in the dark (when the shutter is closed) are followed by the primary reinforcer. Under these conditions, the pigeon responds to Key B whenever the light intensity is below his threshold, as if pecking on it were being reinforced on an intermittent schedule, *because the animal cannot discriminate the difference between the closed shutter condition and when he cannot "see" the light.*

Thus, the experimental situation can be summarized in the following way: in the presence of superliminal light, the pigeon responds on Key A. Each response reduces the intensity of light by a small amount. When the light is below the seeing threshold, the pigeon is essentially being exposed to the S^D for pecking Key B. Each peck on Key B then increases the intensity of the light. On a random basis and while the pigeon is responding on Key B, the shutter is closed, i.e., the no-light condition occurs and responding on Key B is reinforced by making food available to him. By keep-

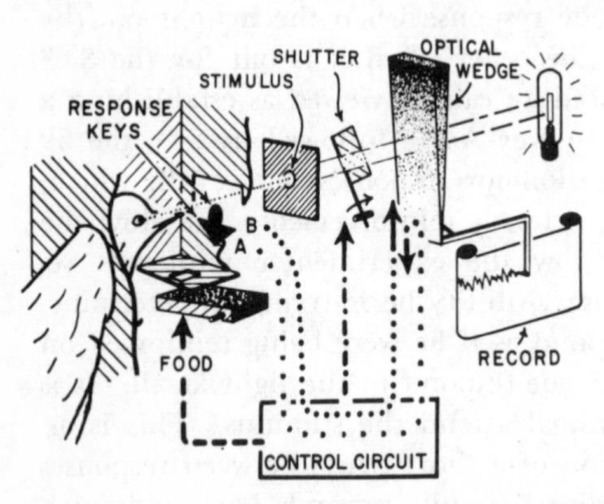

Fig. 6-5. A schematic picture of the tracking apparatus. (Blough, 1958, Fig. 1.)

ing track of when the pigeon switches from one key to another (leaving out his responses when the shutter is closed), it is possible to trace the absolute threshold of the pigeon. The procedure has been applied to other species besides the pigeon and has been utilized in the area of audition. It has also been found that the procedure can be improved by making primary reinforcers, on an intermittent basis, available for responses on both keys. In general, this procedure has been quite useful. Lest the reader think it has no problems, however, let him review some of the difficulties such a procedure can entail (Blough, 1966); there is the problem of unconditioned stimulus preferences, such as preference for one wavelength over another, or a higher response rate to a more intense than to a less intense stimulus; there is the problem of the reinforcer itself constituting an S^D for the next response, i.e., whether the animal should make the "I see" or the "I don't see" response; next, there is the problem of the so-called proprioceptive chain where one response controls the emission of the next response, independent of external stimulation.

It should be noted that many of these problems also occur in human psychophysical procedures, some of them being hidden in the instructions given the subject. Experiments with animals force the experimenter to make the contingency more explicit than is often the case with human subjects.

Application of the same general technique to the problem of monitoring depth of sleep was attempted by Lindsley (1957). The sleeping subject's task consisted of closing a microswitch taped onto his preferred hand. Each response reduced the intensity of a sound which, if no response was made, increased up to a maximum. The experiment showed that rate of operant responding to turn off an aversive sound during the subject's sleep is sensitive to such conditions as sleep deprivation and drug effects.

A recent experiment (Herrnstein & van Sommers, 1962) in operant conditioning employed Stevens's technique of magnitude estimation with two pigeons. The authors had to face the problem of the "instruction," namely that the reinforcement procedure rather than the discriminative stimuli might determine the magnitude estimation. They resolved the problem by reinforcing different rates of response in the presence of different intensities of light.

Responding in the presence of five different intensities was reinforced; responding in the presence of another four intensities was used for testing later without special training. The interresponse times required for the dimmest "training" light were 195 to 214 seconds and 1.35 to 1.48 for the brightest light. The four "testing" stimuli bisected logarithmically the intensity differences between successive members of pairs of the training stimuli. The responses to the testing stimuli were never reinforced. Resulting rates of response for these testing stimuli appeared to follow the psychophysical curve predicted by Stevens, although the authors felt that Fechner's law could not definitely be discounted on the basis of their results. When working with animals, the need for the initial *conditioning* of different response rates to various stimuli is obvious for this kind of experiment; undoubtedly a conditioning process must be involved in human estimation responses as well, thus raising an objection to the magnitude estimation technique in general as simply reflecting a prior conditioning process. If this is so (and not everyone agrees), it still remains necessary to specify why the conditioning process might better be reflected by Steven's rather than Fechner's formulation.

What the animal studies so clearly demonstrate is the possible influence on the response of variables other than the sensory ones. It is obvious that there are such interfering variables in human research as well. One way in which experimenters deal with this problem is by using "trained" subjects. However, since it is clear that reinforcement parameters are critical in animal studies, why therefore should they not be important in human studies? In fact, as the reader must have realized by now, the process of reinforcement does indeed make a difference. Not very long ago a group of psychologists (Swets, Tanner & Birdsall, 1961) were led to doubt the very existence of a threshold by their apparent ability to move threshold values up and down by a number of factors usually viewed as being unrelated to the sensory process. They began with the fact that the subject is allowed, on any given trial in a typical psychophysical experiment, which uses the method of constant stimuli, to make only one of two responses to one of two stimulus conditions. They then superimposed a payoff matrix on this choice situation which is actually the reinforcement contingencies acting upon the responses. Inspection of Figure 6-6 shows a four-cell table which might be considered to cause a bias.

		Stimulus	
		Present	*Absent*
Response	*"Yes"*	+2¢	−10¢
	"No"	−2¢	+2¢

Fig. 6-6. Payoff matrix introducing a bias by the use of a relatively high negative reinforcer for "Yes" responses.

Examination of the matrix makes it clear that a subject has a lower probability of losing money if he says "No" than if he says "Yes." The same matrix can, of course, be biased in the direction of increasing "Yes" responses by making "Yes" in the presence of the stimulus reinforced by the delivery of 50¢ to the subject and all the other event-response combinations followed by the loss or reward of 1¢. The reader might well ask why the experimenter would want to introduce such biases into an experiment. The answer is that the attempt is being made here to simulate, in an explicit manner, some of the effects that are undoubtedly present and which influence the subject's responses when only general verbal instructions are given during the course of a typical psychophysical experiment. Despite the fact that no explicit feedback is given to a subject, reinforcement contingencies either from the instructions (e.g., "Take a chance if you are not sure" may be assumed to increase the frequency of "Yes" responses in the absence of the stimulus) or from the subject's past reinforcement history (e.g., saying he sees something only if he is absolutely certain) or most likely from some complicated combination of both are in effect during the course of psychophysical experiments. Another variable which has been shown to influence a threshold determination is the probability of a signal being present. Obviously, a subject whose past observations have shown him only a small number of trials during which stimuli were present, would be inclined to guess "No" most of the time (cf. Holland, 1958 in Chapter 1). The effect of the payoff matrix must be controlled by sufficient monitoring of the responses a subject makes. Typically the experimenter uses just enough no-stimulus or "catch" trials to make sure the subject does not emit too many false alarm responses ("Yes" responses in the absence of the stimulus). It should be clear, however, that catch trials (their very existence constitutes an important effect on the probability of the presence of the stimulus) are critical if we wish to distinguish a subject whose "low threshold" is due to sensory factors from one whose threshold is determined by a generally higher probability of saying "Yes."

Examination of animal studies as well as studies on human subjects points up the need for the thorough investigation of the role of reinforcement in the measurement of sensory functions.

Respondent Conditioning in Psychophysics

We have talked about the fluctuation of the threshold as a result of the parameters of operant conditioning. Research in the Soviet Union has suggested that the absolute light threshold can be conditioned by means of the respondent conditioning paradigm. Recently, Aiba (1963) repeated a modified version of one of these experiments. First, subjects were familiarized with the experimental situation. The tone (to be used as the CS later on) was presented a few times to eliminate the orienting reaction. Then, after the subjects had been dark adapted, their absolute thresholds were determined by the method of constant stimuli. The 60 per cent seeing point, instead of the 50 per cent point, was used as the threshold value, since a change in value can be more easily detected here. Only those subjects were retained in the experiment who showed less than 10 per cent false alarm rate to the catch trials (catch trials were presented approximately the same number of times as the stimulus-present trials). After determination of the 60 per cent threshold values, the subjects were conditioned in the following way: A 1,000 cps tone (CS) was sounded for 15 seconds and paired with a 10-second bright light (US) for subjects in the experimental group. The bright light (US), by itself raises the absolute threshold for light. A period of darkness between trials dark adapted the eye for the next trial. For the control group, the 1,000 cps tone was paired with a dim deep red light. At random times the CS was followed by test flashes at about the intensity of the predetermined threshold value, and the subject's task was to report, as before, whether he saw, or did not see, the light. A comparison of the two groups showed a relatively small but statistically significant difference between the frequency of seeing the test stimuli. Figure 6-7 shows the relative stability of the frequency of seeing in the control

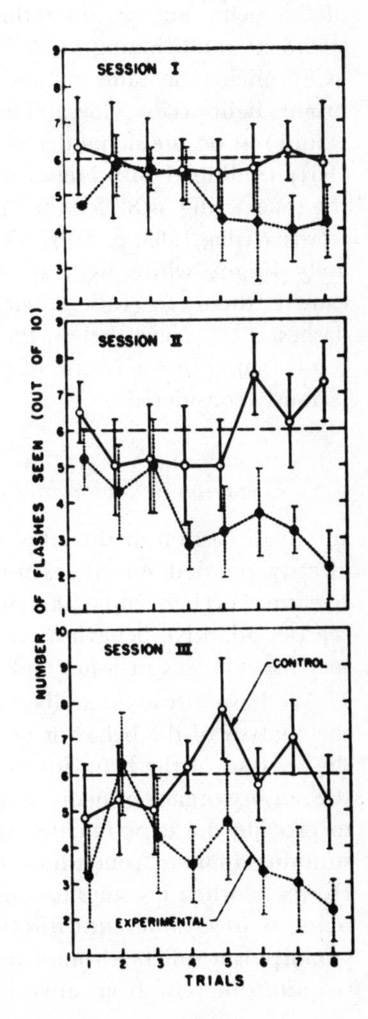

Fig. 6-7. Number of flashes seen in each of the trials in Sessions I-III. (Each point is the average of 6 *Ss*. The vertical bars show the variability among the *Ss* by *SD*. The horizontal line in each figure indicates the original level of seeing, prior to conditioning, in that session. There were, on the average, 1.5 pairings of the light and the tone between each pair of trials, and the first trial was also preceded by an average of 1.5 pairings. Consequently, the number of trials multiplied by 1.5 gives the number of pairings completed on that day. (Aiba, 1963, Fig. 1.)

group (open circles) at the previous 6 out of 10 level, and the gradual reduction of seeing (increase of threshold values) over trials for the experimental group. Not entirely clear is the reason for the apparent lack of carry-over of the effect from one day to the next. One possibility is that extinction took place between experimental sessions in the course of the subject's daily activities. It is of some interest to note that the investigator himself suggests the possibility of this being an operant rather than a respondent effect. The respondent conditioning model would have to assume that the tone (CS) elicits the same or a similar light adaptation effect as the bright light (US) does. The operant conditioning explanation would rest on the signal detection model (Swets, Tanner & Birdsall, 1961) combined with Helson's (1964) adaptation level model, with the tone acting as S^D for the "I don't see" response. In the author's words (Aiba, 1963, p. 239), "The repeated presentation of a moderately bright white light to the experimental groups may have caused them to raise their criterion for reporting the test flashes. . . ." Nevertheless, the possible involvement of respondent conditioning in the course of psychophysical experiments should be seriously considered.

Innate Behavior in Psychophysics

In our discussion of the ethological approach to behavior, we have already pointed out the significance of the fact that the innate releasing mechanism is differentially sensitive to critical stimuli and releases adaptive behavior. Here we will describe two special sensory mechanisms in fishes and dolphins.

We have already described the dangers of anthropomorphism in the analysis of the behavior of animals, and of clinical intuitions in the analysis of the behavior of man. Nevertheless, the similarity of the sensory organs of many animals to those of man is great enough to provide the experimenter with some hypotheses concerning the stimulus domain from which to sample the independent variable. However, when it comes to sensing objects by means of electric currents, as in *Gymnarchus niloticus,* a fish (Lissman, 1963), anthropomorphism suffers a complete setback, since this type of reception is quite different from anything upon which man depends. The electrical activity of *Gymnarchus* is also different from that of the electric eel, since the latter uses its powerful electric organ to stop predators and to paralyze his prey, while the former's weak electric organ can have no such function. *Gymnarchus* emits weak electrical discharges. During each discharge the tip of the tail becomes momentarily negative with respect to the head, thus forming a dipole electrical field. The field is symmetrical in the absence of surrounding objects. When objects are near, the lines of current are modified in such a way as to converge on objects or areas with higher conductivity and diverge from those with lower conductivity. The resulting change in amplitude of the pulses emitted by the fish constitutes the stimulus at the electrical sense organ. By using the presence of different objects as S^D's for food, Lissman and Machin (Lissman, 1963) were able to demonstrate that *Gymnarchus* can discriminate a nonconductor from a conductor of electricity. The fish was able to detect the presence of a glass rod 2 millimeters in diameter but not one .8 millimeter, suggesting that its electrical sense threshold lies between these two values.

Another marine animal known for his exceptional psychophysical performance is the bottle-nose dolphin, *Tursiops truncatus*. Kellogg (1960) showed that the animal avoids obstacles and finds food by emitting a series of sounds. Closer observation showed that the dolphin engages in oscillating head movements while emitting sounds, provided the target cannot be identified visually because of the turbidity of the water. A picture of the dolphin's pattern of movement is provided in Figure 6-8. Kellogg interpreted the oscillatory movements to be a combination of echolocation and binaural localization. He called this general activity *auditory scanning*.

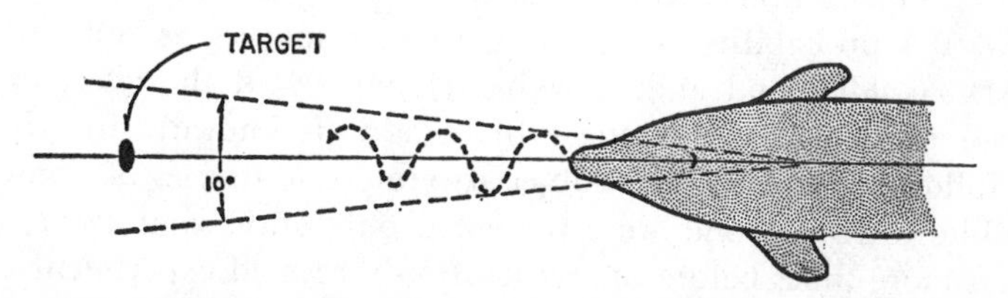

Fig. 6-8. Auditory scanning in the bottlenose dolphin. When echolocating a small target, such as fish, the porpoise approaches by oscillating its head to the right and left through an arc of about 10 degrees. This behavior undoubtedly involves binaural localization as well as echolocation. (Kellogg, 1960, Fig. 1.)

Perception

The Operant Conditioning Approach to Perception

As already pointed out, perception involves many variables in addition to the typical sensory ones. It is for this reason that perception has often been studied in relation to personality variables. Some psychologists have suggested that the way in which people perceive the world around them is determined by their personality. Many investigators have also searched for differences in perception among patients suffering from various forms of psychopathology. Because of the great interest in perception, a series of studies in this area will be reviewed. Essentially, the issue can be described in terms of seeing vs. saying. The problem has revolved about the question of the extent to which a verbal response depends upon the stimulus which is being exposed and the extent to which it depends upon the subject's past emission of that response. McGinnies (1949) reported that the emotional quality of some words (e.g., the word "penis") is such as to raise the recognition threshold for that word above that of neutral words in a situation where it is exposed for a very brief period of time, or at a very low intensity. Typically, such an experiment uses the method of limits. A word is exposed much below the recognition threshold and the subject is required to guess what word is being shown. The time or intensity is increased in small steps until the point at which the subject identifies the stimulus correctly. When emotional and neutral words are exposed by this method the results show that the emotional words have higher thresholds than the neutral words. Subsequent investigators (e.g., Howes & Solomon, 1950) suggested that this difference in threshold did not reflect differences in ability to recognize stimuli but, instead, the probability of emitting some responses as opposed to others. Goldiamond and Hawkins (1958) tested the effect of response probability or response bias (as it is known) directly by the following experiment. Subjects were given a series of nonsense syllables to read. Some were presented only once, some twice, and others more times before the recognition threshold experiment took place. Then the subjects were told that they would be shown the nonsense syllables, one at a time, for very brief periods and that they should guess if in doubt about which one they saw. In fact, the experimenters exposed *no* nonsense syllables at all, showing a Rorschach card at a speed too great to be at all recognizable. The responses were scored in the following way: A given series of "stimulus" presentations was continued until the subject guessed the nonsense syllable which was written down on the experimenter's score sheet for that trial, or until some maximum number of stimulus presentations was made. The results showed that the higher the frequency of preexperimental exposure of a given nonsense syllable, the lower the "threshold"–i.e., the higher the preexperimental frequency of exposure, the fewer the number of trials required to reach "recognition." A later experiment (Zajonc & Nieuwenhuyse, 1964) reopened the question of response bias vs. stimulus process. That experiment showed that, although response bias, as determined by past number of reinforced responses, accounted for a large part of the variance, the stimulus factor itself also exerted an effect apart from the response bias. These investigators found that the function relating frequency of preexperimental exposure to the usual recognition threshold for actual nonsense words was very much like the same function when no words were exposed. However, when the criterion for the recognition threshold was modified so that the subject had to report seeing the same word on two consecutive exposures, the resulting function differed more extensively from the no-stimulus function. In other words, the way in which the method of limits is ordinarily used produces a response bias which can be reduced by simply stipulating that a single correct guess does not terminate the series of stimuli. Thus, here is a clear example of how behavior theory can be used to clarify a problem in perception.

We have already pointed out (Chapter 1) that the observing response (where a subject focuses his attention) is under the control of the reinforcer, the event looked for. Holland (1958) showed that when a subject is asked to monitor the deflection of a pointer on a meter in a dark room by pressing a key which illuminates the meter for .07 second (observing response), the meter deflections constitute the reinforcing event. Holland demonstrated different response rates under different FI schedules (see Figure 6-9). Furthermore, a classical extinction curve was produced by withholding further reinforcement after a FI schedule (Figure 6-10). Holland

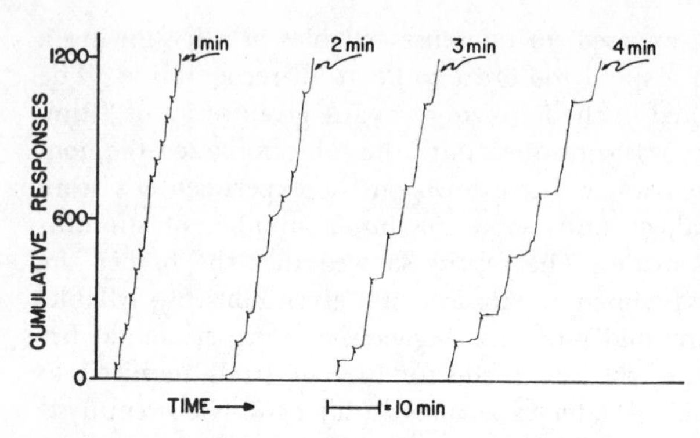

Fig. 6-9. Cumulative response records for 1-, 2-, 3-, and 4-minute fixed-interval schedules of pointer deflections. Detections are indicated by lines cutting across the records. (Holland, 1958, Fig. 1.)

went on to show the effectiveness of VI, DRL, and even a multiple schedule containing FI and FR components. The conclusion that observing responses are controlled by the usual reinforcement schedules seems inescapable. It is of interest to mention in this context an experiment by Schafer and Murphy (1943), who employed ambiguous figures as stimuli. These figures were such that the subject could see either of two faces at any one time in each figure. Before showing these ambiguous figures to the subject (Figure 6-11), the experimenters presented each profile separately, associating one with a positive reinforcer (delivery of money) and one with

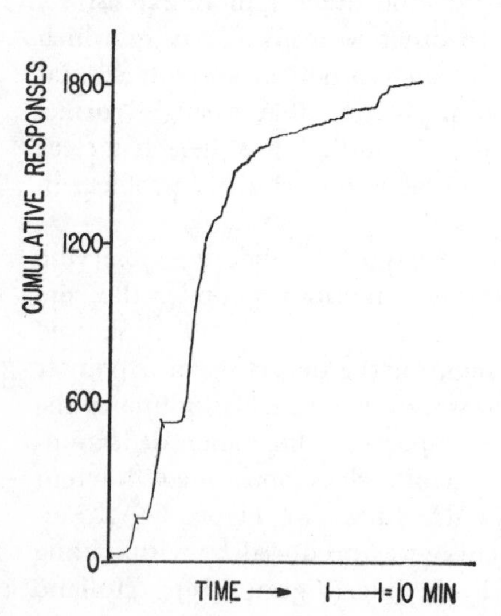

Fig. 6-10. Cumulative response record showing effect of withholding pointer deflections following a fixed-interval schedule. After three detections (indicated by lines cutting across the record) no further pointer deflections occurred. (Holland, 1958, Fig. 2.)

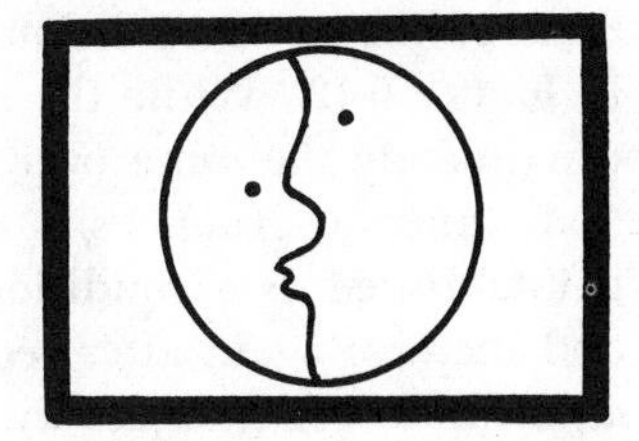
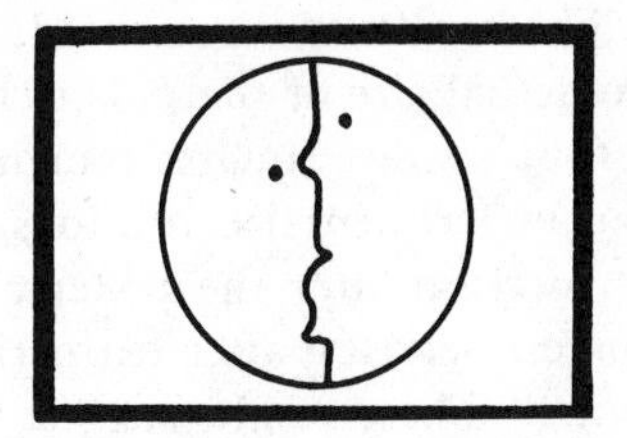

Fig. 6-11. Two ambiguous figures. (Schafer and Murphy, 1943, Fig. 2.)

a negative reinforcer (loss of money). Subsequent presentation of the ambiguous figures containing both the postively and the negatively reinforced profiles resulted in the subject's reporting seeing the postively reinforced face more frequently than the other.

Size estimation, which is the result of a number of determinants including size of retinal image and estimation of distance, was shown by Bruner and Goodman (1947) to vary also with the background of the observer. They found that poor children have a greater tendency to overestimate the size of coins than rich children. That study was followed up by an attempt to modify the background of children, defined in terms of reinforcement history, in order to obtain a clearer understanding of the independent variable. Lambert, Solomon, and Watson (1949) experimentally produced "value" in poker chips analogous to that of coins by establishing the chips as positive conditioned reinforcers. In the experimental group, children were allowed to turn a crank 18 times to receive a white poker chip which could be placed in a slot in exchange for a piece of candy. Each child was administered the reinforcement procedure for 10 days, with one trial given each day. The control group was subjected to the same procedure, except that children in that group received the candy itself rather than the chip for turning the crank. The children were then required to make size estimates (using the method of average error) by adjusting a circular patch of light to match the size of the poker chips. Size estimates of the poker chips were made before the establishment of the conditioned reinforcer, after 10 days of the conditioning procedure, after extinction (children were allowed to turn the crank of the machine without receiving either the candy in the control group or the poker chip in the experimental group), and after one day of reconditioning. The results are presented, in terms of the ratio of estimated size to actual size of the poker chip, in Figure 6-12. While the control group's size estimates remain approximately the same over the various experimental conditions, the experimental group's size estimates increase after the poker chip is established as a conditioned reinforcer, decrease after extinction, and increase again after reconditioning. These results suggest that association of an object with a positive conditioned reinforcer evokes a larger size judgment than an object not so associated. They also suggest that the greater overestimate of the coins displayed by poor children as opposed to that of rich children is related to a greater conditioned reinforcement value for the same coins by poor than by rich children.

The Respondent Conditioning Approach to Perception

The topic of attention (essentially where perception is directed) can be viewed from the point of view of the orienting reflex which we have already discussed in Chapter 2. Maltzman (1967) recently reviewed a series of experiments using the GSR (galvanic skin response, which is a change in conductance on the skin due to sweating activity) as the orienting reflex. The orienting reflex is elicited

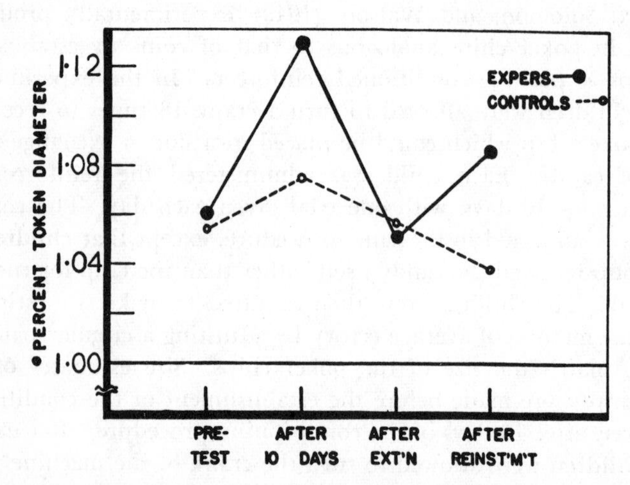

Fig. 6-12. Effects of the experimental conditions upon children's estimates of the diameter of a token when these estimates are taken as percents of the true diameter. (Lambert, Solomon, and Watson, 1949, Fig. 1.)

by stimulus change. When Maltzman separated subjects into two groups (high and low orienting reflex responders), he found that they differed in habituation, conditioning, generalization to stimuli related to the CS, and in extinction (Figure 6-13). He also found that the high orienting reflex subjects produced greater GSR's to the US than the low orienting reflex subjects. Furthermore, he discovered that the orienting reflex performance is related to performance on such different tasks as paired associate learning. Finally, Maltzman pointed out that the orienting reflex, as measured by the GSR, provides a picture of only one of its components, the other component being the operant one (cf. Holland, 1958).

It is of some interest to note that the respondent conditioning paradigm has also been used in the study of subliminal perception. We already discussed this concept at the beginning of the chapter when the word "subliminal" was used to refer to a stimulus which is below threshold, i.e., not necessarily one that is never detected but merely one which is detected less frequently than 50 per cent of the time. The context in which the term "subliminal" comes up now is

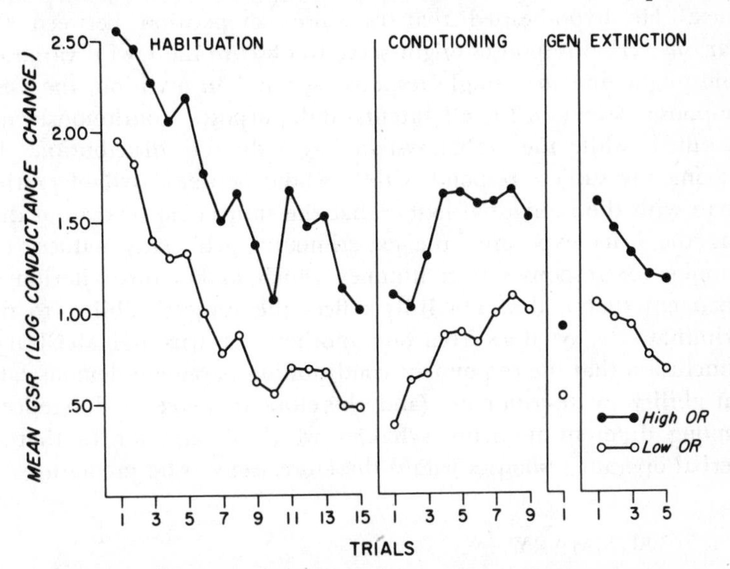

Fig. 6-13. Responses of high and low OR Ss to all words in the habituation phase, the CS word during conditioning, the associated test word in the generalization test, and the CS word during extinction. (Maltzman, 1967, Fig. 2.)

the discrepancy in detection of a nonsense syllable which results from the use of respondent as opposed to operant procedures. Lazarus and McLeary (1951, p. 113) stated that "at tachistoscopic exposure speeds too rapid for correct recognition, subjects are able to give discriminatory responses as measured by their galvanic skin response (GSR)." Thus the respondent conditioning paradigm is here being suggested as a superior index for the absolute threshold in the area of perception.

A few years after the Lazarus-McLeary experiment, Eriksen (1956) reanalyzed the logic of their study and concluded that the assertion of the superiority of the respondent as an index of perception was unwarranted. He pointed out that there are differences of a neurophysiological nature that make the two response systems (verbal and GSR) less than perfectly correlated. He characterized the GSR as essentially a single response, varying only in magnitude, whereas he characterized the verbal response system as consisting of several responses, each varying in magnitude. Any analysis of the verbal response system, therefore, would be considerably more complex. He hypothesized that response competition between the various verbal responses might serve to obscure the lawful variation one might find in a single response system. In addition, the GSR response system is, for all intents and purposes, continuously distributed, while the verbal system has a discrete distribution. By having the subject respond with a whole nonsense syllable rather than with the individual letters that the subject can make out during the brief exposures, the experimenter artificially reduces the number of responses to a number which makes the criterion so stringent that it does not fully reflect the subject's ability to discriminate the syllables from one another. Lazarus and McCleary's conclusion that the respondent conditioning paradigm demonstrates an ability to discriminate (and therefore to perceive differences) among different nonsense syllables which is superior to that of verbal operant responses would therefore seem to be premature.

SUMMARY

The classical areas of psychology, namely, sensation and perception were discussed in this chapter. A comparison of the two areas showed that sensation is primarily, though not completely, controlled by the sensory stimulus, its transduction by the receptor, and its innervation pattern to the brain, while perception is controlled by additional variables consisting of combinations of the sensory stimuli and the perceiver's reinforcement history.

Two psychophysical laws were described to account for the relationship between the physical value of the stimulus and its effect (sensation) on the organism. The first of those laws describes the relationship to be logarithmic, the second a power function.

The behavioral approach to sensation and perception was briefly outlined; the importance of viewing a subject as a source of responses to be measured rather than as a source of information which is *de facto* accepted as a measure was underscored.

We reviewed the concept of the threshold, pointing out its statistical properties, and then described the following methods of measurement: the method of constant stimuli, the method of average error, the method of limits, and the method of single stimuli. These methods are the traditional ones and have given rise to data which support the logarithmic conception of the psychophysical relationship. Other methods yielding data that support the power function include the method of magnitude estimation and cross modality matching.

The operant conditioning approach to sensation was then taken up. Here we described in detail an experiment designed to obtain absolute visual thresholds in the pigeon by means of a tracking procedure. The problem of how to "instruct" the animal without predetermining his discrimination behavior was discussed in relation to this experiment as well as in relation to an experiment on magnitude estimation. The similarity of the problem to that encountered in the study of human discrimination was made explicit.

Signal detection theory was taken up next. This approach to psychophysics can be easily related to operant conditioning studies in the area, since it lays great stress on the payoff matrix (reinforcement contingencies).

Next, an experiment was described demonstrating the possible involvement of respondent conditioning in the determination of the absolute visual threshold. The implications of the presence of unique sensory mechanisms in the adaptive behavior of fish and dolphins was discussed. The electrical activity of *Gymnarchus* helps that fish to locate objects in the water. As for the dolphin, it uses a form of activity known as auditory scanning to locate objects in its environment.

The importance of operant conditioning in perception was evidenced in experiments dealing with the perception of briefly exposed words and nonsense syllables. Such experiments showed that what a subject reports seeing is at least partially determined by his response bias (the extent to which he was previously reinforced for emitting a given response).

The significance of observing responses was demonstrated in studies using complicated perceptual stimuli. It was shown that observing responses can be conditioned by the event to be viewed, and in this way can determine what part of a complex stimulus the subject will attend to. The last example cited of operant conditioning in perception is the effect of an object which is established as a conditioned reinforcer on the judgment of its size. Such an object, when established as an S^{+r}, is judged to be larger in size than the same object as a neutral stimulus.

Finally, the role of respondent conditioning in perception was illustrated with reference to the problems of the orienting response and subliminal perception. We cited some work in which the GSR was used as one aspect of the orienting response in order to show how people differ in the way they attend to their environment, and how this attending response relates to relatively complicated learning tasks. Analysis of the problem of subliminal perception showed that a respondent is not necessarily more sensitive to incoming stimuli than an operant (especially a verbal response).

7

Developmental Psychology

This chapter and the ones to follow deal primarily with the applied areas of psychology. On the basis of the discussions in the preceding chapters, we shall attempt to explicate these applied areas in terms of the basic principles of behavior theory. All of the fundamental techniques described can be applied to developmental psychology. The distinguishing characteristic of this area is the use of the variable of age.

REASONS FOR THE STUDY OF DEVELOPMENTAL PSYCHOLOGY

The first reason for studying this area, as has already been suggested, is to find out what effect the age of an organism has upon its behavior. Investigators who have studied the organism for this reason have posed such questions as: At what age does a child normally begin to perform a given act (e.g., crawling or talking)? Which behavior serves as a prerequisite for which other behavior in the sequence of development? What special therapeutic techniques must one use in helping behaviorally disturbed children as opposed to disturbed adults? Although the study of behavior as a function of age makes sense throughout the lifespan, traditionally the age variable has been limited to study of the period from birth to the end of adolescence. The reason for this is the assumption that after adolescence the changes taking place are smaller and less dependent on age than on learning. Fairly recently the period of old age has been given some attention by psychologists and has given rise to an area termed geriatrics.

The second reason for which investigators study developmental psychology is the particular suitability of children as subjects. Because a younger organism has a shorter reinforcement history, because the reinforcers appropriate to children are easier to administer, and because, by comparison to the response classes of animals, relatively complicated response classes can be conditioned in children, an increasing number of behaviorists are being drawn to the study of child psychology.

The third reason for investigators' interest in developmental psychology stems from the hypothesized importance of the effect of early experience upon later behavior in the adult organism. Although Freud's personality theory appears to decide the fate of the human organism in terms of the experience of the first five years of life, such an extreme view is no longer shared by all psychoanalysts, not to speak of contemporary behavioral psychologists. Nevertheless, this extreme kind of determinism has proved its usefulness in at least one area, namely, that of imprinting, according to which the adult sexual behavior of precocial birds is determined in large part by their "following" behavior evidenced much earlier in life (cf. Chapter 4). There are some very interesting experiments available now to describe the effects of early experience on later behavior.

The fourth source of interest in developmental psychology is a theoretical controversy to which we have already had occasion to refer, namely the nature-nurture or environment-heredity issue. The argument is old, but it continues to crop up in different contexts. In the area of developmental psychology, the issue is concerned with how much of the change which takes place in the child can be attributed to learning, how much to physical maturation, and how much to the interaction of these two factors.

In the remainder of this chapter we will take up studies in each of the four areas described above.

The Study of Developmental Psychology for Its Own Sake

Among the first attempts at a scientific approach to the study of child behavior was the painstaking cataloguing of the normal or typical behavior demonstrated by children at different age levels (e.g., Gesell & Ilg, 1943). Thus we are told when to expect head lifting and when cooing, when creeping and when babbling, when the first word should occur and how sentence length increases, and so on. This kind of description is generally useful in allowing one to locate where a given child appears in comparison to his age mates, but it suffers from the disadvantage of being primarily a description of topographical, rather than functional, response classes. An example of the charting of behavior during the first year of life is given by Aldrich and Norval (1946). These investigators studied a sample of 215 normal infants "from all strata of society in Rochester, Minnesota," and traced their development at monthly intervals from birth to the beginning of their second year. They tested most of the children's abilities in the clinic and relied on mothers' reports for behavior not easily observed in the clinic setting. They established 12 developmental steps, giving the mean age in months, at which the behavior was achieved: smiling in response to the adult at .9 months; vocal response ("ah," "eh," "uh") at 1.7 months; head control at 2.9 months; hand control at 4 months; turning over from back to stomach at 5.1 months; sitting alone "for several moments" at 6.2 months; crawling (actually any kind of movement to another place on the floor) at 7.3 months; picking up objects with thumb and forefinger at 8.1 months; pulling himself up to a standing position at 8.7 months; walking with support (holding on to an adult or a piece of furniture) at 9.5 months; standing alone for several moments at 10.7 months; and, finally, walking alone for several steps at 12 months. In general, these findings agreed very well with a number of other American surveys of these behaviors. The only apparent disagreement with this generalization is that walking alone appeared about two months earlier in this study than in the other studies. One is inclined to attribute this uniformity in development of behavior to physical maturation. However, it should be pointed out that, despite the fact that these infants come from different socioeconomic classes, clearly all of them are raised in the same cultural environment. It has also been found that the variability of the age at which a given behavior is attained increases with age. It may well be that the increased variability is due to the increasing effect of differential handling procedures by the various parents, although one could equally well argue that the greater complexity of behavior by itself allows for the expression of the underlying genetic variability.

Just as there is a question about the possibility of generalizing principles of learning over the entire animal kingdom, so there is a question about generalizing such principles over the entire age range. We have already shown that the principles of respondent conditioning, for example, can be extended to as early an age as the foetus in utero (Spelt, 1948). A comparative study of the conditionability of the eyelid reflex was undertaken by Braun and Geiselhart (1959). Three groups of subjects participated in the experiment: 15 boys, mean age approximately 9 years, 15 male young adults, mean age approximately 21 years, and 13 male old adults, mean age about 71 years. The CS consisted of an increase in light intensity of a disk the subjects were fixating; the US was a puff of air (2 lbs./sq. in.) to the eye. The CS-US interval was 500 milliseconds long during conditioning. Extinction was instituted by increasing the CS-US interval to 1,500 milliseconds. Inspection of Figure 7-1 shows the results for each of three groups. Although the

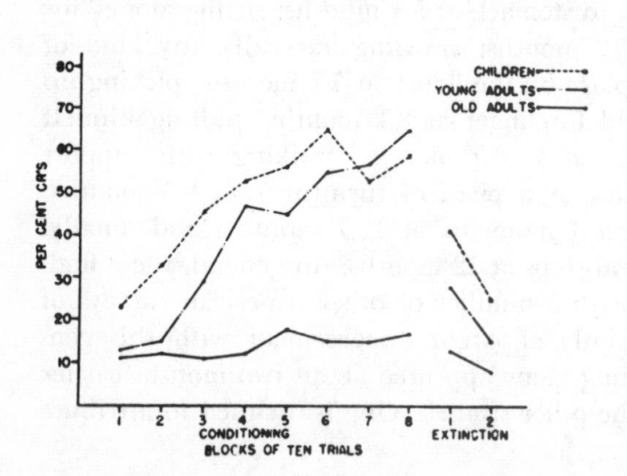

Fig. 7-1. Conditioning and extinction as a function of age. (Braun and Geiselhart, 1959, Fig. 1.)

children appear to produce the largest number of CR's they are, in fact, not statistically significantly different from the young adults. Perhaps a younger group of children would have differed significantly from the adults. On the other hand, both younger groups are statistically significantly different from the old adults. These results hold for both conditioning and extinction. The most striking result of the experiment is, of course, the relative lack of success in conditioning the oldest people. The reader should note also that averaging the curves has, in a sense, obscured the even larger differences (cf. discussion of the analysis of the individual vs. the group in Chapter 1) which obtain for the old-young comparison: Of the 13 old subjects, four gave no CR's at all, seven gave only 1 to 8, while the other two subjects gave 37 and 75 CR's. This is obviously a most varied group of subjects, among whom one could speak of a definite conditioning effect in only two. In contrast to the older group of subjects, all members of the two younger groups gave evidence of conditioning.

Kendler and Kendler (1962), who have used learning theory as a basis for studying the way in which people solve problems, reported a very interesting experiment in which the age variable was ingeniously combined with a special learning problem so as to shed light both on the development of verbal mediation and its effect on the phenomenon of problem solving. The experiment was carried out with four- and seven-year old children and consisted of the following procedure. A child was placed before an apparatus which presented him with two different stimuli varying both in size and brightness. He then had to learn to make a response to one of the two stimuli. If he responded to the correct stimulus he was reinforced by seeing a marble drop down into a cup. Inspection of Figure 7-2 shows the stimuli the subject had to discriminate. The plus sign identifies the stimulus to which responses are positively reinforced. Note that during the first discrimination the child could theoretically respond to the S^D of *black* square along a brightness continuum or to the S^D of a *large* square along a size continuum. The question arises as to what happens when the S^D is changed into an S^Δ. If you look at the second discrimination which subjects face, the aspect of the stimulus which served as the S^D initially makes the second discrimination more or less difficult. Thus, if the initial critical S^D is the large size of the square, then one

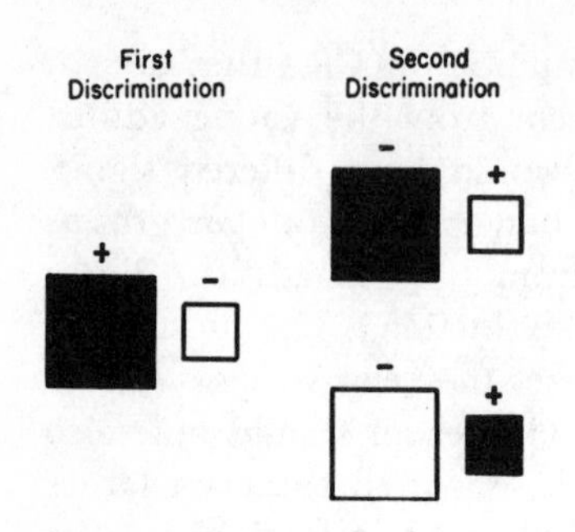

Fig. 7-2. The experimental procedure used to study the influence of verbal habits on a reversal shift. (Kendler and Kendler, 1962, Fig. 6.)

would expect the second discrimination to consist of two simple processes—extinction of responses to the original S^D and conditioning to the new S^D (old S^Δ). If, on the other hand, the S^D in the initial discrimination had been the black color of the square, then the second discrimination would give rise to an intermittent reinforcement situation, which must then be followed by extinction and reconditioning. The intermittency of reinforcement is a result of the fact that the child who responded to the color black initially would be reinforced for making that response in the second discrimination exactly 50 per cent of the time. The Kendlers point out that in human adults such an experiment is accompanied by a mediational process which could be represented by a verbal response. For this reason, they compared the performances of children of two age groups, a four-year-old group which they felt to be too young to use verbal behavior to guide their problem solving ordinarily, and a seven-year-old group which they felt would ordinarily use verbal behavior to guide them. They further decided to isolate the verbal behavior variable by using it as an independent variable for at least part of the group.

The design of the experiment was as follows: Each age group was divided into three subgroups. All were given the same sequence, the first discrimination (until they had all reached a learning criterion) followed by the second discrimination. The "none" groups were given no further instructions. The "relevant verbalization" groups were instructed to say whether the large or the small square was correct. The "irrelevant" groups were required to say whether the black or the white square was correct. Figure 7-3 shows the results in terms of the number of trials the children required to learn the second discrimina-

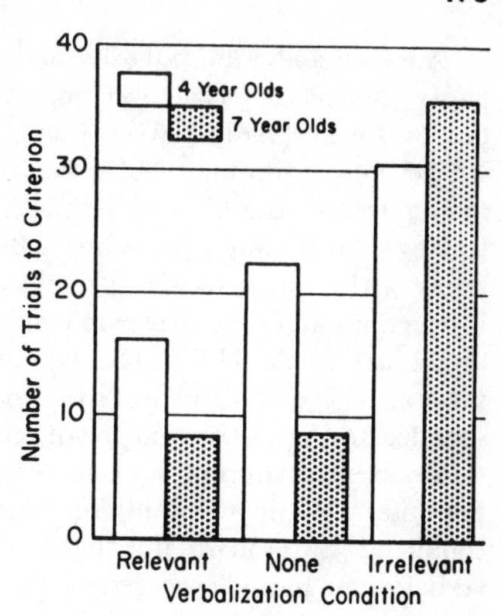

Fig. 7-3. The effect of verbalizations on a reversal shift for 4- and 7-year-old children. (Kendler and Kendler, 1962, Fig. 7.)

tion. The four-year olds performed best (i.e., they needed the smallest number of trials for learning) when they used the verbal response referring to the size dimension, next best when they used no special verbal response, and poorest when their verbal response referred to the brightness dimension. The seven-year olds performed equally well when instructed to use the relevant verbal response as when not instructed to use it, and performed most poorly when instructed to use the irrelevant verbalization. This suggests that a verbal mediation process, possibly in the form of subvocal responses, occurs without special instructions by the time a child reaches the age of seven when he is confronted with this kind of problem. Also of interest is the fact that while the seven-year olds require fewer trials to learn to shift from the first to the second discrimination than the four-year olds need for the relevant and no-verbalization conditions, the irrelevant verbal-response condition appears to affect the older children even more adversely than the four-year olds. Thus, the effect of a verbal response appears to be more powerful in determining the responses of seven-year olds than four-year olds, regardless of whether the verbal response directs towards the correct or incorrect response.

Another and very extensive series of experiments on the regulatory control of verbal over nonverbal behavior has been carried out by Luria (1961; 1967). Using a basic procedure in which a subject must squeeze a rubber bulb, Luria's experiments deal with the analysis of the kind of verbal commands which can exert control over such simple responses. Bulb squeezes are monitored in terms of the extent to which they correspond to a variety of verbal instructions and this correspondence is then examined as a function of the age of the child. He presents the data for three children, varying in age from two to two and a half years of age, who responded to the instruction to squeeze the bulb (Figure 7-4). Note that one instruction to squeeze evokes not one but many repeated responses. While the bulb squeezing can be initiated by verbal command, Luria maintains that at this age it cannot be stopped by verbal command. The successful evocation of the squeezing response at this age demonstrates what Luria calls the impellent or initiating function of speech. The inhibitory function of speech, which marks the second stage, does not appear until the age of about four years. At this time the semantic aspect of the speech rather than its impellent function becomes prepotent, and internal speech begins to control behavior. It is of interest to note, with reference to

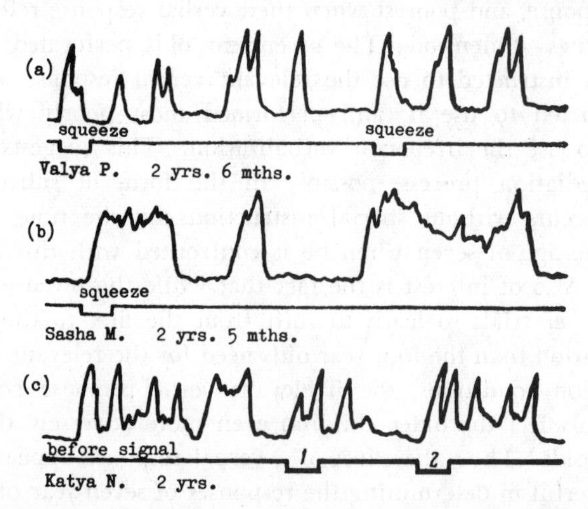

Fig. 7-4. Unregulated motor reactions of pre-school age. Generalized action of a verbal order or instruction. (Luria, 1961, Fig. 1.)

Luria's work, that it is very much an extension of Pavlov's original conditioning model, especially of the second signalling system.

A study which traced the strength of chains of verbal responses in children ranging in age from three to six years was carried out by Salzinger, Salzinger and Hobson (1966). Taking four- and six-word sentences presented in their usual sentence order and in four different nonsentence orders, the authors tested, and about three months later retested, the children for their ability to reproduce these word sequences immediately after hearing them.

In addition, a small group of adults was tested using this procedure. Inspection of Figure 7-5 shows a general increase for all types of verbal stimuli in the ability of the children to correctly reproduce longer sequences with increasing age. This study shows that the sentence chains are sufficiently well-developed even at the age of three years for the grammatical sentence to be more easily reproduced than the various agrammatical sequences. The particular order in which the different sequences enhance reproduction give evidence for the fact that different parts of the sentence cohere with varying degrees of strength. The children's ability to respond in terms of the formal structural cohesiveness of the word sequences remains constant throughout the age range studied and resembles the adults' ability to respond to the same structural cues.

An extension of the operant conditioning paradigm to the practical problem of behavioral geriatrics (science of aged persons) was recently described by Lindsley (1964). Using the approach which is required when a psychologist starts work on a new species, Lindsley suggested a number of improvements in the environment of the aged. Modification of discriminative stimuli in such a way as to make them more suitable for meeting the needs of geriatric people has had some attention, e.g., eyeglasses and hearing aids have made clearer the discriminative stimuli supplied by vision and audition. He added to this list expanded speech, which is apparently more comprehensible to many aged people who cannot understand speech presented at the normal rate. The vocal responses of aged people can be amplified in cases where the individual's voice is too weak to be audible; reduced kinaesthetic feedback for responses can be dealt with by producing feedback by means of special electronic devices. Psychologists have learned that different organisms require

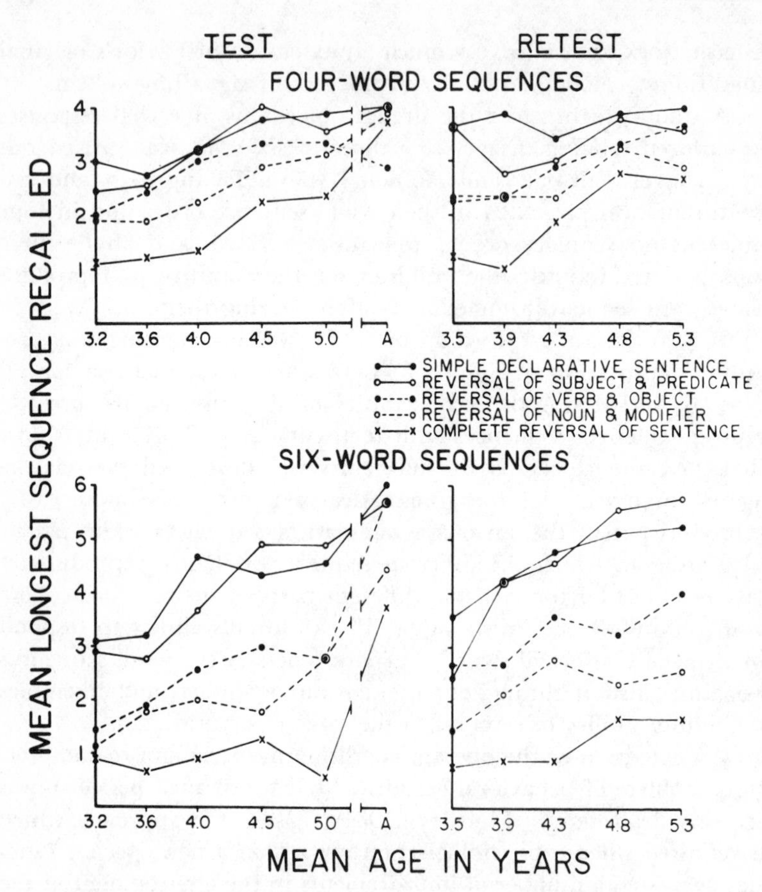

Fig. 7-5. Recall as a function of age with syntactical structure varied as a parameter. (Salzinger, Salzinger, and Hobson, 1966, Fig. 1.)

different reinforcers. It makes a good deal of sense, therefore, to determine what might be the most appropriate reinforcers for the aged. Here Lindsley points to the need for powerful *immediate* reinforcers since long-delayed reinforcers are simply inappropriate to an individual who fears he may not live long enough to receive them. It may also be true that the aged require continuous reinforcement to a greater extent than younger adults. In summary, it would appear that the systematic analysis underlying the behavioral approach leads to useful modification of the environment of man at all ages.

The age variable, so far, has been used to describe the behavior of normal individuals. It is also of importance with respect to modification of disturbed behavior. It is quite evident that psychotherapy, as it is generally practiced (i.e., involving verbal behavior only) has little to offer many disturbed children. Baer (1962) presented an example of the use of operant conditioning in controlling thumbsucking in five-year-old boys, without using any verbal behavior. He first showed the boys cartoons independent of the behavior they exhibited during the cartoons. Then he turned off the movie whenever the boys sucked their thumbs and turned it on again when the boys stopped thumbsucking. A very interesting control group was utilized in this study consisting of a yoked arrangement similar to that employed in the experiment performed by Brady (1966). Figure 7-6 shows the results graphed in the usual cumulative way. Notice that during Session 1, S-1 (the first subject) is the one whose thumbsucking controls the presence or absence of the cartoon for both children, while S-2's behavior is ineffective in controlling the cartoon. In Session 2, however, the positions of the two children are reversed. As a further control, Baer used alternating 5-minute periods, the periods labelled "control" being those where the cartoon reinforcement contingency was in effect and the periods labelled "recovery" where the cartoon was shown without interruption. The results are remarkable in that

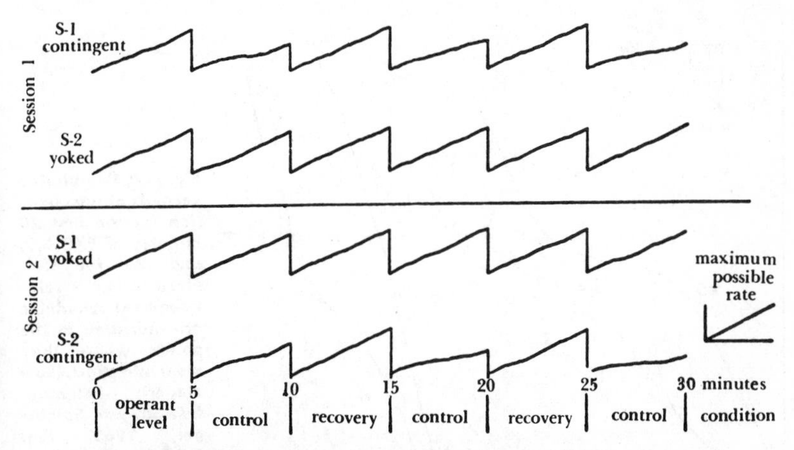

Fig. 7-6. Cumulative thumbsucking curves of two subjects, one experiencing contingent withdrawal/re-presentation and the other yoked, under alternating conditions of Control and Recovery. (Baer, 1962, Fig. 2.)

there is a reduction in thumbsucking only for that subject and period for which the reinforcement contingency holds.

For a more serious case, a three and a half-year-old boy who had acquired no speech at all, and who had to be hospitalized for other asocial behavior as well, the use of candy, peanuts, or spoonfuls of soda proved to be effective reinforcers. The process of instating speech in this child (Salzinger, Feldman, Cowan & Salzinger, 1965) involved reinforcing vocalizations at gradually increasing higher fixed ratios. Eventually, it was possible to reinforce the emission of actual words as well as sounds (see Figures 7-7, 7-8). The figures show steady progress in the rate of response from early to late sessions.

Both of the last two studies cited demonstrate not only the modifiability of aberrant behavior but also show the importance of selecting reinforcers appropriate to the child's age range in order for them to be effective with such disturbed children.

The Study of Developmental Psychology Because of the Advantages of Using Children as Subjects

One of the reasons, although perhaps not the best, that psychologists study certain groups of subjects is the fact that they are easily available and at least approximate the general population which they

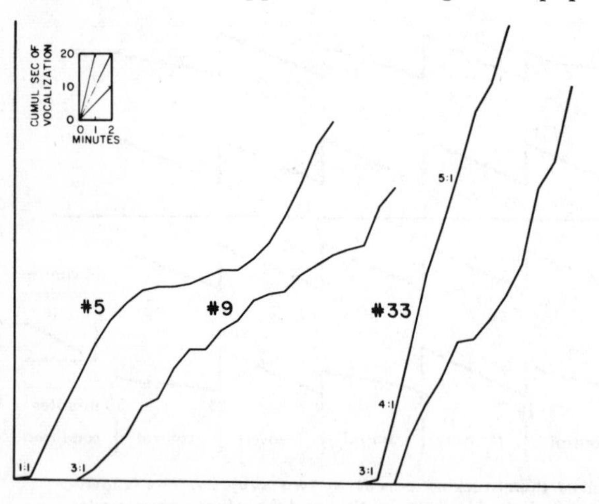

Fig. 7-7. Cumulative seconds of vocalization for the first 20 minutes of EXP 5,9, and 33 for C-1. Fixed-ratio reinforcement schedules are indicated at the points where they went into effect. (Salzinger, Feldman, Cowan, and Salzinger, 1965, Fig. 5-2A.)

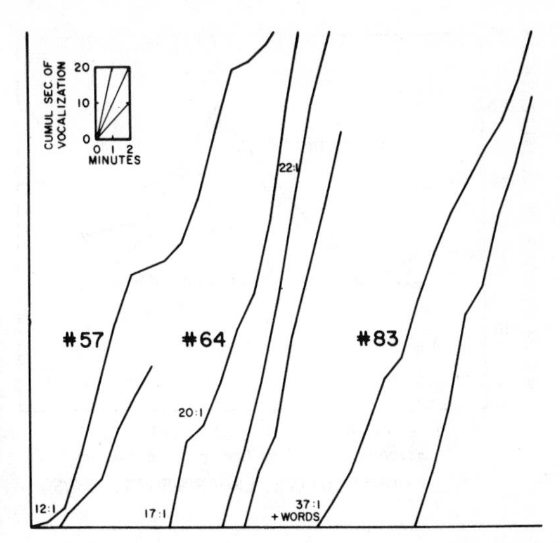

Fig. 7-8. Cumulative seconds of vocalization for the first 20 minutes of EXP 57, 64, and 83 for C-1. Fixed-ratio reinforcement schedules are indicated at the points where they went into effect. (Salzinger, Feldman, Cowan, and Salzinger, 1965, Fig. 5-2B.)

are taken to represent. This describes, for example, the extensive use of the college sophomore as a subject. We have already reviewed the reasons for the use of animals in Chapters 1 and 4. In this section we will describe experiments carried out on children because they are particularly suitable subjects for the study of a particular problem.

Rheingold, Gewirtz and Ross (1959), in pursuing their interest in the question of the importance of the process of reinforcement in the acquisition of language, did an experiment on three-month-old infants. Making use of a rather complex series of events as a reinforcer (a broad smile, three "tsk" sounds, and a light touch applied to the infant's stomach), they were able to demonstrate that vocalization could be conditioned in these infants. Furthermore, they varied the degree of intermittency of reinforcement, and were able to show that the children on the higher VR schedule (Experiment 1) tended to emit a larger number of extinction responses than the children on the lower VR schedule (Experiment 2). Figure 7-9 shows response rate during baseline performance (no reinforcers given), conditioning, and extinction. The graph shows that the mere presence of an observer during baseline determinations causes no change in response rate, the delivery of reinforcement does

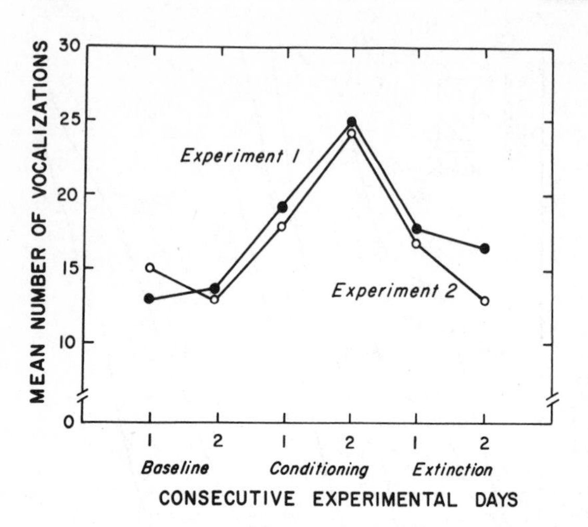

Fig. 7-9. Mean number of vocalizations on consecutive experimental days. (Rheingold, Gewirtz, and Ross, 1959, Fig. 1.)

cause an increase, and the operation of extinction produces a decrease in response rate. This experiment demonstrates that operant control over vocal behavior is possible at three months of age, long before many of the complicating variables found in the study of adults have had an opportunity to appear.

The study of the conditionability of continuous speech in five- to seven-year-olds (Salzinger, Salzinger, Portnoy, Eckman, Bacon, Deutsch & Zubin, 1962) was subsequently carried out, using as reinforcers the flashing of a light-bulb nose of a papier mâché clown and the presentation of trinkets. This study demonstrated that, in organisms of relatively short reinforcement history, verbal behavior is in fact conditionable by the operant paradigm.

Despite the fact that Skinner (1953a) maintains that there are no drives for conditioned reinforcers, he does concede that, if one could demonstrate operations corresponding to deprivation and satiation, a conditioned drive would certainly appear to be feasible. The task of establishing the existence of such a drive was undertaken by Gewirtz and Baer (1958). They used 102 first and second grade children as subjects. The children were divided into three groups in accordance with operations performed preceding the conditioning phase of the experiment. Thirty-four of the children were left alone in a room for a period of 20 minutes; this was the deprivation condition. The second group of 34 children was placed into the conditioning situation as soon as they arrived in the experimental room; this was called the nondeprivation condition. The remaining 34 children were reinforced positively for a period of 20 minutes for drawing and cutting out designs; this was called the satiation condition. All of the children were asked to participate in the same "game" in which they were required to put marbles into one of two holes. During operant level, which lasted for four minutes, the experimenter merely observed the behavior. This was followed by a 10-minute period of conditioning. Reinforcement was administered by the experimenter at increasingly higher FR's, by using such phrases as "good," "mmhm," and "fine." The response which was reinforced was the one each child made with the smaller frequency during the last minute of operant level. It was hypothesized that the deprivation operation would enhance the reinforcer effectiveness while the satiation operation would reduce the effectiveness. The results of this experiment are depicted in Figure 7-10. It shows quite clearly that the hypothesis is confirmed. We have here an example of an experiment with children which is useful for gaining a better understanding of some basic concepts of behavior theory.

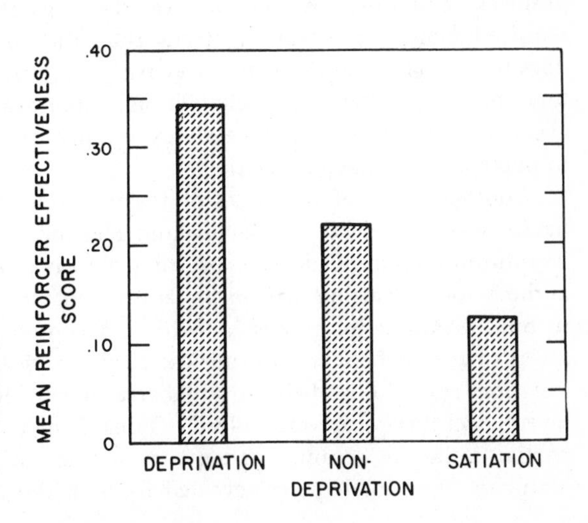

Fig. 7-10. A pictorial representation of the means for the three levels of the experimental variable (34 Ss per condition). (Gewirtz and Baer, 1958, Fig. 2.)

The Study of Developmental Psychology in Order to Explore the Effect of Early Experience upon Later Behavior

There are a great many generalizations abroad about the effects of early experience upon the later behavior of human beings. It might be well to quote from one recent review, substituting the word "behavior" for "personality," to have a fair view of the area (Sluckin, 1966, p. 234):

> Despite the many studies concerning the effects of deprivation of maternal care, our knowledge of the role of early experience in the development of human personality is still very slight. It is important that the extent of this ignorance be fully appreciated.

With this warning in mind, let us look at some experiments. Melzack and Scott (1957) studied dogs raised in isolation from puppyhood (four weeks of age) to maturity (eight months of age) and compared them to dogs raised under more normal conditions in order to determine whether being reared alone would make any difference in the animals' response to aversive (painful) stimuli. Despite the fact that both groups of dogs found the electric shock, pinprick, and nose-burning aversive, the dogs reared in isolation required many more training trials than did the normally raised dogs to learn how to avoid the aversive stimulation. The investigators concluded that even behavior as important as avoidance of aversive stimulation requires early experience with such stimulation to make adult behavior effective.

Another study of the effect of rearing conditions on adult behavior was carried out by Harlow and Harlow (1962) on monkeys. Examining different degrees of early deprivation situations, the authors found various deficits in adult behavior. Monkeys raised in total isolation for two years exhibited complete failure to emit social or sexual behavior during the next two years of life. Partial isolation resulted in behavioral aberrations which, although less severe, were very serious indeed. Thus female infants raised in partial isolation became inadequate mothers when they reached maturity. The inadequacy revealed itself in the mother's behavior by the fact that she ignored and pushed her infant offspring away; in some cases these inadequate mothers actually beat the infants and pushed their faces down into the wire-mesh floor without any apparent provocation.

An interesting experiment on the long-range effect of early learning on later learning was performed by Burtt (1941). He began working with a boy at the age of 15 months, presenting the child with several selections of 20 lines each from Sophocles' *Oedipus Tyrannus* in the original Greek. The selections were presented repeatedly until they totalled 90 times over a period of three months. During the next three months new selections were read to the subject, and then another set for the next three months, and so on until the boy reached the age of three years. At the age of eight and a half, one-third of the selections from the material learned when he was younger, along with new but similar selections for control purposes, were presented for learning. At age 14, another third of the early selections were presented with new control material, and finally, at the age of 18, the last third of the early material was presented with new control material for learning. Using the method of serial anticipation, the experimenter continued to present the material until an entire selection was correctly anticipated. The results showed that at the age of eight and a half years the subject required approximately 30 per cent fewer trials to learn old than to learn new material; at 14 years 8 per cent fewer trials were required for old than for new material; finally, at age 18, old and new material required the same number of trials. Thus, while the effects of early learning are visible years after original exposure, they do not last indefinitely even when the material is in Greek and thus little influenced by other experiences an English speaking subject might have in intervening years.

The Study of Developmental Psychology as Part of the Nature-Nurture Controversy

Despite the fact that the controversy of nature vs. nurture continues, there are some basic undeniable facts on both sides of the argument which force a nature *and* nurture resolution. On the nurture side, it has been found that early learning (both operant and respondent, including even the simple behavior acquisition process of imprinting) as well as the effects of presence or absence of sensory and social stimulation, all indicate the profound influence of the environment upon current and later behavior. We need not repeat these findings here except to mention the additional studies in which the smiling response (Brackbill, 1958) in the four-month old and simple discriminative behavior in 10-month olds (Simmons & Lipsitt, 1961) have been modified by the operant conditioning paradigm.

On the other side of this controversy is the undeniable fact of physical growth following birth which results in an increase in muscular strength. There is also the less obvious but (nonetheless) real growth of the nervous system (Hebb, 1966) to be considered. Although the human brain does not increase in the number of neurons with age, the connecting fibers continue to grow, making it possible for impulses to traverse more elaborate paths. Such elaboration, along with the aid of environmental stimulation, enables learning involving these neural paths to take place. There is also evidence that the process of myelinization continues for some time in the child's nervous system. The myelin sheath is a fatty white covering on many nerve fibers and serves, in part, to insulate one nerve fiber from another. It also facilitates rapid conduction of impulses between points at some distance from each other. Finally, there appears to be an increase in the number of glial cells as a function of age. The glial cells are assumed to hold the neurons in place as well as to aid in the nutrition of the neurons. Information concerning the maturation of the nervous system after birth is gleaned not only from the traditional neurophysiological examination but also from behavioral evidence found in such reflexes as the "Babinski." This reflex, for example, is present in the normal human infant but not in the normally intact adult. It occurs when the sole of the foot in the newborn infant is scratched, causing the toes to curl upward and outward, whereas in the older child and adult the toes curl downward. There are other behavioral phenomena whose occurrence can be attributed primarily to physical maturation rather than to the environment. The development of walking in human beings and the swimming behavior of salamanders can be cited as further examples.

Having pointed out the importance of both nature and nurture in developmental psychology, and having shown that, to be effective, environmental influences must await physical and neurophysiological maturation, it remains for us to demonstrate the importance of early experience in the maintenance of neural structures. As one example, it has been demonstrated that a lack of visual stimulation in chimpanzees for the first 16 months of life results in the loss of nerve cells in the retina. Typically, the nature-nurture issue is investigated by means of experiments showing that when certain physical structures or environmental exposure are absent, behavioral development is absent or at least impaired. The approach used by Kellogg and Kellogg (1933) consisted of inverting the process by taking a nonhuman organism who, because of its *nature,* is not usually *nurtured* in the same way as a human child, and placing it in just that kind of environment. They obtained a seven- and a half-months-old female chimpanzee and raised her along with their own son for a period of nine months, beginning when the baby was 10 months of age. They found some classes of behavior in which the child outdistanced the ape, some in which they were at the same level, and some in which the ape learned to make responses which exceeded in skill those learned by the child. Of all the differences, the ones in which the ape exceeded the child are the most interesting and suggestive. The ape acquired a series of responses peculiar to civilized society and performed them better than the child. Examples of these responses are: skipping, cooperation and obedience, skillful opening of doors, anticipation of bladder and bowel responses, and the ability to eat with a spoon and drink from a glass. It becomes apparent that conclusions concerning the extent to which maturation controls behavior by comparison to the control exerted by the environment can be determined only by utilizing optimal environmental conditions. Certainly, recent developments in operant and respondent conditioning have shown that a large number of response classes, which used to be considered unalterable because of their maturational dependency, are actually dependent upon the environment.

A recent review of cognitive learning (Fowler, 1962) pointed out that it is at least in part the neglect of research in learning in early childhood which has resulted in stress on maturational factors.

By sampling behavior at different age levels of *different* children, learning effects could not be easily discovered and consequently the changes were attributed to maturation. Furthermore, those studies which were carried out on learning utilized relatively short periods of training and resulted in negligible learning effects because the learning variables simply were not applied long enough. In contrast to this maturational approach, those working with operant conditioning have recently applied their well-developed methods to child psychology. Bijou and Baer (1966) reviewed this area of research and showed that there was a large increase in techniques that were being successfully applied to control the behavior of children. Since the practical application of these techniques is just beginning, it may well turn out that more behavior that is now attributed to the control of physical factors will show itself to be amenable to environmental control.

SUMMARY

This review of developmental psychology showed that there is an area of study whose major focus is the analysis of behavior in relation to the age variable. Within this area a number of investigators have estimated the effect of the age variable directly. Some have catalogued the occurrence of various topographically defined classes of behavior at different ages in cross-sections of the population. Others have investigated the degree of conditionability of simple responses in relation to age. Still others have investigated the effects of age on the control of nonverbal by verbal behavior. The change in the strength of chains of verbal responses was charted in relation to the age of the young child, and proposals based upon behavior theory were made with reference to the aged.

The importance of the age variable in the modification of undesirable behavior was made clear by the fact that the effectiveness of reinforcers depends in part upon their suitability to the age of the subject to whom they are applied.

The chapter also described a series of studies which were carried out with children because they were particularly well-suited as subjects for the research questions asked. Thus the conditionability of verbal behavior was illustrated in studies of three-month-old infants and five- to seven-year-old children. The application of the operations of deprivation and satiation to conditioned reinforcers was investigated in young children because such reinforcers are particularly well-established even in young children when compared to animals.

A number of studies were cited to illustrate the effect of early experience upon the later behavior of organisms. These studies showed the importance of a normal early environment in the subsequent acquisition of efficient avoidance behavior in dogs; monkeys raised in isolation or with various types of mother surrogates were found to be inadequate mothers themselves after they gave birth. Finally, the systematic follow-up of an early learning experience of a young child showed a later effect through the age of 14 but no apparent trace of the early learning by the time he reached the age of 18.

The last series of studies covered in this chapter dealt with the nature-nurture controversy. It was made clear that any resolution of the controversy had to admit a nature *and* nurture determination of behavior. Evidence was produced for early learning, as well as for continued physical development of the nervous system after birth. The effect of an improved, or at least more humanoid, environment on the development of an ape was described, showing that the mere observation of the behavior of an organism in its natural environment does not necessarily reveal whether the lack of other behavior stems from maturational or environmental deficiency.

The chapter was ended with the prediction that present developments in operant conditioning will show many behaviors to be environmentally determined which, until the present time, have been considered to be controlled by maturational factors alone.

8

Complex Stimuli and Complex Responses: Education

The oldest, most concerted and systematic process of behavior modification in civilized society is the process of education. Until very recently (Skinner, 1954), although psychologists were experts in the field of learning, they were laymen in the field of teaching. In much of educational psychology, the vague and general terms of "motivation," "needs," "Gestalt," the "whole child," and the like continue to be significant in descriptions of the process of education, while the new and promising behavioral approaches are still given but scant attention, their explication often including a general sprinkling of such opprobrious adjectives as "machine-like," "overly limited," "artificial," and "impractical." A recent book in education (Lindgren, 1967, pp. 260-261) says, "Such explanations [theories of learning] work best when one tries to explain the learning of animals, small children, and older children and adults who are for some reason unwilling or unable to function intelligently. However, they are of little practical value when it comes to explaining learning of a more complex nature." The student of behavior will recognize immediately the problematic nature of such terms as "unwilling," since here the behavior is attributed to a cause of unknown origin. The meaning of the term "unwilling" may perhaps be best restated as, "I don't know why he is not learning." In any case it requires further analysis. The validity of the rest of the quotation is, at least in part, a matter for empirical investigation. The degree of complexity of behavior which can be conditioned has already been indicated in the preceding parts of the book, but we will show additional examples in this chapter. Once more we will discuss the concept of intelligence in an attempt to define what it means to "function intelligently." Finally, we will try to show that the analysis of behavior is powerful enough to be relevant to young, old, and middle aged alike, and that the functional relations between the subject's responses and the environment remain the same, regardless of the population chosen for study, except for some lawful changes in the parameters of learning. The fact that operant conditioning has been successfully applied to the behavior of the exceptional child (brain damaged, mentally retarded, or autistic) should not be used to infer that it is relevant only to this type of child, but rather, that if it can help a child who has great difficulty in learning, it should have at least an even chance of helping a child who displays only the normal amount of difficulty in learning. And finally, there is evidence for the success of behavior theory, not only in generating specific techniques for effective learning, but also in analyzing and explaining those techniques which are currently in effect.

Behavioral Analysis of What Is to Be Learned

Despite the fact that education itself is ancient, a behavioral analysis of what the student is expected to learn has only recently been undertaken. In the study of animal learning, on the other hand, the explicit behavioral approach is a must. Each step of a conditioning process must be programmed with animals. As in the study of sensation and perception (cf. Chapter 6), one cannot use imprecise instructions with animals if one is interested in training them to perform a specific task. For this reason it might be well to look at the way in which animals are conditioned in the acquisition of a complex behavior repertoire. This might then serve as an example for behavioral analysis in education. A recent example of a program of complex behavior acquisition in animals is to be found in a study by Ferster and Hammer (1966).

These investigators chose to teach binary arithmetic, an example of a complex behavior repertoire, to chimpanzees. They used binary arithmetic because it contains response-response relations of the kind which Skinner (1957b) posited for verbal behavior in general. In addition, the binary system of arithmetic allowed them to represent all numbers by the simple device of having "1" represented by a light being on, and the other element of the binary system, "0," represented by the light being off. The utilization of only two elements instead of 10, as in the decimal system, does not reduce the complexity of the repertoire, but only the number of individual responses which are required. For those readers who are unacquainted with the binary system of arithmetic, we will give the binary equivalents of the decimal numbers, 0 through 10: 0000 = 0; 0001 = 1; 0010 = 2; 0011 = 3; 0100 = 4; 0101 = 5; 0110 = 6; 0111 = 7; 1000 = 8; 1001 = 9; 1010 = 10. Although the training of the animals was not brought to the point of teaching them addition, it is of interest to trace the process in behavioral terms. The analysis shows that for consideration of any given column of binary numbers there are 4 basic discriminations: when the two numbers to be added have 0's in the same column, then S = (0 + 0) and R = 0; when they have 0 and 1 in the same column, then S = 0 + 1 or 1 + 0 and R = 1; and when they have 1's in the same column then S = 1 + 1 and R = 10. The last response converts the last column into a 0 and allows a response for a "carry" operation (as in the decimal system when 1 or more is added to 9).

The actual training procedure was quite involved and long. It used as a basic technique the matching-to-sample device where the organism must select which of a number of stimuli matches the sample stimulus. The operation of matching was taught to the chimpanzee by first training him to perform a task which was relatively simple, i.e., he was reinforced for pressing a switch which matched the sample in color. When the chimpanzees had mastered this task, they were trained to match the binary numbers.

This matching operation is shown in Figure 8-1 under the letter A. The center stimulus is the sample, the stimuli to the right and left, the potential matches. If the animal makes a correct match, a conditioned reinforcer, consisting of a tone, is sounded; if the wrong match is chosen, a time-out period occurs, i.e., for a short period of

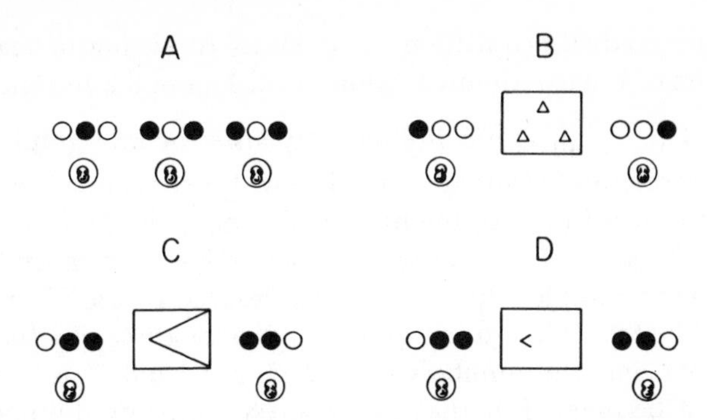

Fig. 8-1. Diagrams of the various paradigms used in matching to sample. A: Matching identical stimuli. B: Matching a binary sample to a numerosity stimulus. C & D: the sample consists of an instruction which determines which of the binary stimuli is to be reinforced. A response to the larger or smaller binary stimulus is reinforced depending upon whether the symbol in the center window is large or small. (Ferster and Hammer, 1966, Fig. 1.)

time nothing the animal does will result in reinforcement. Primary reinforcers consisting of banana pellets and other foods were then placed on a ratio schedule and administered for numerosity matching. Under B in Figure 8-1 is shown the numerosity matching for which the animal had to match a binary number to the corresponding number of objects, in this case, triangles. Under C and D, the sample indicates that the response is to be made to the larger or smaller number. The operations indicated under C and D had not been attempted at the time of publication of that paper. Operations under B, the numerosity matching, have been successfully modified in such a way that, after the animal had learned to match the number response to the number of objects, he learned to "write" his count of the number of objects. The first step in this procedure was accomplished by having a switch control a pattern of lights. Whenever the switch was pressed, a new pattern of lights appeared. The animal continued to press the switch until the resulting number matched the number of objects. After the animal learned this response, he was then trained to "write" the binary number by having him turn each light of the binary number on or off to achieve the pattern which represented the number of stimulus objects. The results of the various phases of the procedure were shown as follows: The gradual acquisition of responses consisting of matching seven pairs of binary stimuli is depicted in Figure 8-2 for one chimpanzee. The S^{Δ}/S^{D} ratio is essentially an error rate graph. Note that the error rate eventually falls below .01. Examination of the data on the acquisition of the numerosity responses, however, made clear the importance of checking to determine how much of the control over a complex discrimination is exerted by the S^{D} and how much by the S^{Δ}. When using only one, two, or three objects as the sample S^{D}'s, but the numbers 0, 1, 2, 3, 5, 6, and 7 as potential matches, it becomes clear that the progress shown by the low ratio of S^{Δ} to S^{D} responses is only apparent and is, in large measure, due to those S^{Δ} responses which are never reinforced. Figure 8-3 shows that the first decrease in S^{Δ}/S^{D} (curve under A) does not reveal S^{D}

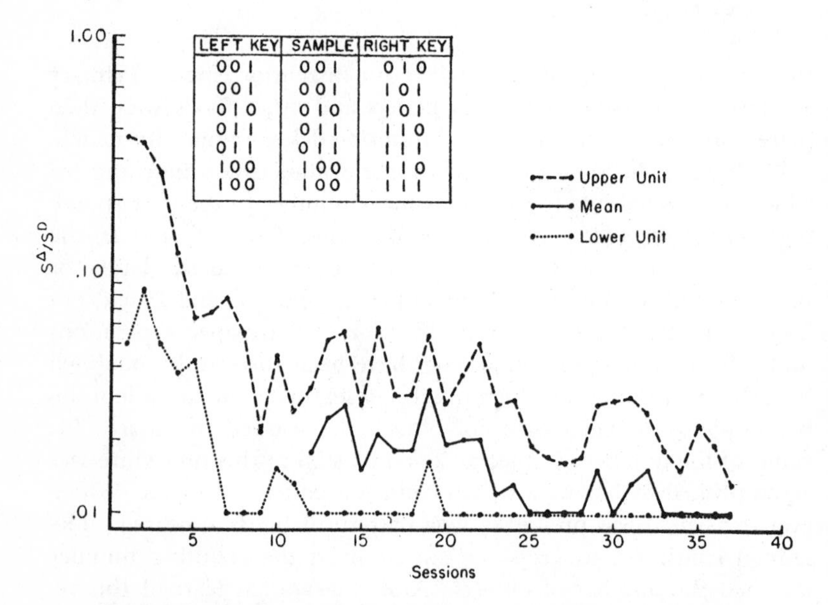

Fig. 8-2. Dennis: Development of matching-to-sample performances with seven pairs of binary stimuli, programmed concurrently. The dashed curve gives the S^{Δ} levels for the least accurate stimuli, and the dotted curves for the most accurate. Values less than .01 are indicated as .01. The mean value is not recorded for the first 12 sessions. (Ferster and Hammer, 1966, Fig. 12.)

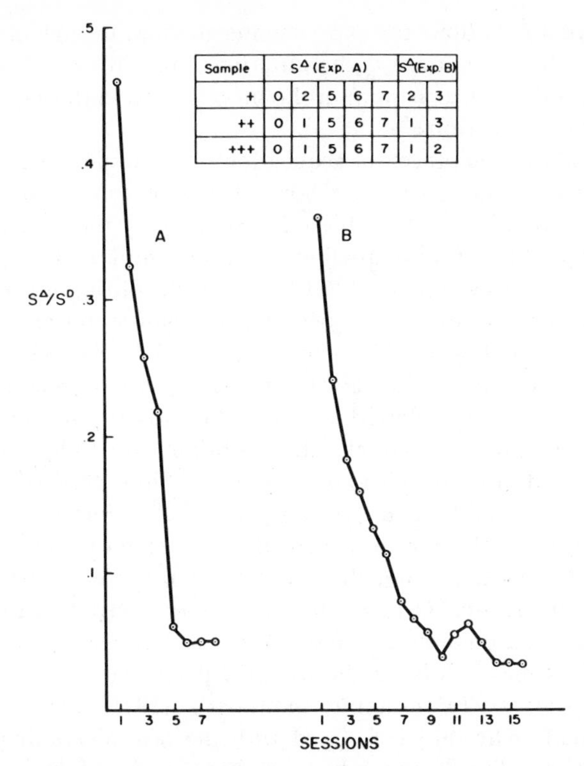

Sample	S^{Δ} (Exp. A)					S^{Δ} (Exp. B)	
+	0	2	5	6	7	2	3
++	0	1	5	6	7	1	3
+++	0	1	5	6	7	1	2

Fig. 8-3. Dennis: The first development of numerosity control by the binary stimuli. In the left curve, the S^{Δ} binary stimuli include 5,6, and 7, which do not correspond with any of the numerosity samples. In the right curve, all of the binary stimuli correspond with the numerosity samples. (Ferster and Hammer, 1966, Fig. 14.)

control, since when only those S^{Δ} numbers are used (1, 2 and 3) which do, in fact, get reinforced sometime during the experiment (curve under B) the $\frac{S^{\Delta}}{S^{D}}$ starts quite high again before the error rate is reduced to a new low level. It is of added interest to note that this discrimination still was not completely under the control of numerosity, as evidenced by the large increase in the $\frac{S^{\Delta}}{S^{D}}$ ratio when the shapes of the objects to be counted were changed. Without going into any further detail concerning these experiments, we can make the point that the rather slow acquisition of the complex response repertoire allows the experimenter to view, in slow motion, the various discriminations, generalizations, and response chains that the organism has to acquire in the process of assimilating a particular response repertoire.

Having shown the process of acquisition of a complex behavioral repertoire in an animal, let us see how a behavioral analysis can be applied to a complex form of behavior emitted by the human organism. Orginality certainly qualifies as being complex. In a paper on the training of originality, Maltzman (1960) distinguished, for purposes of clarity of discussion, between originality and creativity. He defined originality as "behavior which occurs relatively infrequently, is uncommon under given conditions, and is relevant to those conditions." He referred the term "creativity" to products (e.g., an invention) of original behavior which are judged so by the "reactions of other members of a society." Thus, originality depends on fewer variables than creativity and is therefore simpler to analyze. Original behavior, unlike creativity, does not depend upon recognition by society, although it is defined relative to behavior normal for the group. Original behavior is involved in problem solving where uncommon responses often lead the subject to a solution. This may consist of the use of a particular object in an uncommon way, as, for example, in Maier's (1931) famous two string problem. The subject is faced with the task of holding two strings together. The strings, which are hanging from the ceiling, are placed sufficiently far from each other so that if the subject holds one string he cannot reach the other. The solutions consist of using other available objects in an uncommon way. Thus, by tying a pair of pliers to one string and swinging it like a pendulum, the subject can bring the other string to the center, catching the first string as it swings towards him. Another solution is to rest the string against the back of a chair and move the chair towards the other string; thus, while the subject moves one string towards the center the other string is waiting for him within reach.

For the task of training originality, Maltzman (1960) made use of the technique of free association. Since there are free association norms available (Russell & Jenkins, 1954), it is possible to estimate precisely what an original response would be by comparing it to those norms. Free association norms are obtained in the following manner: A large group of subjects is presented with a list of words and instructed to respond with the first word which occurs to them. On the basis of their responses, it is then possible to arrive at a response distribution showing the proportion of subjects who give any one response. An original response is then defined as one given by very few or none of the norm group. Maltzman (1960) trained his subjects in originality by the repeated presentation of the same list of stimulus words, with an instruction to the subject to emit a new association each time. This procedure produced original behavior not only in response to the stimulus words themselves (to be expected, perhaps), but also in an entirely different situation where the subjects had to provide different uses for a number of named objects. In one of his control groups he instructed subjects to respond with the same word every time the same stimulus occurred. This group showed a definite reduction in originality as a function of the "unoriginality" training. Maltzman further demonstrated in another study that the effect of the originality training, short as it is, lasts for at least two days. Finally, he showed that the mere evocation of original responses, by having the subject read them in response to the stimulus words, does not produce as much originality in subsequent tasks as does the situation where the subject emits the words directly in response to the stimulus words.

This very interesting series of studies should serve as an introduction to the idea that behavioral analysis can furnish us with a solid basis for education. The first task in the application of behavioral analysis to education consists of the empirical and explicit definition of what it is that the subject or student is to learn; the second consists of investigating the extent to which the acquired responses then generalize to other behavior; the third is to determine what stimulus is to control the emission of that response or what chains of responses the subjects are to emit; the fourth consists of finding the appropriate reinforcement contingencies. For example, the fact that originality training that consists of reading the responses to stimuli is not as effective as emitting them in response to the stimuli directly, is not surprising when we analyze the conditions under which we might expect original behavior to occur. Such conditions require that the name of the object act as an S^D for the description of a unique use for it. In the case of reading the responses, the printed material is acting as the S^D for the responses. Nevertheless, as we shall see later when we discuss programmed learning, the reading of a desired response may conceivably be used initially and then slowly faded out, much as Terrace's (1966) technique prescribes for the transfer of control over a response from a stimulus which has current control to a stimulus which the experimenter wants to have control.

The detailed behavioral analyses presented in this section should make clear the fact that any consideration of education as an experiment in learning immediately points up the fact that many courses which now form an important part of the school curriculum have never undergone a behavioral analysis. Even an activity as fundamental to other areas in education as that of reading has, it seems, so far defied adequate analysis. Despite the fact that many investigators are working on reading, many basic questions are as yet unanswered. Is it any wonder that Johnny can't read? While it is quite clear that reading consists of discriminative responses, neither the size nor the exact boundaries of the stimulus nor the size of the response is known. In fact, the continuing battle between proponents of the phonetic vs. the whole-word approach testifies to the viability of the controversy. In addition, we might point out that the discriminative responses we have so far ascribed to reading are patently incomplete. This is so because the discriminative responses could, in the same manner, have been to objects in the room—perhaps less so for the phonetically trained child, but certainly for the child trained to recognize whole words. We shall see below that reading includes other things as well. In reading or responding to the discriminative stimuli—the parts of letters, whole letters, syllables, words, phrases, clauses, and complete sentences—the child is presented with stimuli whose general occurrence as well as whose sequential occurrence have certain probability levels. Thus, one of the determinants of his reading response has to do with the stimuli and their probabilities. That the relative frequency characteristics of stimulus exposures are critical in determining responses has already been shown (cf. Chapter 6). There is, in addition, the probability of one response following another, i.e., the response chains which have already been established in the speaking and hearing repertoire of the child. In other words, one would expect a response under discriminative control to be influenced by the general response strength of that response. A child used to saying "they is here" might have more trouble in reading "they are here" than a child who speaks correctly (i.e., whose verbal response is more likely to be congruent with the written stimulus) in the first place. An analysis of the responses a child brings to his initial reading experience might well shed some light on the problems of teaching reading to diverse groups of children. A little thought about reading makes it clear, however, that this is still not all there is to reading. For one thing, it is quite clear that speed reading does not consist of "naming" each word; for another, except in proofreading, a reader should be responding in such a manner that he combines the responses in some way. This combination may serve the purpose of storing information, coming up with refutations of the material read, comparing it with other information, applying it to a practical situation, and so on. What is the response which we call reading under these circumstances? The answer to the last question is still a matter for future research which will undoubtedly be helped along by the more systematic view of behavior theory.

The reader might wonder why the process of reinforcement has not yet been explicated in this section. It was decided to postpone its explication in education to show that, alone, its usefulness is limited. In fact, the unthinking utilization of reinforcement in education has consisted of a concentration, on the part of some, on making learning "pleasurable," sometimes at the expense of learning. While the whole-word method of reading has the immediate advantage of allowing the child to make out meaningful material soon after he starts to learn reading, it does not provide the child with the discriminative responses which allow him to read new words. Furthermore, the method may well reinforce responding to words easily read, with the subsequent reading of more difficult words coming under the control, not of these harder words, but of chaining to the more easily deciphered words. Having been forewarned about the importance of using reinforcement procedures only in conjunction with a well-worked-out behavioral analysis, let us examine this variable briefly.

The problem of reinforcement can be stated no better than in Skinner's (1953a) introductory remarks to his chapter on education (p. 402): "In an American school if you ask for the salt in good French, you get an A. In France you get the salt." Educational reinforcers are probably among the least powerful reinforcers used by our society. This point is also made explicit by Staats and Staats (1962), who ascribe at least part of the difficulty which children experience in learning to read (as opposed to learning to speak) to the difference in the reinforcers which are made available. Following up this theoretical discussion, Staats, Staats, Schultz, and Wolf (1962) conditioned the reading of words in six four-year-olds, using two different reinforcement sequences. Figure 8-4 shows the rate of reading words for three of the children who were first given social reinforcers only (the typical reinforcers used in school) and then, when they refused to continue (marked by the letter "a"), were given reinforcers consisting of candy, trinkets, and tokens which could be exchanged for small plastic toys. The three other children were reinforced initially by objects, then switched to social approval, and then returned to the object reinforcers. Their behavior is shown in Figure 8-5. Note that one child (D. L.) did not continue working after a period of being given only social rein-

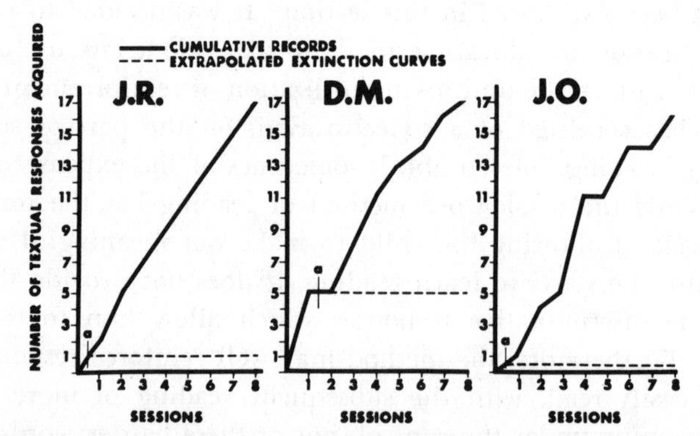

Fig. 8-4. The curves shown here were generated under a beginning period of no "extrinsic" reinforcement. When subject would no longer remain in the experimental situation, reinforcement was reinstated as indicated by the mark on the curve. The dotted line commences at the point where S would no longer remain in the experiment and indicates the curve which would have resulted if reinforcement was not introduced. (Staats, Staats, Schutz, and Wolf, 1962, Fig. 1.)

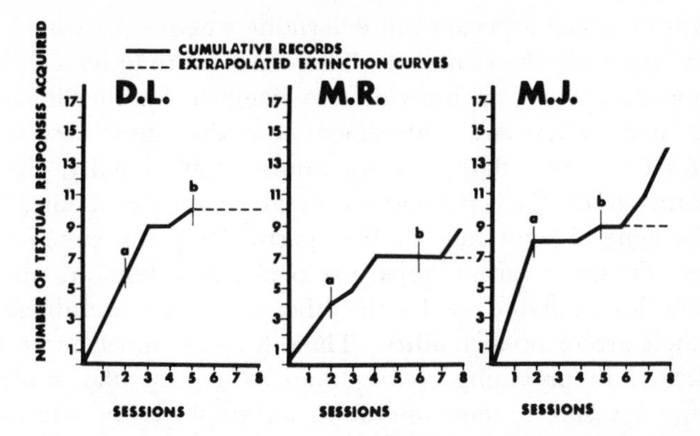

Fig. 8-5. For these Ss, the first condition included reinforcement, which was discontinued at the point of the first mark on the curve. When S would no longer remain in the experimental situation, reinforcement was reinstated, as the second mark on the curve indicates. The dotted line commences at the point where the S would no longer remain in the experiment and depicts the curve which would have resulted if reinforcement was not reinstated. (Staats, Staats, Schutz, and Wolf, 1962, Fig. 2.)

forcers, even though restoration of the object reinforcers was promised. Both Figures 8-4 and 8-5 show the importance of using strong and appropriate reinforcers for educating children.

The Learner

While the behavioristic psychologist is inclined to suggest that the subject (in this case the learner) is always right, and that some modification of the procedure would train the subject to execute the desired response, the educator is typically (and most unfortunately) in the position of having to apply a fixed procedure to a group of children rather than to the individual pupil. For this reason, the educator has had to rely on instruments (tests) which enable him to evaluate the effect of his procedure on different children's behavior as well as to predict which standard procedure might be most appropriate for a certain group of children. The intelligence test, it is of interest to note, was specifically designed by Binet to take out of the Paris school system those children who would be unable to profit by the education offered them. Today tests are employed for many purposes. There are interest tests on the basis of which a person can determine whether he would enjoy one activity more than another. There are aptitude tests which reveal how competent an individual is likely to become in a given subject area. There are achievement tests that show how well an individual has assimilated certain information. Finally, there are personality tests which purport to reveal something about an individual's general approach to life, particularly his emotional responses. Of these various tests, the personality tests are the least valid and least reliable. As for the other tests, their usefulness stems from their group predictability. These tests are much more useful to a school in providing courses than to a particular student in planning his career, more useful to an employer in selecting an employee than to the individual worker in finding out which particular job he is best fitted for.

As a result, the problem of individual differences persists and must be studied. Despite the fact that intelligence tests are presumed to be able to predict later learning, a recent review (Zeaman & House, 1967) shows very little evidence for a strong relation between intelligence test performance (the scores varying widely) and learning in a variety of tasks. Furthermore, while intelligence test scores under certain conditions allow one to predict school performance, recent research has shown that, despite evidence for a genetic component of intelligence (Erlenmeyer-Kimling & Jarvik, 1963), a great many environmental conditions appear to influence intelligence test performance. In a recent survey of some of these conditions, Pettigrew (1964) showed that variables ranging from diet during pregnancy, to race of the tester, to socioeconomic level of parents, etc., all influence test performance. The fact that so many of these variables are not genetic indicates, of course, that alteration of these variables could cause a change in test performance and presumably a change in school performance as well. That variation occurs in intelligence test scores should not be surprising in view of the analysis of behavior presented in this book.

Organisms up and down the phylogenetic scale and throughout the entire age range appear to be conditionable. Furthermore, a change from one discriminative stimulus to another (from one situation to another) has been used to alter behavior quite radically, as we have shown in our discussion of schedules of reinforcement.

The ability to cause large changes in an individual's behavior immediately suggests the possibility of applying operant conditioning directly to education.

Programmed Instruction

Programmed instruction (two examples in psychology are Holland & Skinner, 1961, and Geiss, Stebbins & Lundin, 1965) consists of arranging a learning sequence in such a way as to promote the emission of new responses, or old responses under the control of new discriminative stimuli, without the learner making incorrect responses along the way. Such a program includes immediate reinforcement of correct responses and allows each learner to proceed at his own rate. It presupposes a behavioral analysis of the material which is to be learned, so that the programmer can state what the terminal behavior of the program should be, i.e., what behavior the learner should be able to emit after he has completed the program. For example, the writing of a program in reading must be preceded by an operational statement of what reading consists of. A program must make explicit the entering behavior, i.e., the behavior which a learner already has in his repertoire when he starts the program. Among the basic principles of a program is that of gradualness, which is achieved by means of response shaping and stimulus fading. And finally, since the program includes built-in reinforcements, each student can proceed at his own pace, thus eliminating the problem raised by the typically inflexible lecture method which requires all students to be at the same level.

A recent study by Sidman and Stoddard (1967) examined the acquisition of a circle-ellipse discrimination in retarded children, using stimulus fading techniques with one group and no gradual introductory techniques with another. Two groups of retarded boys, matched in terms of observed behavior in the institution, intelligence test scores, and chronological age, were given the two different training programs. Each child was seated in front of a key matrix (Figure 8-6). Each key displayed either an ellipse or a circle and the child's task was to press the key with the circle on it, i.e., the circle was the S^D for key pressing. The procedure for the Program Group, i.e., the group for whom the fading technique was

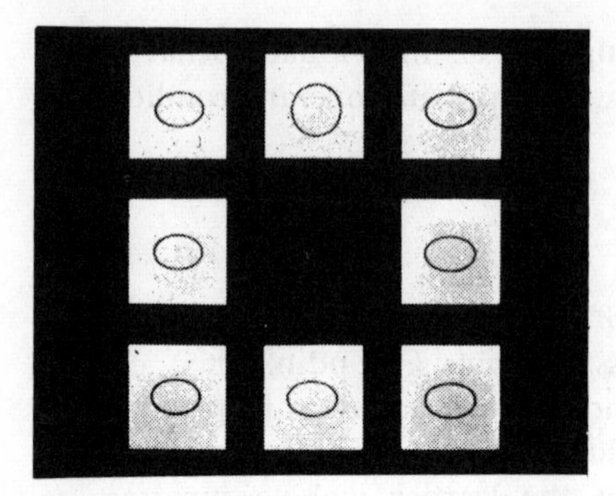

Fig. 8-6. The key matrix. (Sidman and Stoddard, 1967, Fig. 1.)

used, consisted of the following: Only one key was lit initially and that one displayed a circle. The background illumination of the other keys was then gradually increased in brightness (Figure 8-7). It can also be seen from Figure 8-7 that the first discrimination was based on a brightness difference which, by the last step, had been transferred to a difference between keys displaying a form vs. keys with no form. The next step in the program consisted of gradually making the ellipses more visibile on the other keys. Figure 8-8 shows the gradual increase in visibility of the ellipses while the response to the circle still remains correct. Note that in both Figures 8-7 and 8-8 the particular key which has the circle on it changes so that the subject does not respond to the position of the key rather than the shape of the figure. The other group, to be known as the Test Group, was given the circle vs. ellipse discrimination to learn without any prior fading, i.e., they were exposed to the D condition of Figure 8-8; those children who failed on this discrimination were given the D condition of Figure 8-7, i.e., circle vs. no circle discrimination; those children who learned this discrimination were given the circle-ellipse test again. Failing children were then given the

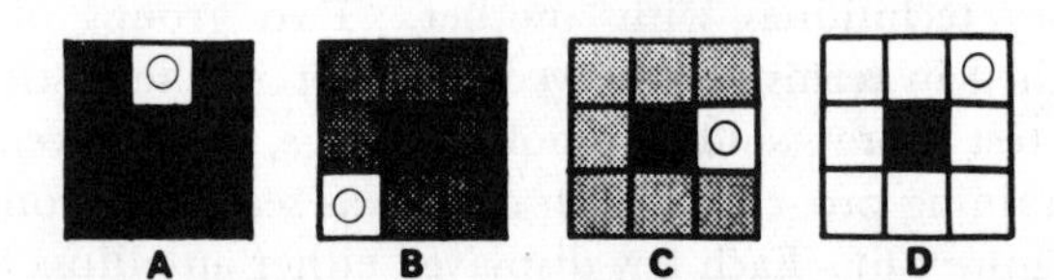

Fig. 8-7. Schematic illustration of a few steps in the background-fading portion of the program. The correct key always had the circle on a bright background. The incorrect keys were dark at first (A) and gradually became brighter (B,C,D). (Sidman and Stoddard, 1967, Fig. 2.)

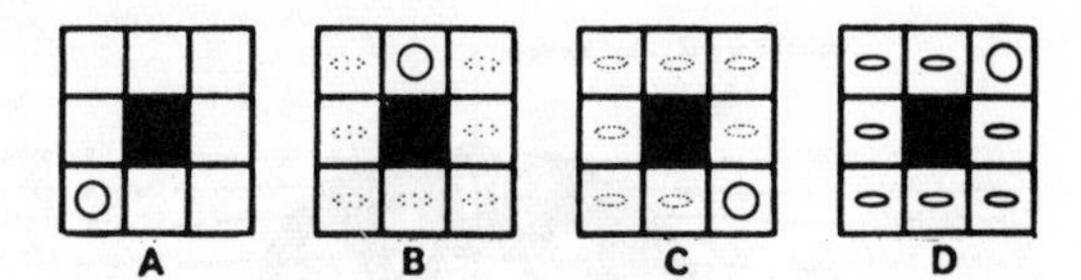

Fig. 8-8. Schematic illustration of a few steps in the ellipse-fading portion of the program. The ellipses appeared gradually (B,C,D) on the bright backgrounds of the incorrect keys. (The ellipses were not actually dotted; they were drawn that way here for convenience in reproduction.) (Sidman and Stoddard, 1967, Fig. 3.)

ellipse fading, and failing that, the background fading procedure. All correct responses were reinforced by the automatic delivery of candy. Seven of the 10 Program Group children learned the discrimination, while only one of the nine Test Group children learned the discrimination without subsequent application of the program. The authors noted that analysis of the error patterns showed that they "were nearly always traceable to reinforcement contingencies inherent in the teaching techniques and conflicting with contingencies deliberately designed to help the children to learn" (Sidman & Stoddard, 1967, p. 14). Those errors showed that all the children did learn something, e.g., when their responses were not controlled by the stimulus property of form, which should have been the basis for their responding, systematic circling around the matrix brought some of them to the correct key more rapidly than did random responding. The authors also pointed out that error patterns, which occurred when the subject could not cope with the new stimulus discrimination task, showed that extinction is basically an ineffective procedure for teaching. Extinction allows the subject to emit other responses and response patterns until these other responses also are extinguished.

The use of fading techniques for more sophisticated course work has been illustrated in a neuroanatomy program (Holland, 1960). Figure 8-9 shows a fully labelled cross section (A) of a part of the central nervous system, the *medulla oblongata*. Initially, in the discussion of this structure, the student has the A drawing in front of him while he is describing the spatial arrangement of the structures in response to various questions. After a large number of items concerning this drawing are discussed, he is given the B drawing, which is the same as the A drawing except that the structures are labelled

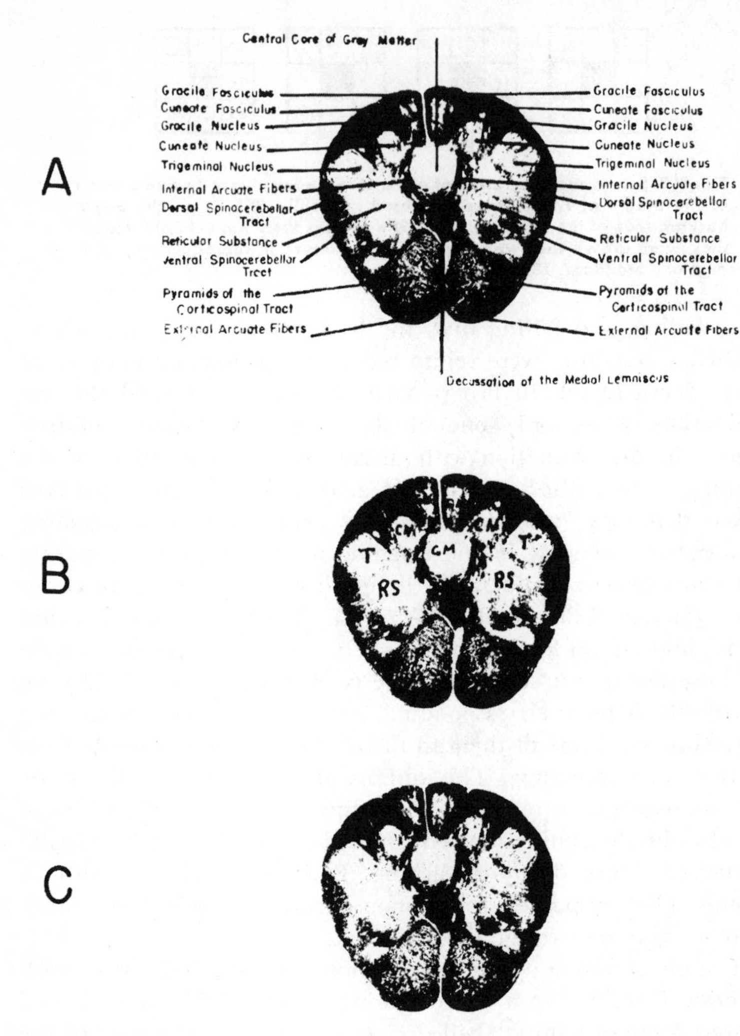

Fig. 8-9. An illustration of the technique of fading. Section A is in front or the student while he is working on the earliest items of a neuroanatomy program; Section B is in front of the student for later items; and Section C for still later items. (Holland, 1960, Fig. 4.)

only with initials. The final drawing about which he must answer questions is C; it contains no labels and yet if the student has gone through the entire program, he can now label the figure correctly simply by looking at the drawing.

An example of a program sequence for teaching a behavior chain is given by Gilbert (1962). Figure 8-10 provides the skeleton of a lesson plan. A behavior chain consists of a series of stimuli and responses where each response, except for the last, produces a stimulus which marks the occasion for emission of the next response. The term "demonstrate" in the figure means that the response required is shown to the student; the term "prompt" means that instructions are given about the response to be made, but the response itself must be executed by the learner. The term "spontaneously completed" means that the learner has executed the next step in the sequence without any special stimuli except for the last part of the behavior chain. Finally, the reader should note that the behavior chain is learned from the last step backwards. Figure 8-11 demonstrates the application of a program for learning such a behavior chain to the problem of long division. Still another sample of exercises from a program is given by Gilbert (1962). These are items for learning the color codes of electrical resistors. Of special interest is the use of mediating responses to facilitate the learning process. Figure 8-12, Exercise 1b, shows how a mediating response can be used to circumvent the problem posed by the fact that the association between the ten colors and numbers is initially very weak and that the responses themselves compete with each other. An analysis of the problem reveals that an additional response is needed which is highly probable as an association to a given color, e.g., brown, and which, as a stimulus, evokes the response "one" with a high probability. The response which satisfies both of these requirements is the word "penny." The reader can demonstrate the great ease with which the color bands can be learned by going through the sample exercises himself.

Programmed instruction has been used, not only for academic instruction for children, but also for industry. To take but one example, let us look at a study (Hughes & McNamara, 1961) which compared the learning of part of a 16-week course on the IBM 7070 Data Processing System by means of programmed instruction

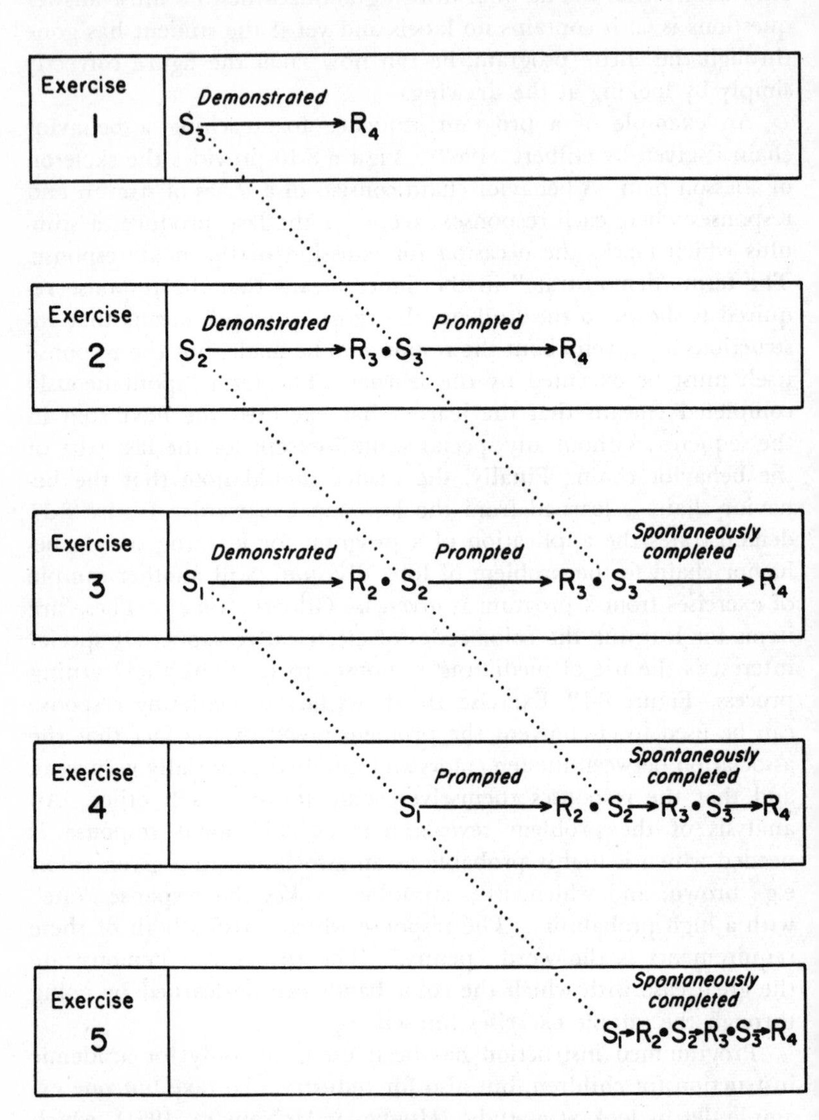

Fig. 8-10. Skeleton of mathetical lesson plan. Beginning with terminal operant, each operant is (1) introduced with full demonstration, (2) prompted in the next exercise, (3) performed spontaneously thereafter. (Gilbert, 1962, Fig. 3.)

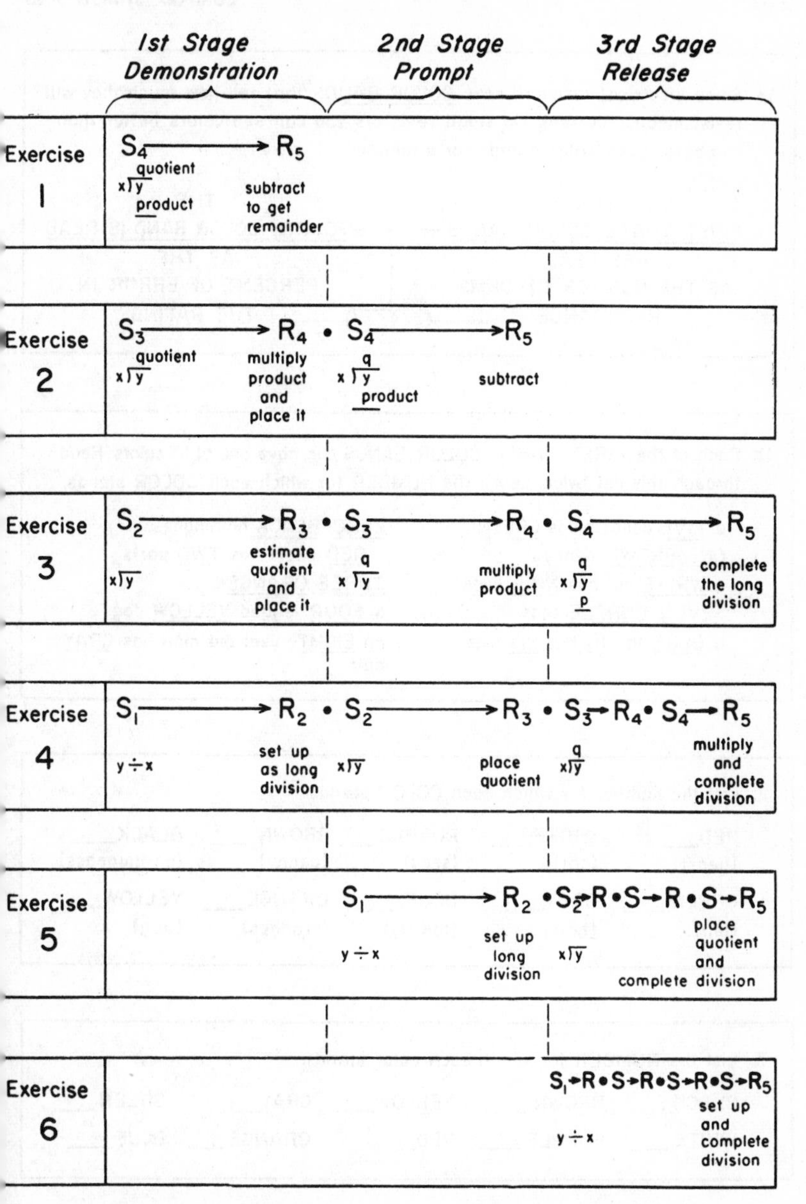

Fig. 8-11. Schematic of lesson plan for long division, indicating the three stages of each exercise in developing a behavior chain. (Gilbert, 1962, Fig. 4.)

1a. Some electrical resistors have COLOR BANDS that tell how much they will resist electric current. On small resistors you can see colors better than numbers. Each color stands for a number.

THE FIRST THREE COLOR BANDS ARE READ AS THE NUMBER OF OHMS RESISTANCE

THE FOURTH COLOR BAND IS READ AS THE PERCENT OF ERROR IN THE RATING

1b. Each of the FIRST THREE COLOR BANDS can have one of 10 colors. Read through this list twice. Learn the NUMBER for which each COLOR stands.

a FIVE dollar bill is GREEN
ONE BROWN penny
a WHITE cat has NINE lives
SEVEN PURPLE seas
a BLUE tail fly has SIX legs

ZERO: BLACK nothingness
a RED heart has TWO parts
THREE ORANGEs
a FOUR legged YELLOW dog
an EIGHTy year old man has GRAY hair

2. List the number for which each COLOR stands:

RED____ (heart)	WHITE____ (cat)	PURPLE___ (seas)	BROWN ____ (penny)	BLACK____ (nothingness)
GREEN____ (bill)	GRAY____ (hair)	BLUE____ (tail fly)	ORANGE____ (oranges)	YELLOW____ (dog)

3. List the NUMBER for which each color stands:

BLACK____	BROWN____	YELLOW____	GRAY____	GREEN____
WHITE____	PURPLE____	RED____	ORANGE____	BLUE____

Fig. 8-12. Sample exercises. From lesson on color codes of electrical resistors. (Gilbert, 1962, Fig. 5.)

with that of conventional classroom instruction. The Programmed Instruction Group used only programmed textbooks in the regular classrooms and at home. The results showed that programmed instruction required 11 hours of class time while conventional instruction took 15 hours. Thus, in teaching only part of one course as many as 4 hours learning time was saved, not to speak of all the instructor time. In addition, the Programmed Instruction Group had significantly higher scores on the same achievement test. A questionnaire given to the Programmed Instruction Group before the achievement test showed that 100% of the students believed that programmed instruction was more effective than conventional instruction, and 93% found it to be less difficult. Furthermore, 83% wanted to see more programmed instruction used in place of conventional instruction in the future.

Before leaving the discussion of programmed instruction, we should mention the teaching machine. The latter term is often used synonymously with programmed instruction but this usage is incorrect. A teaching machine is a device for presenting the instructional material while preventing the learner from looking at the answer before he has generated it himself. It also adds further interest to the learning situation, particularly for children. No machine, however, is any better than the instructional material which is programmed for it. Furthermore, programmed textbooks have been designed to simulate machine presentation. These books have, of course, the obvious advantage of being usable in a wide variety of situations (the home as well as the school) and require a much smaller investment of money. On the other hand, there are certain subject matters which require a machine for presentation of the material, e.g., material dealing with the problem of learning to pronounce words in a foreign language or learning to read.

Writing a good program is a difficult undertaking. It requires a careful behavioral analysis of the subject matter, the construction of a well-organized sequence of behaviors to be learned, presented in such a way as to insure that the learner, while emitting correct responses to all of the items, is constantly learning something new. Finally, it requires that the program be tested and retested until errors made during the course of the program are very close to zero and the learner has learned the terminal behaviors which were set as goals, as shown by an achievement test. Due to the amount of time and effort which must go into the writing of a program, only certain types of subject matter are more efficiently presented by means of a program. Schools can make most efficient use of programs in teaching students much basic material which is more successfully taught by these techniques, while they continue to use teachers employing the more conventional methods for other subjects. As to instruction given by teachers, it has become clear that the lecture technique, which requires the least amount of response on the part of the student, is the least efficient. The problem is that the student gets no opportunity to respond during the course of a lecture and therefore no learning, or very little, can take place in the course of a lecture. Reading also is not a very efficient way of learning. For all of the conventional instruction materials (lectures or books), therefore, the learner must adopt efficient study habits to adequately master the subject matter.

Fox (1962) presented a paper on the subject of learning more efficient study habits. Using behavior theory for purposes of analysis he made a list of problems in the area. The first problem dealt with the inadequacy of stimulus control over the response of studying. Typically the student works at odd times, thereby exposing himself to the competing responses which these occasions might evoke. A student who tries to study at a time when he typically meets friends for coffee is less likely to be able to concentrate on studying. The physical setting in which he works is also a determining factor. Thus, it is more than likely that a student who brings textbooks to the same desk at which he reads novels and the newspaper, solves crossword puzzles and writes letters to his girlfriend will engage in those activities instead of studying even though he has set out to study. Studying must become associated exclusively with certain stimuli in order for them to maintain control. Many responses which the typical student emits when he is "studying" are only indirectly related to learning. Under this heading belong underlining and copying. The response the student must learn is, of course, to recite the material on the basis of minimal cues, not on the basis of reading. Fox suggests that the student outline material he has read, while sitting on the book to prevent copying. In a pilot study on improving the study habits of students, he made use of the principles of gradualness, reinforcement, and stimulus control. The student with inadequate study habits was required to begin working with one subject matter (gradualness), to go to a specific room at a specific time equipped only with material relevant to that subject (stimulus control), and to work for only a short period of time, leaving the room immediately after quitting (reinforcement of studying). The student was then supposed to gradually increase the amount of time he spent working. If he found himself daydreaming (engaging in competing behavior which might be reinforced in the presence of stimuli which should be controlling his studying by relieving him of the aversive nature of the study material), he was instructed to study another page or problem and then to leave the room, thus assuring that his studying behavior would receive reinforcement by its termination. Then after one subject matter had been brought under study control, other subjects were gradually introduced into the student's repertoire. The interesting point to note here is that the cessation of the very activity we are trying to strengthen serves as a reinforcer for the occurrence of that behavior.

By this time the reader himself should be able to make use of the concepts of behavior theory to control his own behavior and perhaps apply it to improve his study habits.

SUMMARY

The application of behavior theory to education is not merely feasible, but desirable as well. Nevertheless, such application has not come into practice until the last decade or so. The influence which behavior theory had exerted on education until that time was the result of an emphasis on the variable of reinforcement. This emphasis often turned out to be deleterious to the learning process, since the delivery of reinforcers was not necessarily made contingent upon learning responses. Underlying any reinforcement of learning must be an analysis of the behavior to be learned. After the subject matter has undergone such analysis—so that the teacher knows what responses must be produced and strengthened, what kinds of stimulus control must be instated, what stimulus generalization must be generated, what response class must be established—

only then can appropriate sequences of study material be set up and appropriate responses be reinforced.

A number of studies were described showing the importance of analyzing the behavior which is to be taught the organism in question. A study was cited on counting in chimpanzees as well as one on the behavioral analysis of originality in human beings. We also listed some of the problems involved in a behavioral analysis of reading.

The importance of the characteristics of the learner was mentioned with respect to the practical problem faced by educators who work with relatively inflexible curricula. Some of the limitations of the measurement of learner characteristics were pointed out.

Programmed instruction was described as a technique of teaching which makes best use of the principles of behavior theory. The advantage in having a program for acquiring a discrimination as simple as that between a circle and an ellipse was clearly demonstrated in a study of retarded children. Further examples of programming techniques were given for the study of neuroanatomy, long division, and color coding. Finally, a study was presented which compared programmed and conventional instruction under controlled conditions. The function of the teaching machine in programmed learning was briefly described.

A discussion of the amount of time and effort which must go into the writing of a program provoked consideration of the application of behavior theory to the study response itself, which is still necessitated by the continuing use of old teaching methods as adjunct techniques to programmed instruction.

9

Abnormal Behavior

The first man to build a bridge knew very little of engineering and still less of the physical laws which might have helped him to build a stronger bridge with sturdier materials. And yet the building of bridges proceeded anyway, simply because the bridges were needed. In a similar way, man had to deal with abnormal behavior before he knew much of psychotherapy and still less of the behavioral laws underlying the successful outcome of the therapeutic process. Many of these older procedures are still with us. In fact, anyone who has ever tried to introduce a fundamentally better procedure based on research, *but* a new one, has learned to expect the greatest resistance from those who have practiced a less efficient, *but* older procedure. This is true even if the older procedure was successful in only a small fraction of the cases to which it was applied. The reader might well expect this resistance to extinction simply on the basis of the effect of intermittent reinforcement (cf. Chapter 3).

Models of Abnormal Behavior

In abnormal psychology, the older procedures have come essentially from a combination of the medical disease model and the conviction that talking can ameliorate abnormal behavior. The medical disease model relies, first of all, on the procedure of diagnosis. Diagnosis in the area of abnormal psychology has been, at best, disappointing. Schemes for classification of behavior disorders are continuously being revised and improved, and research in this area, as indicated by a recent review (Zubin, 1967), appears to be undiminished. Nevertheless, the continuing research activity shows us that the reliability of diagnosis is very low indeed (Ash, 1949). Bandura and Walters (1963) maintain that the categorizations made have not been based on empirical research, since categorization into "normal" and "abnormal" involves value judgments. In a recent book on scientific approaches to the study of abnormal behavior, Inglis (1966) also decries the use of psychiatric diagnosis, suggesting that what is needed is not examination of schemes of diagnosis, but more precise and objective study of the abnormal behavior itself. We shall return to the question of diagnosis below.

The Medical Disease Model

What exactly does the medical disease model imply? The use of this model in psychology assumes that abnormal behavior is merely a symptom of some more important underlying cause. As in physical disease, where the physican might use the symptoms of temperature, cough, and inflamed throat to prescribe some medicine to counteract the effect of the underlying germ or virus, so the psychologist, psychiatrist, or social worker (all of these disciplines practice psychotherapy) tries to deal with the underlying psychological cause. As indicated by Ullmann and Krasner (1965), this model represented a major medical breakthrough in the nineteenth century and it later formed the basis for the model of psychoanalysis developed by

Freud. Unfortunately, Freud's use of the concept of an underlying cause restricted not only the kind of research to be done but would allow only well-initiated psychoanalysts to determine those underlying causes. In summarizing, the point of the model is that abnormal behavior cannot be treated directly and even a change in the behavior is viewed as unimportant unless the underlying cause has been dealt with also.

The medical model, used in its physical sense, has given rise to a significant amount of information in the study of the nervous system and the endocrine system, in biochemical studies, and in genetic studies. However, although the pursuit of the physical causes of abnormal behavior has given rise to a few outstanding discoveries of underlying causes (e.g., syphilis of the brain), this line of research has, in most cases, been disappointingly unproductive in explaining abnormal behavior. The model led, at one time, to a rash of operations performed on various parts of the brain; more often to electro-shock and insulin shock therapy; and recently to widespread use of drugs. With the exception of the reduction in length of depression in patients given electro-shock therapy, no convincing evidence for the effectiveness of these various somatic treatments exists when compared to samples of patients given no therapy (see, for example, Staudt & Zubin, 1957). Nevertheless, continuing research on the effect of drugs on specific behavioral functions in animals (Boren, 1966) may yet prove their worth beyond the general tranquilizing function which they presently serve as used in mental hospitals.

One line of research which the medical model has stimulated is the examination of the genetic variable in abnormal behavior. Perhaps the most outstanding name in this field is Kallmann (1946), who over the years traced the genetic variable in schizophrenia. Schizophrenia is a psychosis (extreme form of abnormal behavior marked by bizarre behavior which is difficult to modify) of relatively high incidence. The results of one study carried out by Kallmann are presented in Figure 9-1. Inspection of Figure 9-1 shows a systematic increase in the incidence of schizophrenia and schizoid personality (characteristic of the general manner of a schizophrenic patient without a psychotic breakdown which would prevent the person from functioning in society) with an increase in the degree

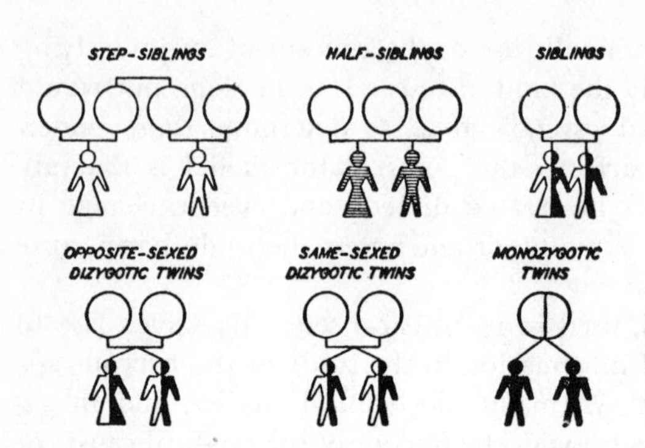

Fig. 9-1. Degree of consanguinity in twin family method. (Kallmann, 1946, Fig. 4.)

of relationship to schizophrenic patients. Monozygotic twins, offspring of one egg and therefore of identical genetic make-up showed, by far, the highest amount of concordance. The effect of the environment in this case, appears to be relatively small as evidenced by a comparison of the monozygotic twins who lived together and those who lived apart. Dizygotic twins show less concordance than monozygotes and about as much as full siblings, which might be expected on the basis of the fact that dizygotic twins come from two different eggs as full siblings do. Half-siblings have one parent in common while step-siblings have no blood relatives in common but are raised in the same environment. Dramatic as these results are, the reader should be cautioned about a number of possible artifacts in such a study. As mentioned above, diagnostic categories are typically unreliable and therefore some bias might have entered into judgments of concordance of schizophrenia due to the investigator's basic genetic hypothesis. There is the additional problem of possible bias in the selection of the twins for study. Since the mental hospital population constituted the basic sample for the study, it is possible that only those characterized by more severe, or at least more asocial, abnormality were studied.

The Behavior Theory Model

Attempts to make use of behavior theory in explaining the etiology (the study of the cause) of abnormal behavior and its modification have been reported for some years. Thus, the production of a phobia by respondent conditioning was first reported by Watson and Rayner (1920) in an 11-month old boy. They conditioned a fear reaction to the presence of a rat by pairing rat presentation with a loud aversive sound. The fear response, consisting of an avoidance component (turning and moving away from the aversive object) and a respondent component (crying), generalized to a rabbit, somewhat less to a dog, and even to a fur coat. Four years later Mary Cover Jones (1924) treated a 3-year old boy by means of respondent conditioning. The boy showed fear reactions to animals, furry objects, cotton, and hair. The therapeutic procedure consisted of pairing the presentation of a rabbit with food that the child liked. At first the rabbit was presented at a distance, and caged, while the child was eating. With successive trials, the rabbit was brought closer to the child and even taken out of the cage. The procedure was based on the premise that, by initially presenting the aversive object far away, only a part of the respondent component of the fear response would be elicited, and probably no avoidance responses would be emitted. Pairing the aversive object with positive reinforcers, viz., the food, an attempt was made to establish the rabbit as a positive conditioned reinforcer. The treatment procedure was not only successful in eliminating the fear of the rabbit, but also produced generalization to the other feared objects. The two studies thus demonstrated the usefulness of the conditioning model in etiology and in therapy of abnormal behavior. Other studies followed. Mowrer and Mowrer (1938), for example, had complete success in the elimination of enuresis by means of a respondent conditioning technique. Whenever the child wet his bed, a buzzer (US) went off automatically, waking (UR) the child. Eventually bladder pressure (CS) alone, which regularly preceded bed wetting, and therefore the buzzer, woke (CR) the child. The response of awaking in turn controlled the sphincter contraction. Eventually the bladder pressure itself became the controlling stimulus for the sphincter contraction, thus keeping the child dry without waking. There are numerous other examples of the early utilization of behavior theory in abnormal psychology (viz. Ullmann and Krasner, 1965).

Work in a somewhat different, although relevant, vein was done by Pavlov (Kaplan, 1966), who reported on the production of what he termed experimental neuroses in his dogs. The basic paradigm which he used was relatively straightforward (cf. Chapter 2) and is credited to have been developed by Dr. Shenger-Krestovnikova. The dog was confronted by a circle (CS+) and this stimulus was followed by food (US) in the mouth. After the CR of salivation was established, an ellipse (CS⁻) was introduced which was never followed by feeding. The first ellipse presented had a ratio of its semiaxes of 2:1; in subsequent trials a gradual change was made in the ellipse, the modification being made in the direction of a circle, with the ratios of the semiaxes varying from 3:2, 4:3, and so on, until the ellipse reached the ratio of 9:8. At first the dog discriminated between the circle and the ellipse, salivating as many as 10 drops to the circle and as few as 1 to the ellipse. After some three weeks of further trials on the discrimination procedure, the behavior broke down, with salivation occurring equally to the circle and ellipse; the dog also behaved in a most unusual manner. The formerly quiet dog began to squeal, tore off some of the apparatus attached to it, and, in subsequent sessions, barked violently upon being brought to the experimental room. At this point, even the discrimination between the circle and the ellipse having a 2:1 ratio of its semiaxes was not successful. A period of retraining, although initially quieting the animal again, took twice as long as before to bring him to the discrimination between the 9:8 ellipse and the circle. Furthermore, even though the animal succeeded in discriminating the two stimuli on the first presentation, subsequent presentations ceased to yield further discrimination and once again elicited the excited behavior described above. Pavlov's interpretation was based on a hypothetical clash between excitatory and inhibitory processes within the nervous system. The elicitation of so-called neurotic behavior as a function of the difficulty of discrimination is the most well-known model of the inception of abnormal behavior, but it is not the only one by any means. Pavlov reported an experiment by Dr. Erofeeva (Kaplan, 1966), in which the experimenter used an electric shock that under normal circumstances elicits withdrawal (called the defensive reflex by Pavlov) as a CS for the salivary response. The final CS was a very high shock, although it was first presented as a weak shock which was gradually increased. Conditioning using this stimulus was successful. Then the CS was applied to new places on the dog's body. While at first stimulation of neighboring areas elicited the salivary response, there came a point (the furthest from the original site yet tested), at which the dog abruptly changed his behavior. The salivary response disappeared completely and a violent defense reflex took over. Even applications of weak currents to the original site produced only the most violent defense reflexes. Variations of this procedure were applied to two additional dogs, with very similar results. Even more interesting perhaps, was the fact that only one of the dogs could be retrained by using electric shock as a CS, and that became possible only after a three-month rest. Pavlov interpreted this experiment to mean that the nervous system had suffered from being in a chronic pathological state. As in the circle-ellipse discrimination procedure, the dog suffered from a conflict between two antagonistic processes; in this case the unconditioned excitatory defense reflex, which had to be inhibited, was opposed to the conditioned salivary reflex.

Of some interest with respect to Pavlov's experiments on the production of neurotic or abnormal behavior is his stress on the fact that the nervous system of each dog determines in large part the type and degree of abnormal behavior which the experimental procedure produces. Thus, he arrived at a temporary classification of nervous systems into two types. One he called "sanguine"—represented by the type of dog that responds when there are quick changes of stimuli but becomes inactive and does not condition rapidly when the environment becomes relatively monotonous. The other type he called "melancholic"—represented by the type of dog that is very restrained in its movements when stimuli change rapidly, but which conditions well when the stimulus conditions are restricted. A similar and more recent classification of individuals into extraverts and introverts has been suggested by Eysenck (1957). Thus, we have here at least one connecting link between the medical model approach and the behavior theory approach. As we have stated in preceding chapters, both nature and nurture must be considered in assessing variables which control behavior. It is no different for abnormal behavior.

Let us look at some more recent formulations of the behavior theory model of abnormal behavior. Dollard and Miller (1950), who may be considered the scientists who sparked the current interest in the application of the behavior theory model to abnormal behavior, went about their theorizing more by way of translation from psychoanalytic theory to learning theory than from behavioral data (whether animal or human) to learning theory. Nevertheless, they constructed the scaffold for the behavior theory model as we accept it today. They listed four so-called critical training situations to be observed in the production of neurosis: feeding, cleanliness training, early sex training, and anger-anxiety conflicts. These situations they deemed to be critical on the basis of psychoanalytic theory and case studies. Behavior theory enters only in providing the mechanism by means of which the abnormal behavior might be acquired. In describing what the infant learns in the feeding situation, they point out that if his cry is reinforced by feeding, he is learning at least one way of controlling his environment; if on the other hand, the cry is not reinforced by feeding, he might become "apathetic"; finally, if the child is fed only after crying violently for a long time, he might learn to "overreact" to deprivation situations. The authors also describe how specific abnormal responses are learned, pointing to the likelihood of an avoidance response being learned when a positively reinforced response is punished. Thus, a little boy who is punished for masturbating (a response resulting in positive reinforcement) while in bed, learned the avoidance responses of staying up late, getting up out of bed and so on.

A more recent attempt to show how behavior theory could be applied to abnormal behavior comes from Bridger (1964). He ascribes abnormal behavior to a shift in control from the second signalling system (verbal control) to the first signalling system (nonverbal stimuli such as those controlling animals' behavior). He explains hallucinations ("sensing" something for which there is no actual physical evidence) in schizophrenic patients as being due to prepotency of the first signalling system over that of the second signalling system. When only the first signalling system is in control (and the second signalling system cannot modify the effect of the first), one might also expect the CS (a stimulus often associated with a given US) to elicit responses like those elicited by the US, and hence the hallucinatory behavior.

An explanation of the origin of schizophrenia in terms of behavior theory was provided by Mednick (1958). Beginning with the assumption that the preschizophrenic individual suffers from greater anxiety than the normal individual, and that this anxiety acts as a drive (in the terms of this book we would say that the preschizophrenic finds a larger number of stimuli to be more aversive), he goes on to show how bizarre, tangential verbal responses are reinforced because they constitute the responses which completely avoid the aversive stimuli of the schizophrenic's environment.

Let us consider some of the general characteristics and implications of the behavior theory model of abnormal behavior. First, this model considers behavior (once its abnormality has been established to be functional rather than due to purely organic causes) as the only valid object for study and modification. It makes no attempt to seek out inner causes for the behavior, although it does, of course, allow for the case where one behavior abnormality is the outcome of another. In some cases, even where the original cause is established as a physiological defect, the behavior theory model still suggests the lines along which behavior modification can be pursued. We have already reviewed studies which show that the behavior of retarded children (cf. Chapter 8), to take but one example, can be modified, provided appropriate techniques are employed. Abnormal behavior is considered to be lawful behavior, basically subject to the same controlling variables as normal behavior, but where the relative and/or absolute effectiveness of these variables differ, thus producing abnormal behavior, or where the environment alone conspires to condition behavior which society at large views as being abnormal. It also implies that while the history of the origin of the abnormal behavior may be critical in its treatment, in many cases only the variables currently controlling that undesirable behavior need be manipulated to cause a change in the patient.

The acceptance of a behavior theory model poses very clearly problems concerning the definition of abnormal behavior. Of course, this is also a problem which psychologists utilizing the medical disease model must face, since for most abnormal behavior the hypothesized microorganism or nervous system deficit, or endocrine system malfunction cannot actually be located. The term "abnormal," within the context of behavior theory, may be attributed to an individual because of a deficit in behavior, as for example in a child over four years old who does not yet speak, or because of the maladaptive nature of a response he *does* emit, such as temper tantrums. What is abnormal or maladaptive can be described in terms of the individual's success or failure in obtaining the positive reinforcers and averting the negative reinforcers, which his station in life, determined by the culture in which he lives, entitles him to. Such a definition is surely culture bound and therefore relative, with the exception of such essential primary reinforcers as food and drink which any culture must allow to control behavior even though these too can, for short periods of time (e.g., during periods of hunger strikes), be culture modified and act as negative rather than positive reinforcers. While this definition of abnormality sounds quite vague, it is, in fact, quite serviceable on a practical basis. The question of abnormality need not be posed for each individual. It need arise only for those people who, themselves, question the normality of their own behavior and seek help, or for those whose behavior is deemed abnormal by the key people controlling the reinforcers in their environment. Ferster (1965), in a discussion of the definition of abnormal behavior, indicated that what is really needed is a functional analysis of the people and the agencies who designate particular people as abnormal. Lest the reader become confused about what extreme abnormal behavior is, let him be reassured that, in fact, very few people would have difficulty in recognizing extreme forms of such behavior in psychotic patients as being abnormal and, furthermore, that many persons who are supposed to detect abnormal behavior during the course of their daily activities (e.g., policemen) do in fact recognize such abnormality. In addition, many hospitalizations are made by members of patients' families. On the other hand, the reader should realize that, on the basis of the preceding discussion, the final arbiter of what constitutes abnormal behavior is a human value judgment. Thus, society decides that stealing (which, when the thief is caught, results in the loss of positive reinforcers and an increase in negative ones), is criminal, that suicidal behavior is abnormal, and that a person who kills another man in the course of a military battle is heroic.

Diagnosis or Behavioral Analysis

We have already indicated that diagnosis is a term which comes from the medical disease model. Its continued widespread use requires that we discuss the processes involved in it; its many failures requires that we describe an alternative approach. The process of diagnosis generally consists of interviewing the patient and closely observing his behavior, sometimes by means of testing procedures. Typically, the behavior, since it is viewed as being *only* symptomatic, is interpreted, which is to say its "real significance" is indicated. We shall first cite a study on interpretation.

Problems in Interpretation

Haughton and Ayllon (1965) worked on a special ward in which the behavior of psychotic patients was systematically observed and controlled. Selecting a 54-year old female patient who had been hospitalized for 23 years, they obtained base-line data which indicated that she spent 60 per cent of her waking time lying in bed, 20 per cent sitting and walking, and the remainder in behavior related to meals, cleaning herself, and elimination. They then chose to reinforce a response consisting of "holding the broom while standing up." The reinforcer consisted of cigarettes and tokens exchangeable for cigarettes. The delivery of reinforcement by the nurses caused an increase in frequency of occurrence of broom-holding and the cessation of reinforcement brought about complete extinction of the broom-holding response, as evidenced by a two-year follow-up. During the course of her conditioning period, the broom-holding gained such strength that she did not allow other patients to even hold the broom. At the time, the experimenters asked two board-certified psychiatrists, without providing them with information about the development of the behavior, to observe the behavior of the patient and to evaluate it. Here are some of the interpretations given by one of the psychiatrists (Haughton & Ayllon, 1965, p. 97):

> Her constant and compulsive pacing holding a broom in the manner she does could be seen as a ritualistic pro-

> cedure, a magical action. When regression conquers the associative process, primitive and archaic forms of thinking control the behavior. . . . By magic, she controls others, cosmic powers are at her disposal and inanimate objects become living creatures.
>
> Her broom could be then:
>
> 1. a child that gives her love and she gives him in return her devotion;
> 2. a phallic symbol;
> 3. the sceptre of an omnipotent queen.
>
> Her rhythmic and prearranged pacing in a certain space are not similar to the compulsion of a neurotic; but because this is a far more irrational, far more controlled behavior from a primitive thinking, this is a magical procedure in which the patient carries out her wishes. . . .

Need we say any more about the dangers attendant on interpretation of behavior?

The Effect of the Interviewer

The conduct of the interview, a basic form of inquiry in widespread use, has only recently undergone scientific scrutiny. In a series of studies conducted by the author and his associates (Salzinger & Pisoni, 1958, 1960, 1961; Salzinger & Portnoy, 1964; Salzinger, Portnoy, & Feldman, 1964), the conduct of the interview was analyzed, viewing the behavior of the interviewer as the independent variable and the behavior of the patient as the dependent variable. The first task in the experimental examination of the interview required the establishment of a reliable response class. The experimenters chose the class of self-referred affect because the amount of affect (emotion) expressed by a patient is supposed to be diagnostic of schizophrenia; presence of little affect or "shallowness of affect," as it is described in clinical studies, is considered to be indicative of schizophrenia. The investigators defined affect operationally, in terms of a list of statements such as "I love," "I hate," "I'm happy," "We're sad" and so on. The response class was limited to self-referred statements in order to make certain that the statements related to the patient. It was demonstrated that the response class, defined in an operational manner, could be reliably recognized, since two independent observers agreed on their counts of the frequency of occurrence of the response in the patient's speech. After reliability of the response class had been established, the experiment went on to determine whether the interviewer's behavior could cause a change in the frequency of occurrence of the selected behavior. Questions which act as S^D's (Salzinger, S., 1956), obviously increase or decrease the frequency of the response class, but this variable was believed to be easily controllable by the interviewer since it is so obviously a factor in any interview. It was therefore assumed that the typical diagnostic interviewer would not bias his results in such an obvious way.

Any observation of a conversation makes it clear that it continues only as long as the participants attend to each other's speech. This attending behavior can be viewed as constituting reinforcing events (Verplanck, 1955) and generally consists of such verbal remarks as "Mmhm," "Yeah," "Yes," "I see." Following up this interpretation of attending behavior, Salzinger and his associates were able to determine what effect such reinforcement had on the emission of self-referred affect statements in interviews with schizophrenics. The procedure consisted of 10 minutes of operant level, 10 minutes of conditioning, and 10 minutes of extinction. Throughout the interview only general questions were asked and then only when the patient ceased talking for more than two seconds. Figure 9-2 shows the behavior of 3 schizophrenic patients selected because they had a high, medium, or low operant level for self-referred affect statements. The results show that the delivery of reinforcement definitely influenced the number of self-referred affect statements emitted. Similar results were obtained by a male and female interviewer. Further study showed that a comparable group of schizophrenic subjects, put through the same interview procedure, but without any administration of reinforcement, showed no significant variation in frequency of self-referred affect statements during corresponding periods of the interview. Furthermore, starting the interview with a reinforcement period followed by extinction produced the greatest number of self-referred affect statements dur-

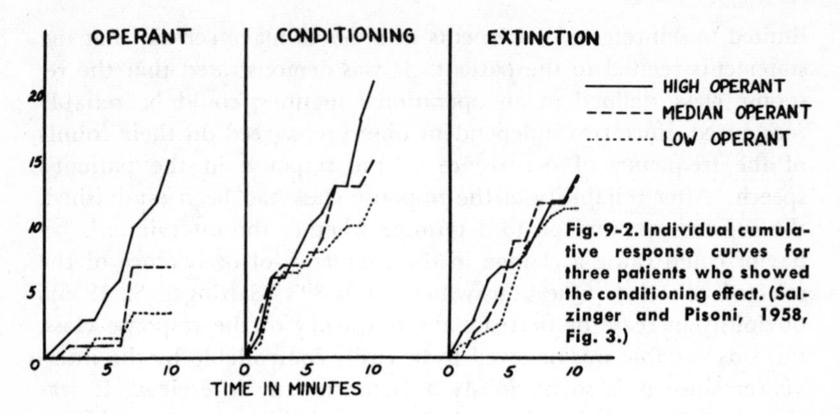

Fig. 9-2. Individual cumulative response curves for three patients who showed the conditioning effect. (Salzinger and Pisoni, 1958, Fig. 3.)

ing the first 10-minute period of the interview. These studies demonstrated quite clearly that typical "attending" behavior when systematically administered can change the verbal behavior of a patient even in as short a period of time as 10 minutes.

In order to make certain that the questions asked of the patient during the course of the interview, even though they were of a general nature, did not somehow produce conditioning through an artifact, a further experiment was performed. Patients were placed behind a screen so that they could not see the interviewer and so that he, in turn, could program more complicated schedules of reinforcement than he could in the above described face-to-face interviews. The patients were then told that a light would flash whenever they said something of importance and that saying things of importance would make them feel better. In this manner, the light was established as a positive reinforcer. Finally, they were asked to deliver monologues on topics usually discussed during the typical intake interview, thus eliminating the need for questions altogether. Three comparable groups of subjects were used. One group was reinforced for self-referred affect for the entire 30-minute period; a second group was reinforced for all speech on a FI 30″ schedule for 30 minutes; the third group received no reinforcement at all. This study enabled the investigators, under conditions which controlled for possible artifactual effects of the questions, change in facial expression of the interviewer, and the influence of intonation on the verbal reinforcers, to examine the specificity of the reinforcement effect by tracing the change in speech rate and the change in self-referred affect statements. Figure 9-3 shows the results of representative subjects of the three groups. The subject who was reinforced for self-referred affect emits a noticeably larger proportion of such statements than either of the subjects in the other groups. Inspection of Figure 9-4 shows two interesting effects. The subject who was reinforced for speech in general emits the largest number of words. The subject who was reinforced for self-referred affect also shows an increase in word rate initially, but subsequently, after response differentiation has taken place, his rate drops to the level of the control group subject. The significant differences between the experimental and control groups indicate quite clearly that the conditioning effect achieved in the course of the interview was correctly attributed to the administration of reinforcement. It therefore seems fair to conclude that the interviewer can, by his reinforcement operation, determine what it is that the patient will tell him. Taking this finding in conjunction with the fact that the typical interviewer makes no planned effort to control his own emission of reinforcers, it remains for us to make explicit what does, in fact, determine the reinforcing behavior of the interviewer. The answer to this appears to be that statements made by the patient which are concordant with the interviewer's general theory of be-

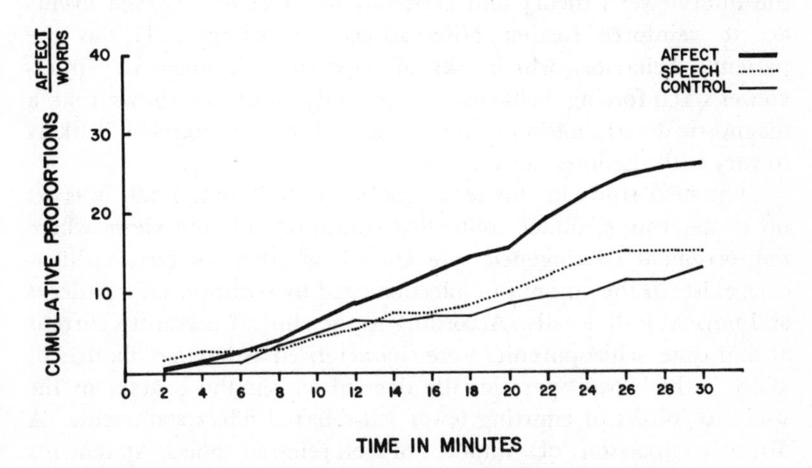

Fig. 9-3. Individual cumulative response curves of the proportion of affect to words for three subjects selected at the median of each of the three groups. (Salzinger, Portnoy, Feldman, 1964 (a), Fig. 1.)

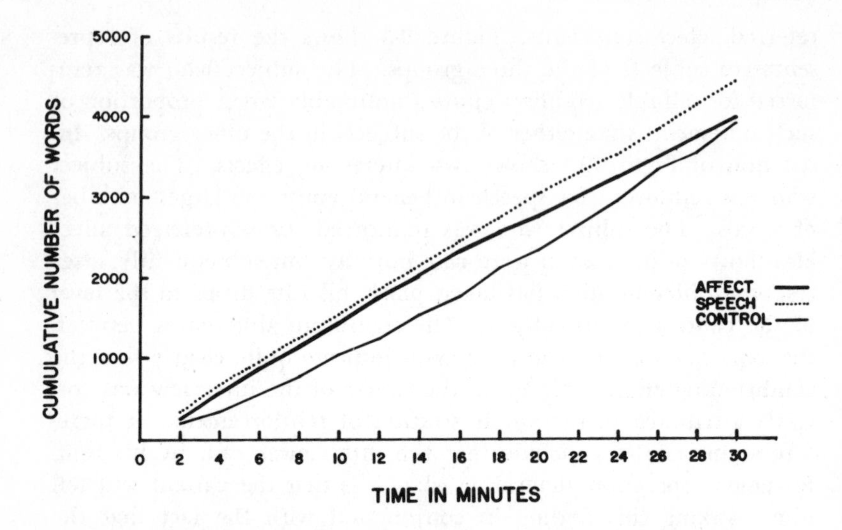

Fig. 9-4. Individual cumulative response curves of total number of words for three subjects selected at the median of each of the three groups. (Salzinger, Portnoy, and Feldman, 1964 (a), Fig. 2.)

havior, or which conform to his expectations of the patient, are most likely to be reinforced and to act as reinforcers themselves for the interviewer's theory and expectations. Just as observed events act to reinforce further observations (cf. Chapter 1), so the patient's behavior, which was anticipated, reinforces the interviewer's reinforcing behavior. This study therefore shows that a diagnostic determination made on the basis of the interview is likely to vary with the interviewer.

The next study in this series (Salzinger & Pisoni, 1960) was set up to determine, under controlled conditions of interviews where reinforcement contingencies are known, whether, in fact, a difference exists in the amount of affect emitted by schizophrenic patients and normal individuals. According to the clinical literature current at that time, schizophrenics were characterized as having "flatness of affect," which was operationally defined within the context of the study to consist of emitting fewer self-referred affect statements. A direct comparison of number of self-referred affect statements emitted during operant level revealed no difference between the two groups. Nor was there a significant difference in conditionability, i.e., both normal and schizophrenic subjects responded to reinforcement. A difference in number of affect responses occurred only when schizophrenics and normals were matched in terms of sex, number of responses emitted during operant level and number of reinforcers received, and then only in the extinction period. Two representative matched pairs of subjects are pictured in Figure 9-5. The clinically reported result of shallowness of affect in schizophrenics, therefore, has to be attributed to an extinction effect on the response class in question. Only research with other, nonaffect response classes can tell us whether the difference between normals and schizophrenics should be wholly attributed to differences in rates of extinction or to the difference in rate of extinction of the particular response class of affect.

Another possible criticism of these studies was that the schizophrenic patients used as subjects were not severely ill, i.e., none of them had been in the hospital for a long time. For that reason, another study was undertaken (Salzinger & Portnoy, 1964) in which chronic patients constituted the sample. Although the chronic patients emitted a smaller number of self-referred affect statements

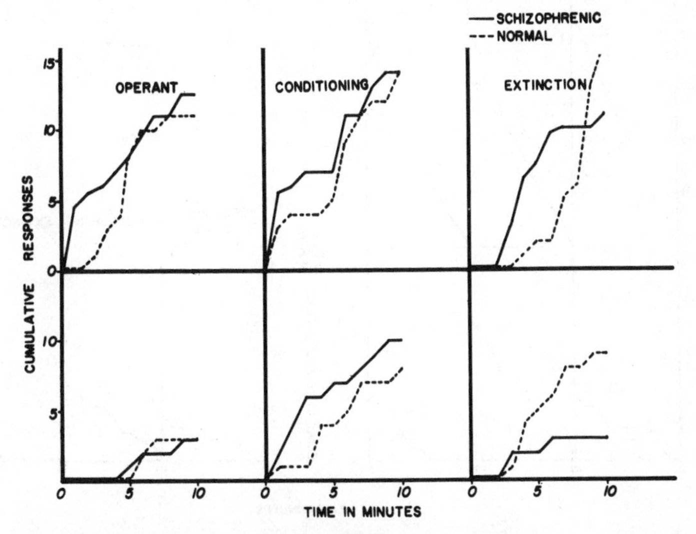

Fig. 9-5. Individual cumulative affect response curves for two pairs of matched schizophrenics and normals. The top pair shows two subjects with high operant levels, while the bottom pair shows two subjects with low operant levels. (Salzinger and Pisoni, 1960, Fig. 1.)

than the acute patients, and therefore less than the normal subjects, closer scrutiny of the results also showed a significant difference in amount of general speech. When the amount of speech was taken into account, no significant difference between the chronic and acute patient groups remained. Figure 9-6 shows an acute and a chronic schizophrenic patient. They differ both in speech rate and in number of affect statements. When the ratio of affect to speech is plotted, however, the difference is considerably reduced. This study shows that chronic schizophrenic patients cannot be generally characterized as being flat in affect but that they are better described as talking at a lower rate.

Some Objective Measures of Abnormality

In our discussion of a definition of abnormality, we indicated the importance of society in determining how a given behavior should be characterized. The next technique utilizes the reaction of society

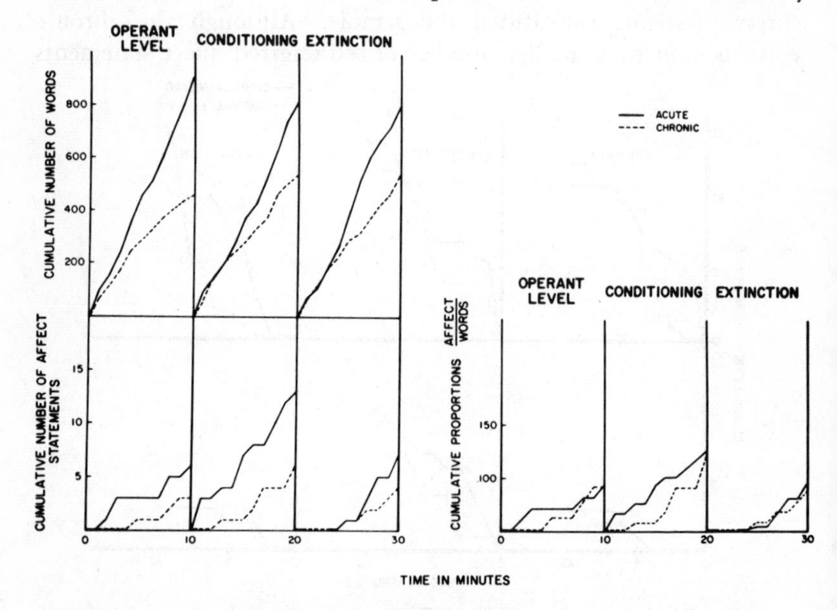

Fig. 9-6. Individual cumulative response curves for one acute and one chronic schizophrenic patient for three measures of verbal behavior. (Salzinger and Portnoy, 1964, Fig. 1.)

to objectively quantify some specific abnormal characteristics. The application of the technique, called the cloze procedure, was based on the general observation that the speech of schizophrenic patients is difficult to comprehend. Extreme difficulty in comprehension is evidenced dramatically in the cases of muteness or echolalia (a tendency to repeat everything that is heard). Recognition of these abnormalities is relatively simple and requires no special technique. Recognition of other communication difficulties in patients is not as simple. With the exception of a few patients (and even those are perhaps more affected by their long stay in the hospital than by their illness), no patient displays his abnormal behavior all of the time. The task before us, then, consisted of devising a technique for detecting communication difficulties which are not very obvious. The cloze procedure was originated by Taylor (1953) and is based on the following reasoning: In listening to someone talk, the listener occasionally misses a word. Nevertheless, he still has enough context to enable him to guess what the missing word is. If a speaker is very clear, then filling in these missing words is relatively easy; if, on the other hand, the speaker is hard to understand in the first place, then the listener cannot fill these words in correctly. The cloze procedure consists of deleting words systematically (according to common practice, every fifth word) from some text and requiring a group of subjects who speak the same language as that used in the text to guess what words were originally emitted by the speaker. The studies comparing schizophrenic and normal speech (Salzinger, Portnoy, & Feldman, 1964b, 1966) used portions of the monologues and continuous speech of interviews obtained prior to the use of reinforcement in the studies cited above. Taking the first 200 words of schizophrenic and normal speech samples and matching them in terms of sex, age, education, and where possible, for ethnic group of the subjects, comparisons were made in terms of the proportion of words correctly guessed. Figure 9-7 shows that more words were guessed correctly for normal than for schizophrenic speech samples in 12 out of 13 pairs; in only one pair were more words correctly guessed for the schizophrenic than for the normal speech.

Two other techniques were used by these investigators (Salzinger, Portnoy, & Feldman, 1966) to measure the relative com-

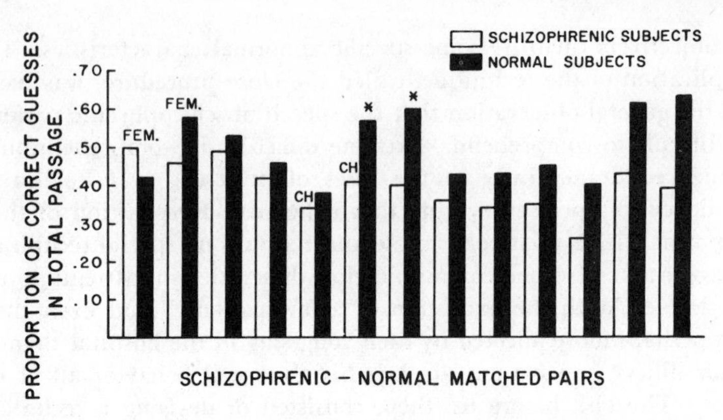

Fig. 9-7. Proportion of correct guesses to total guesses (C score) in total passage for each schizophrenic-normal matched pair. The two female pairs are indicated by *FEM.*, the two chronic schizophrenics are indicated by *CH.*, and the normal subject used in two pairs is indicated by (*). (Salzinger, Portnoy, Feldman, 1964 (b), Fig. 2.)

municability of schizophrenic and normal speech. One of them was called the method of reconstruction. It consisted of the following procedure: The first 200 words of a given speech sample were divided into 10 successive 20-word segments without punctuation, and typed on separate cards. The ten cards were then placed in random order and each subject was asked to restore the cards to their initial order. The speech samples of the schizophrenics were restored correctly less often than those of the matched normals (11 vs. 2 pairs). In addition, the time it took subjects to put the cards into an order which satisfied them (independent of how correct the order was), was longer for the schizophrenic speech samples than for the samples of the normal members (Figure 9-8) of the pairs.

The final technique of evaluating the communicability of schizophrenic speech was the method of unitization. In this method, the subject was given a typescript, without punctuation, and was instructed to divide the script into sentences, crossing out any words which did not seem to fit at all. Out of 10 matched pairs, the material of 9 schizophrenic members had more words crossed out than their normal matches.

Thus, even the seemingly vague definition of abnormal behavior in terms of how society responds and reinforces is amenable to operational definition, whether we are referring to the reinforcing

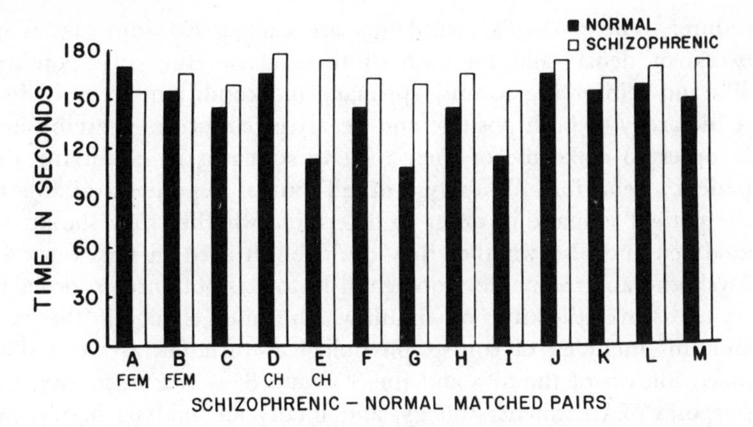

Fig. 9-8. Reconstruction technique. Time (geometric mean of subjects' reconstruction times for a given speech sample) taken by subjects to complete the reconstruction of samples of normal and schizophrenic speech. Results are shown separately for each schizophrenic-normal matched pair. Pairs A and B are females; pairs D and E each include a chronic schizophrenic. (Salzinger, Portnoy, Feldman, 1966, Fig. 4.)

behavior of the interviewer or to the "comprehension" behavior measured by the above techniques.

Behavioral Analysis

As an alternative to the diagnostic classification derived from the medical-disease-model, Kanfer and Saslow (1965), in a provocative paper, suggested behavioral analysis. Pointing out the fact that current diagnoses are based upon their purported relations to etiology, symptom description, and prognosis, the authors showed that, in fact, they fulfill none of these functions adequately. Behavioral analysis, on the other hand, is based essentially on "an attempt to identify classes of dependent variables in human behavior which would allow inferences about the particular controlling factors, the social stimuli, the physiological stimuli, and the reinforcing stimuli, of which they are a function." It is important to realize that a behavioral analysis does not imply a topographical description of responses (criticism of topographical descriptions has already been made earlier in the book) but rather a functional description. This functional description is arrived at by means of the following procedure: The patient's complaints are categorized into classes of excess or deficit and for each of these classes the corresponding S^D's and reinforcing stimuli (primary and conditioned) are listed. A hierarchy of both positive and negative reinforcers is established in order to make use of their relative strengths in modifying the patient's behavior. An analysis of self-control responses available to the patient is made in order to determine whether they should be modified and also whether they could be utilized in the course of psychotherapy. Some developmental history is obtained in order to try to discover the kinds of stimuli which caused change in the past, and this includes, of course, physiological variables as well. The social sources of the S^D's and the S^r's (and S^R's) are uncovered for purposes of treatment strategy, and finally an analysis of the patient's environment (social, cultural and physical) is undertaken in order to formulate treatment goals appropriate to the patient's current environment. While it is still too early to say how widely accepted the behavioral analysis scheme will be in general practice with patients, its very appearance in a psychiatric journal (psychiatrists do most of the diagnoses in this country) augurs well for its future.

Prognosis

One of the important determinations made in a medical examination consists of a prediction as to the course and outcome of an illness. Despite the fact that proper obeisance has been made towards prognosis, there is relatively little available by way of reliable data to indicate much actual success in predicting the outcome of mental illness. Factors which have shown significant correlations with outcome of illness have included such measures as marital status and suddenness of onset of illness. Such correlations are not puzzling when one considers their functional meaning. An individual who exhibits abnormal behavior and who is married has a better prognosis (a higher probability of a favorable outcome) than one who is not married because the stimuli which produced (or which help to maintain) his abnormal behavior have had less of a chance of influencing him for as long a time (hence a shorter reinforcement history) as it has influenced the bachelor patient.

(This also assumes that an individual who gets married is less likely to emit abnormal behavior before that time than one who does not.) The better prognosis for the patient whose behavior becomes suddenly abnormal would most likely be due to the fact that fewer stimuli have had the chance to develop control over his abnormal behavior, and therefore his behavior would require fewer modification procedures.

It should be stressed that the functional dependence of behavior upon the environment must be dealt with (as discussed above) regardless of whether the precipitating cause of the abnormal behavior is a physiological lesion or an unfavorable environment. In both cases, the abnormal behavior emitted not only evokes consequences from the environment but also becomes associated with that environment because of the fact that the environment functions as a discriminative stimulus for the emission of the behavior. It is for this reason that no drug or brain operation can, by itself, produce new or adaptive behavior. The drug's effect must be viewed in terms of making certain environmental effects more or less probable. Thus a drug may augment stimulus input effects or it may reduce the rate or strength of responses, but it cannot produce new behavior; that must be learned.

Having discussed the importance of the functional relations between the patient's responses and his environment for prognosis, we will now present two techniques which take advantage of the fact that they are sensitive to this relationship. Both have already been discussed with respect to diagnosis.

Salzinger and Portnoy (1964) first examined the hypothesis that those schizophrenic patients who emit little affect have a poorer prognosis than those who emit more. This hypothesis, derived from the clinical literature, is stated, the reader should note, in a noncontingent manner. A comparison of the interviews of schizophrenic patients out of the hospital with those still in the hospital six months after the interviews, in terms of number of self-referred affect statements emitted, showed no significant differences at all. On the other hand, when the two groups were compared in terms of the rate of conditioning self-referred affect, independent of operant level, the patients who left the hospital showed a significant conditioning effect while those remaining hospitalized did not.

This implies that the patients who were still relatively receptive to the effects of verbal reinforcers when they first came to the hospital showed a better outcome than those who were not.

The other set of techniques used to predict the outcome of abnormal behavior was based on an evaluation of the comprehensibility of the speech of the schizophrenic patients. In a study already cited, Salzinger, Portnoy and Feldman (1966) used the cloze procedure to obtain data on the kinds of responses which the speech of schizophrenic patients evokes. Figure 9-9 presents two different scores. The C-score, which was discussed in the section on "Diagnosis or Behavioral Analysis," is the proportion of correct responses made, a correct response being one which matches precisely the word deleted. The D-score was defined as the proportion of all the different incorrectly guessed words. Thus, the larger the C-score the more comprehensible the speech, since it means that a large number of subjects guessed the correct word; on the other hand, the lower the D-score, the less confusing the speech, for it means that even when incorrect guesses were made, there was at least some consensus about what word might fit rather than the situation in which

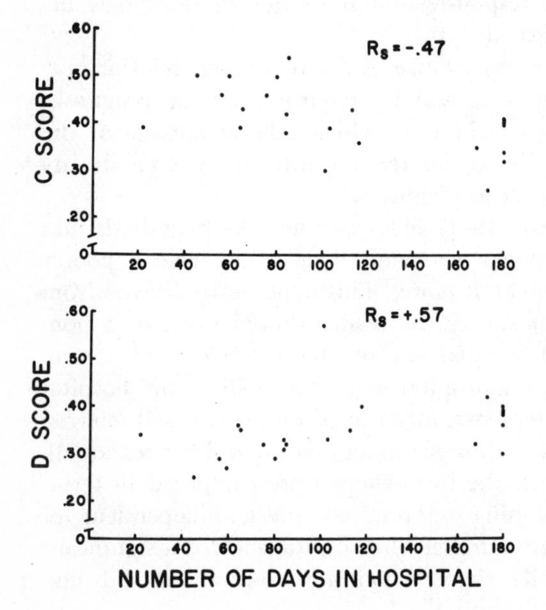

Fig. 9-9. Rank order correlation scatter diagrams relating cloze procedure scores to outcome of illness (as measured by number of days in hospital during 180-day follow-up period) for 23 acute schizophrenic patients. The correlation is −.47 with C score (top) and +.57 with D score (bottom). (Salzinger, Portnoy, and Feldman, 1966, Fig. 6.)

almost any word would fit equally well. Inspection of the graphs shows again the importance of the functional relationship in the matter of evaluating abnormal behavior. Thus, for prognosis as for diagnosis, the response of society to the behavior of the patient is critical in determining what measure will be useful.

THERAPY

The usefulness of behavior theory in the treatment of abnormal behavior must seem quite obvious to the reader by now. In fact, we have already briefly described (see Chapter 7) a study (Salzinger, Feldman, Cowan, & Salzinger, 1965) demonstrating the feasibility of conditioning speech in speech-deficient children. One of the children included in that study had a history indicating almost complete deprivation of reinforcement for practically any behavior except remaining quiet and staying out of the way of his parents. The subsequent treatment program consisted, in large part, of establishing people and speech as conditioned reinforcers and subsequently reinforcing the child's speech to match, ever more closely, the speech of adults. Both the etiology (as far as it could be determined from the case history) and the treatment process were derivable from behavior theory.

In recent years, many investigators and some clinicians have applied the principles of behavior theory to the treatment of a wide variety of abnormal behaviors. The interested reader should consult Eysenck (1960), Krasner and Ullmann (1965), Ullmann and Krasner (1965) and Wolpe, Salter and Reyna (1964) for more examples than we have space for here.

Treatment of Psychotic Behavior

Let us look first at an example of the use of operant conditioning in the control of the behavior of a schizophrenic female patient who had been hospitalized for a period of seven months (Ayllon & Michael, 1959). This patient refused to eat by herself and, consequently, had to be spoonfed by a nurse. Some investigation of the patient's response to her environment indicated that she was indifferent to social contacts, including the nurses, but that she was concerned about the neatness of her appearance. It was thereupon decided to make use of an escape and avoidance conditioning procedure in which the positive reinforcement was made contingent upon the response class of self-feeding. The aversive stimulus consisted of occasionally deliberately dropping food on the patient's dress. This was accomplished by simply instructing the nurses that, although they were to continue spoon feeding, they were to do it carelessly, so that sometimes (though not so often as to make the patient think that the nurse was being mean) food was dropped on the patient. Whenever the patient fed herself, the nurses were instructed to remain with her for about three minutes, talking to her and otherwise keeping her company, for whatever positive reinforcement value that procedure had. The number of meals which the patient ate by herself and the number she had to be spoonfed are plotted in Figure 9-10. The relapse during the sixth week of the study was attributed to the suspicion that someone had informed the patient that the spilling of food was deliberate. Nevertheless, the relapse lasted only for a few days. After the eighth week, self-feeding continued for at least the 10 months of follow-up indicated. Of particular interest is the fact that the patient's statements about the food being poisoned, which had originally accompanied her unwillingness to eat, dropped out. The experimenters report that, when the patient was released from hospitalization as a result of the elimination of these behaviors, she had gained some 21 pounds.

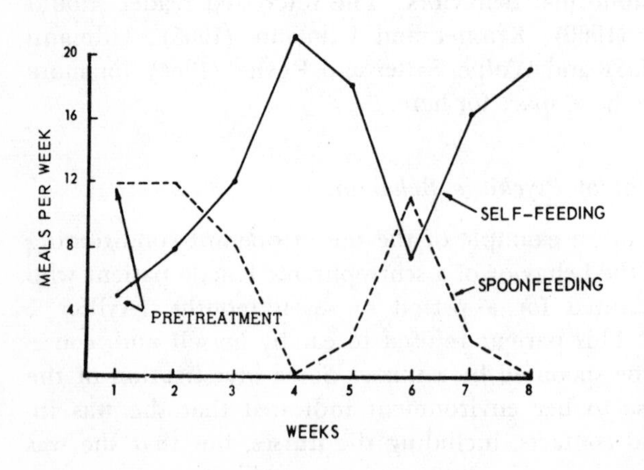

Fig. 9-10. Escape and avoidance conditioning of self-feeding. (Ayllon and Michael, 1959, Fig. 4.)

Treatment of Stuttering

Although stuttering is not to be classified in the same category of severity as a schizophrenic's refusal to eat, it is nevertheless a form of behavior which, aside from its direct effects in reducing the possibility of receiving a variety of positive reinforcers, also sometimes provokes avoidance or escape responses which constitute additional abnormal behavior. An active investigator in the field, Goldiamond (1965), viewed stuttering and fluency as operant response classes and embarked upon a series of studies to test their reactivity to variables specified by behavior theory. Of particular interest in his experiments was his approach to the attenuation of stuttering. Rather than making use of the various well-known methods of reducing the strength of an undesirable response, such as punishment and extinction, or any other techniques for *correcting* the response, he embarked upon the alternative course of *substituting* a response pattern which excluded stuttering. The techniques he used for establishing this alternative response pattern consisted of delaying the stutterer's auditory feedback. Under normal circumstances when an individual speaks, he hears what he says as he says it. It is possible, however, by the use of a specially constructed tape recorder and earphones, to return the speaker's speech to his own ears only after a short delay (e.g., .2 seconds). Normal speech becomes disrupted under these conditions. One adaptive response consequent upon the fact that the speech is delayed is a prolongation of the medial units of speech as in "ca- - - -me." Goldiamond made use of this effect by having the delay in effect continuously, with each stuttering response restoring immediate feedback conditions for 10 seconds. There are thus three possible consequences to the three types of speech: (1) normally fluent speech (i.e., speech without prolongation) is followed by delayed feedback and consequent speech disruption, which is aversive to the stutterer; (2) stuttering speech eliminates the delay, thus allowing the stutterer to hear his stutter, which is aversive also; (3) the third speech type (prolonged but fluent speech) is followed by the delay, and, because the speech prolongation essentially makes the stutterer's feedback immediate, this speech is not disrupted and therefore maintains itself under these conditions. Having established a new pattern of speech which was fluent, but only under special circumstances, Goldiamond used the fading (cf. Chapter 3) method to slowly restore the speech to immediate feedback conditions. The next step was then to increase the response rate by machine pacing (which is *slowly* increased). Special procedures were also introduced, for purposes of generalization, where the stutterer had to practice, at home, reading and speaking to different people in the new pattern, at first for short periods and then for longer ones. The final aspect of this treatment of stuttering consisted of the instatement of self-control procedures in which the person learns to analyze his behavior and the conditions under which it occurs. Thus, the college student who stutters in class may require training in better study habits so that he may know how to respond when called upon, as well as direct training to eliminate stuttering. Figure 9-11 shows the progressive changes in stuttering and reading rate as a function of the training procedure. The subject, a stutterer of long standing, was put through the procedure in 27 sessions. At first he was simply instructed to read, and his stuttering and reading rates were monitored. Then he was instructed to press a button whenever he stuttered and, as indicated by S/DF, he showed a temporary drop in reading and stuttering rates. At the fourteenth session, marked by the letters DFB, the delayed auditory feedback condition was put into effect. Note the large drop in stuttering rate to *0*. On the following day (T/C in the figure), the reading material was presented by a controlled timer which determined how much he could read. The reading rate was set at 20 words/minute on Session 16 and increased to 34 words/minute on the twentieth session. The numbers 200, 150, etc., indicate the rate of fading out of the delay; the numbers refer to milliseconds of delay between speech and feedback. At Session 23 his reading rate was increased to 204 words/minute without stuttering. On the next day, he started stuttering at the 204 words/minute rate; his rate was immediately reduced to 110 words/minute and then gradually raised again, without further stuttering. At the time of publication, Goldiamond made known the fact that he had treated some 30 stutterers and that, "In all 30 cases, at a specified 50-minute period in the program there has emerged a fluent pattern of reading which is well-articulated, rapid, and devoid of blockages" (Goldiamond, 1965, p. 156).

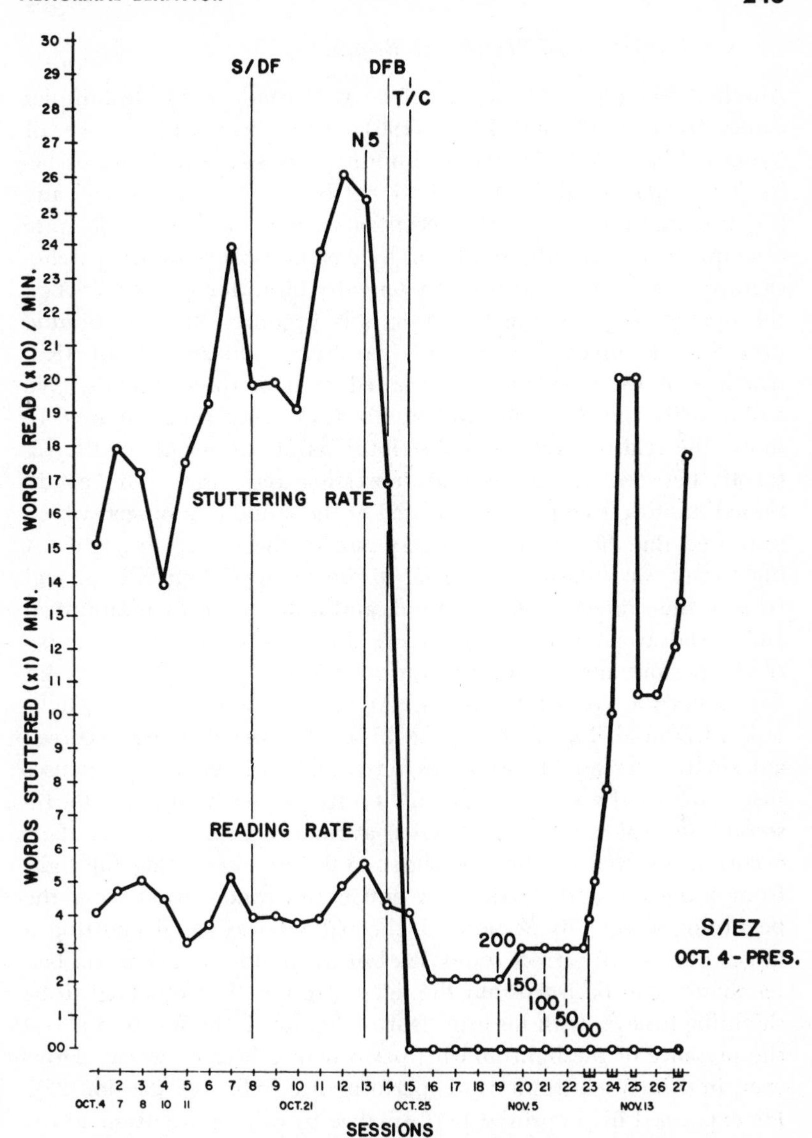

Fig. 9-11. Laboratory elimination of stuttering and quadrupling of reading rate in a very severe stutterer, the third *S* tried. (Goldiamond, 1965, Fig. 6-25.)

Treatment of Hysterical Blindness

Another example of the utility of operant conditioning techniques comes from Brady and Lind (1961) who dealt with a case of hysterical blindness. Hysterical blindness consists essentially of behavior similar to that of a blind person, in the absence of any physical malfunction in the receptor or nervous system. Despite attempts to alleviate the condition by means of conventional psychotherapy, the patient had been hysterically blind for two years when the operant conditioning program was begun. The conditioning procedure involved the patient's pressing a button on an IRT schedule of 18 seconds with a limited hold of three seconds. We will describe the procedure and results at the same time. Figure 9-12 shows the relative frequency distributions of the length of the intervals between successive button-pressing responses. The conditioned reinforcer employed consisted of the sound of a buzzer, which indicated that he had made a response in the correct interval. A high score was followed by social approval, special privileges, and trips to the canteen in the hospital, and a low score by disapproval and withdrawal of these. In Figure 9-12, Session 6 shows the patient's performance before the introduction of the light; the solid bar shows the correct responses. At Session 7, when a dim light was introduced during the 18- to 21-second period, there occurred a dramatic decrease in correct responses and an increase in responses just prior to the onset of the light. Responses in the 15- to 18-second interval can be considered as avoidance responses, since their occurrence served to reset the timer to 0, thus preventing the light from going on, and starting the entire 18-second period from the beginning again. By Session 16, the patient was again emitting a larger number of correct responses, but his performance was no better than it had been without the light. He was then observed to be shielding his eyes with his arm. During Session 17 he was told about the presence of the light and his performance became worse. However, in subsequent sessions his performance improved (Session 23). He explained his improved performance by calling attention to the heat of the light. The intensity of the light was therefore reduced and his performance still improved in Session 33. To make certain that he was responding to the light rather than the time period

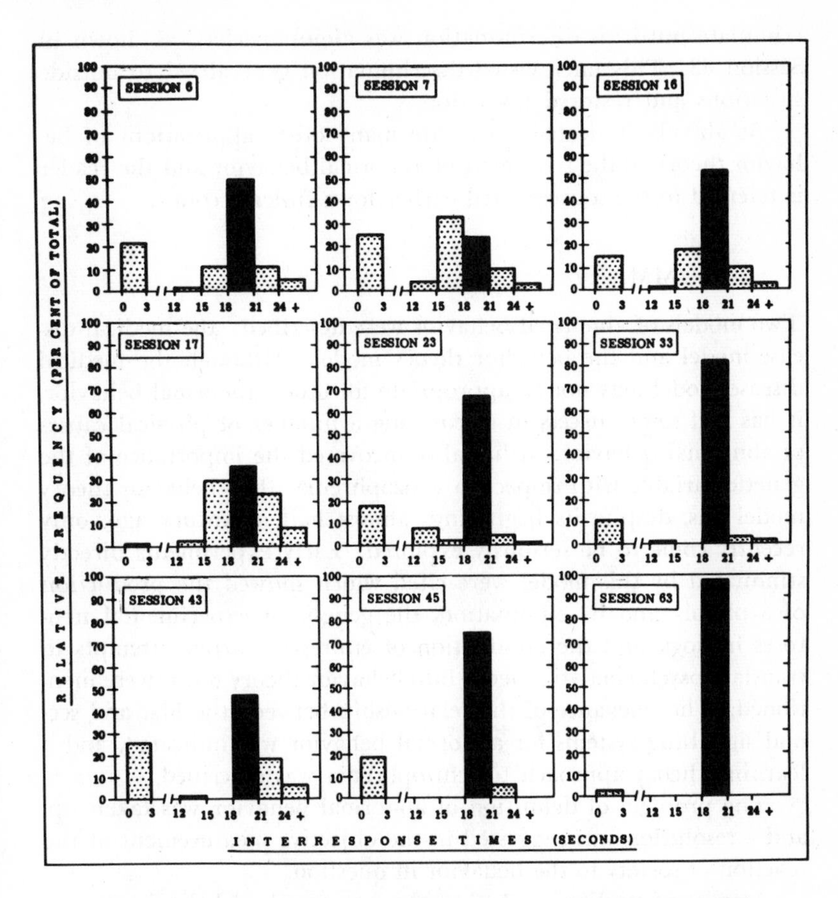

Fig. 9-12. Relative frequency distributions of interresponse times (IRT's) grouped into class intervals of 3 seconds each. Responses falling in the 18-to-21 second interval (black) are reinforced. IRT's between 3 and 12 seconds (occurring only rarely) have been omitted. (Brady and Lind, 1961, Fig. 2.)

alone, the light was turned on during other intervals and his responses followed. During Session 43, the number of correct responses decreased dramatically and the patient explained that he could see the light and that it had excited him so that he forgot to respond some of the time. From Session 46 through 63 he was given increasingly more complex visual stimulus configurations to discriminate until his discrimination was almost perfect, as shown in Session 63. This finer visual discrimination generalized to outside situations and restored his vision.

As already indicated, there are many other applications of behavior theory to the treatment of abnormal behavior and the reader is referred to the sources cited earlier for a fuller account.

SUMMARY

Two models of abnormal behavior were described: the medical disease model and the behavior theory model. Although the medical disease model may not be appropriate for much abnormal behavior, it has had some success in discovering a number of physical causes of abnormal behavior. It has also uncovered the importance of the genetic variable with respect to schizophrenia. The behavior theory model has, despite its beginnings almost half a century ago, only recently come to be seriously explored. Early experiments directly stimulated by this model were cited which showed the production of a phobia and its elimination, the genesis of experimental neuroses in dogs, and the elimination of enuresis. Earlier attempts to translate psychoanalytic theory into behavior theory terms were mentioned. The relevance of the relationship between the first and second signalling systems for abnormal behavior was indicated, and a learning theory approach to schizophrenia was described.

The problem of definition of abnormal behavior was taken up, and a resolution was suggested in the objective measurement of the reaction of society to the behavior in question.

A series of studies couched in the framework of behavior theory examined the effect of the interviewer on what the patient says and the effect of the reinforcing behavior of the interviewer was shown to be critical in distinguishing normals from schizophrenic patients.

Some objective measures of abnormal behavior were described. These measures dealt with the comprehensibility of schizophrenic speech and indicated some of the difficulties schizophrenic patients might have in getting along in society.

Diagnosis was also discussed. The danger of interpretation of symptoms rather than their empirical functional analysis was shown.

An alternative to the medical diagnostic approach was presented in behavior analysis. It consists of a functional description of behavior, i.e., the conditions which prevail when the behavior is emitted and the consequences which follow it. Such an analysis has the advantage of providing the therapist with the knowledge of what stimuli he can manipulate to change the behavior.

Some methods of measuring prognosis were briefly described and related to behavior theory.

Several examples of treatment based upon behavior theory were given. The examples included a feeding problem in a psychotic patient, stuttering, and hysterical blindness.

10

Social Behavior

THEORY

ANIMAL STUDIES
Social Facilitation
Superstitious Behavior
Cooperation

PSYCHOPHYSICAL STUDIES

THE DIRECT APPLICATION OF BEHAVIOR THEORY TO SOCIAL PSYCHOLOGICAL PROBLEMS

VERBAL BEHAVIOR
The Measurement of Attitudes
Verbal Behavior and Linguistics

APPLICATIONS OF THE KNOWLEDGE OF PSYCHOLOGY TO THE PROBLEMS OF SOCIETY

The phenomenon of birth imposes upon man a relatively long period of helplessness—originally exclusively biological, but eventually social as well. It is at this point that he begins his long social conditioning history. His dependence on other people may lessen and his dependent behavior may change in form, but the class of behavior most generally labeled social behavior remains, and in many ways becomes more firmly controlled by other people. In our complex society the lack of social behavior is unheard of except in the extreme cases of the psychotic and the retarded, and even here there is most often evidence for some minimal social behavior. Living together is of course not restricted to man; animals also display social behavior. The definition of social behavior is then quite simple: It is behavior which varies as a function of other organisms—other organisms may elicit the behavior, set the occasion for it, or reinforce it. Furthermore, the behavior need not occur in the presence of other organisms to be called social—it may be related to other organisms only through stimuli which were once associated with them.

Simple as the definition of social psychology is, its actual study is complicated indeed. For, whereas the inanimate environment can be manipulated systematically, at will, and, perhaps even more important, along well-known, quantifiable, physical dimensions, modification of social variables has required all the ingenuity psychologists could muster. Social psychologists have traditionally been under social pressure to apply their knowledge and experience to "real" problem situations, with the consequence that they often made use of common-sense terms to explain social phenomena. The development of behavior theory in recent years is beginning to have an important influence in this area of psychology, thus obviating the need to use the less well-defined, common-sense terms. It might be well to begin this chapter by pointing out that much of social behavior consists of verbal behavior, and that what distinguishes social responses from physical ones is the former's lower reliability in being followed by reinforcement. Thus, the verbal response, "Please pass the salt," is less likely to be reinforced by your possession of the salt than is the nonverbal response of reaching for it yourself. Such verbal responses, however, resist extinction, which can be explained, of course, by the principle of intermittent reinforcement which is so important in social behavior.

Theory

Some ten years ago, when the social psychologist, Festinger (1957), evolved a theory (dissonance theory) which facilitated the prediction of attitudes (i.e., verbal responses) toward certain tasks, social psychologists flocked to it from far and wide. As a result, a large body of data has been collected concerning a circumscribed area of research and lends itself to interpretation, not only in accordance with the theory which stimulated it, but also according to other systematic views of behavior. Festinger's dissonance theory states essentially that an individual holding two views (cognitions) which are inconsistent with each other is in an aversive motivational state that will cause him to reduce or eliminate that state. One way in which the individual reduces that state is by changing one of his cognitions. This theory thus makes use of a hypothesized internal state as a primary explanatory concept to predict behavior. It might be well to describe at least one of the experiments used as evidence for Festinger's theory. The experiment was carried out by Festinger and Carlsmith (1959). Subjects were placed in one of three groups. In one group, each subject was required to do a long, repetitive, and ostensibly boring task. At the end, he was paid $1.00 to tell the next subject (who was actually a stooge) that the task was enjoyable and interesting. In the second group, each subject performed the task and was paid $20.00 for doing the same thing. In the third group (control), each subject was simply required to do the task. After the end of the experiment, all subjects were asked to indicate (under circumstances calculated to evoke frank replies) how enjoyable they found the tasks. The results showed that the subjects who were paid less ($1.00) to describe the boring task in glowing terms, expressed more favorable attitudes towards the task than those who were paid more ($20.00) and the latter did not differ from the control group in the extent to which they said they enjoyed the task. Dissonance theory psychologists have maintained that behavior theory would predict the reverse, since those who received the bigger reinforcer, namely $20.00, should have been more positively influenced in the same direction as that in which they verbalized arguments. Dissonance theory, on the other hand, points out that, while the boring nature of the task produced the cognition that the task was boring, the fact that the subjects had to maintain to other students that the task was enjoyable produced an additional cognition that resulted in a favorable attitude toward the task. These two cognitions were dissonant and therefore aversive for the subjects paid only $1.00 because neither the task nor the small size of the compensation was consonant with their saying they enjoyed the task. The subjects therefore reduce the dissonance by changing the cognition toward the task and finding it more interesting. The subjects paid $20.00 experienced no dissonance because the large amount of money was entirely consonant with the idea that what they say may differ from what they believe to be true about the task.

Let us now see how behavior theory explains the above data. While it is undeniable that $20.00 makes for a larger reinforcer than $1.00, the above experiment was complicated by other factors as well. In the experiment we described, the money was actually given to the subject before he described the task as enjoyable. The money may therefore be viewed as a reinforcer only for agreeing to co-operate, and as an S^D for how truthful that description was going to be. In this respect, the receipt of $20.00 by an undergraduate student might well act as an S^D for his categorizing his statement as untrue, while receipt of $1.00 might well act as an S^D for the description to be true. A recent and much more detailed analysis of the data coming from dissonance studies in terms of behavior theory was undertaken by Bem (1967). He suggested that the subjects' attitude statements could be best understood by assuming that the subjects could observe themselves pretty much the way they might observe others. He pointed out that an outside observer would judge a person who described an event to be enjoyable for $20.00 to be under the control of that $20.00 rather than under the discriminative control of the task itself. He might therefore infer that the task was boring to the subject. On the other hand, for only $1.00 a person might more likely be considered to be under the discriminative control of the task itself, and his judgment of the task would be considered more valid, resulting in the inference that the task was at least somewhat enjoyable. Bem proceeded to test his interpretation by describing the task the subject had to perform to a group of students, telling them that the subject had received $20.00 (or $1.00) for describing the task as enjoyable to a prospective subject, and letting them listen to a tape-recorded conversation between the two subjects. Then the students were asked to rate how favorably inclined the paid subjects actually were toward the task they had performed. The results of this study were essentially the same as for the self-ratings. High-compensation subjects were rated to have enjoyed the task less than low-compensation subjects. Bem (1967, p. 189) concludes, "The original *S*s (subjects) may be viewed as simply making self-judgments based on the same kinds of public evidence that the community originally employed in training them to infer the attitudes of any communicator, themselves included. It is not necessary to postulate an aversive motivational drive toward consistency."

Again we find that a careful functional analysis of behavior reveals the controlling variables without the need for positing unobserved and unobservable states.

For the rest of the chapter we shall attempt to demonstrate the value of viewing social phenomena in terms of behavior theory.

Animal Studies

The general usefulness of animals for clarification of experimental questions has already been amply evidenced. Use of animals in social psychology has, with rare and outstanding exceptions (such as Miller and Dollard's (1941) work on imitation), been conspicuous by its absence. This work, the reader will recall, demonstrated in rats and in children that imitation is a response class which can be learned by the usual operant conditioning paradigm.

It should also be noted, as already indicated in Chapter 4, that distinct classes of social behavior can be observed in animals under natural conditions. Such social behavior as that found, for example, in certain insects can often be shown to be elicited or released behavior. There is in addition, however, social behavior, which appears to be under the control of operant contingencies.

Social Facilitation

In a recent review of the phenomenon of social facilitation (effect of the mere presence of other organisms upon the behavior of a given organism), Zajonc (1965) reported increases in eating (which, at least for animals, has traditionally been assumed to be under the control of physiological variables only) in chickens, rats, and dogs. He also reported finding increases in the amount of work done by ants when in groups over the amount done when alone. On the other hand, he noted that paired birds, on being trained to make a discrimination, learned less quickly than birds trained alone. Zajonc summarized these results in the following way: The presence of other organisms facilitates the emission of learned responses but interferes with the learning of new responses or new stimulus-response relationships. He attributes these results to the concept of arousal (somewhat akin to drive), a state of the organism which enhances responses that are dominant. In the case of the situation where responses have already been learned, they are facilitated because they are dominant; in the case where learning is just beginning to take place, incorrect responses are dominant to begin with, and hence the higher arousal produced by the presence of another organism interferes with the task at hand. Zajonc presented some independent evidence (though admittedly scanty) from studies of the endocrine system which indicated that the presence of other organisms does, in fact, raise the level of arousal.

Whether the increase in occurrence of the dominant response is to be attributed to the intervening arousal state or not, the generalization of the observed results remains to be tested under other circumstances. An experiment by Hake and Laws (1967) tested the effect of social facilitation upon response rate emitted under the conditioned suppression paradigm (cf. Chapter 3). If Zajonc's summarizing statement is correct, namely, that well-learned responses will be facilitated in the presence of other organisms, then one would expect a higher response rate in the presence of, rather than in the absence of, another organism during the CS-US interval. The subjects used in this experiment were pigeons. The experimental birds were conditioned on a VI:1 minute schedule over which the conditioned suppression paradigm was imposed at a rate of approximately once every 15 minutes. The socially facilitating birds were conditioned to respond on a FR:1 schedule during the conditioned suppression periods, i.e., the CS of these periods was the S^D for responding in the socially facilitating birds, and the other periods (i.e., "safe" periods for the experimental birds), constituted the S^Δ periods for the socially facilitating birds. A comparison of the rate of response of the experimental birds during the safe periods when the socially facilitating bird was present with the rate of response when that bird was absent showed very little difference, thus suggesting that the mere presence of another bird is not, by itself, facilitating for response rate. It is possible, however, since the facilitating bird responded only during the period constituting the CS-US interval, but not during the safe period, that the lack of response constitutes an S$^{\Delta}$ for the experimental bird. More research will have to be done on this question. The results on the experimental birds' performance during the conditioned suppression periods are much more clear-cut. Inspection of Figure 10-1 shows the suppression ratio (rate of response during the conditioned suppression period divided by the rate during the safe periods) (1) before shock was introduced (CS only), (2) after the CS-US paradigm had been instated, and (3) after the US was removed. Of interest to us here is the consistently higher suppression ratio (actually meaning *less* suppression) when the facilitating bird was working within view over that when he was absent. This experiment, it must be noted, is also relevant to the issue of emotional behavior, since the higher suppression ratio can also be interpreted as due to mitigation of the respondents underlying the operant response suppression.

Before leaving this topic, it should be mentioned that studies on social facilitation originated with Floyd Allport (1924), who first discovered the phenomenon when he compared human subjects working alone with those working together on a number of different tasks.

Superstitious Behavior

The process of conditioning requires only that the organism's response be in a particular temporal relationship with its reinforcer. Although conditioning is more rapid when the reinforcer follows every response, acquisition of behavior can take place even if reinforcement is intermittent from the beginning. Furthermore, a response maintained by intermittent reinforcement results in greater response strength than one maintained by continuous reinforcement. Therefore, given an event which occurs regularly, a response which accidentally occurs before it may come to be controlled by it. Superstitious behavior may then be defined as behavior conditioned by a reinforcer whose occurrence is independent of, i.e., not contingent on, that behavior.

The phenomenon was first described by Skinner (1948) when he used the following procedure: A pigeon was deprived of food and was placed in an experimental cage for a few minutes each day.

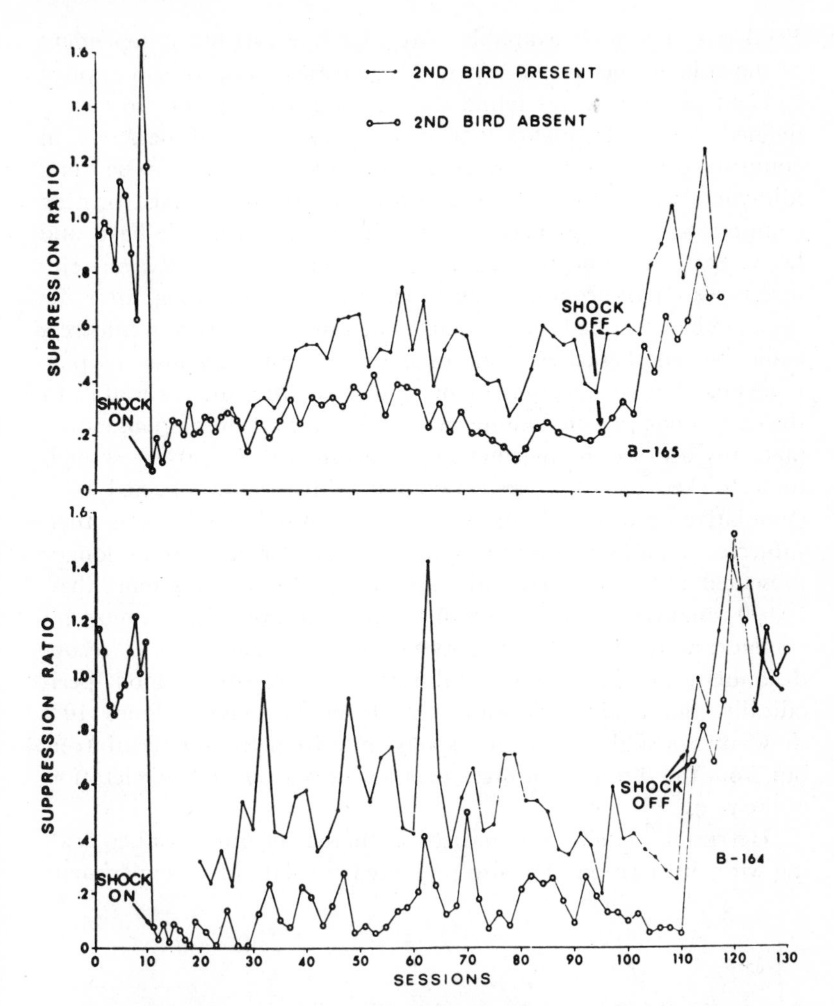

Fig. 10-1. Daily suppression ratios before shock, during the criterion shock intensity, and after shock was removed. The criterion shock intensity was 400 v for Bird 165 and 160 v for Bird 164. The second bird was present (solid circles) on alternate days. Several sessions have been omitted between the sessions designated as 10 (no shock) and 11 (shock on). During that period, the shock intensity was being gradually increased to the criterion intensity. (Hake and Laws, 1967, Fig. 2.)

Food was then made available at regular intervals but independent of the animal's behavior. When this general procedure was applied to eight pigeons, it was found that six emitted responses so clearly defined and so frequent, that two observers agreed perfectly in counting occurrences. The resulting responses were, to be sure, idiosyncratic, but they did occur with great regularity, e.g., turning counterclockwise, and making a pendular motion of the head and body. Skinner found that, although shorter intervals between reinforcers were more conducive to superstitious conditioning, after the response had attained some strength the interval between reinforcers could be lengthened without extinguishing the response (a phenomenon that is characteristic of regular conditioning as well). In the case of one pigeon, Skinner was able to record the response automatically because the pigeon's stepping response was strong enough to be picked up by a large tambour which was connected to a cumulative recorder. This animal's stepping response was then subjected to an extinction procedure, i.e., reinforcers were no longer presented and, in this particular case, the pigeon emitted more than 10,000 responses before responding reached a level where almost no responses were emitted in twenty minutes. At that point a "reconditioning" procedure was established by presenting food periodically, but again independently of the behavior. Figure 10-2 shows only a slight effect on response rate from the first reinforcer, but from the second reinforcer on there was a positive acceleration of the rate.

Herrnstein (1966) summarized a number of other studies dealing with superstition. He also presented the data of an experiment

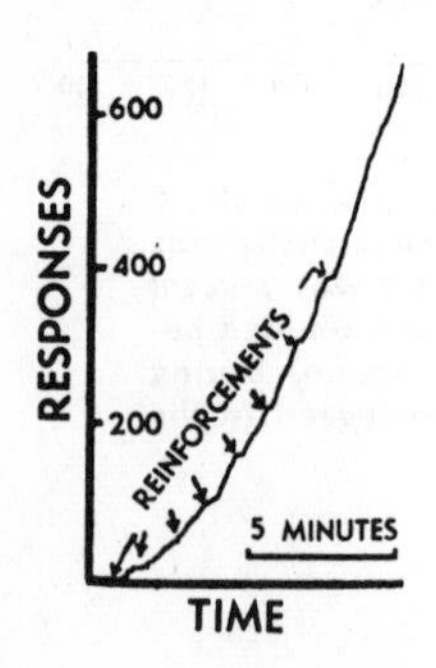

Fig. 10-2. "Reconditioning" of a superstitious response after extinction. The response of hopping from right to left had been thoroughly extinguished just before the record was taken. The arrows indicate the automatic presentation of food at one-minute intervals without reference to the pigeon's behavior. (Skinner, 1948, Fig. 1.)

he did with Morse, using pecking as the superstitious response to be conditioned. The procedure was based on the assumption that whatever response is dominant at the time is likely to become conditioned by the regular but noncontingent reinforcer presentation. Figure 10-3 is a presentation of a sequence of experimental conditions which demonstrates the phenomenon of superstition in the pigeon. The pigeon was first put on a FI:11 seconds schedule and then, from the tenth session through the thirty-first, food was delivered every 11 seconds, independent of its behavior; this was followed by a return to the FI schedule and finally by extinction. Note that while the rate of response is higher during FI than during the noncontingent feeding schedule, it is considerably higher during the latter than during extinction.

Herrnstein also points out that superstition forms one aspect of any response class, namely, that the response which is conditioned has some properties which are not part of the reinforcement contingency (cf., topographical aspects of responses in Chapter 3). Thus,

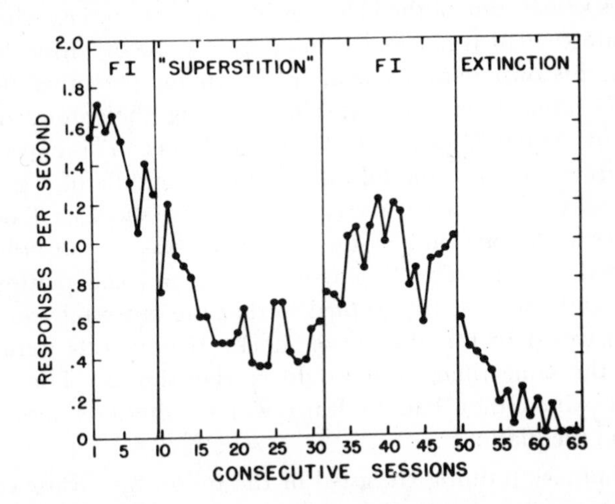

Fig. 10-3. A pigeon's rate of pecking at a key over the course of 65 daily experimental sessions. During the first portion of the experiment (sessions 1-9), the pigeon received food for the first peck that occurred at least 11 seconds after the preceding delivery of food. During the second portion (sessions 10-31), food was delivered every 11 seconds, independent of the pigeon's behavior. During the third portion (sessions 32-49), the conditions of the first portion were duplicated. During the last portion (sessions 50-65), food was no longer delivered. (Herrnstein, 1966, Fig. 1.)

a pigeon learns to peck in a particular way, despite the fact that the bird would receive reinforcement even if it changed its pecking style.

In social behavior, where much, if not all, behavior is reinforced on an intermittent basis, where reinforcers come from many different sources, and where the conditioned reinforcers often consist of large classes of stimuli, there is much room for the accidental juxtaposition of response and reinforcer to produce superstitious conditioning. A good example of such superstitious behavior is to be found in the mannerisms which public speakers emit while they are emitting the responses which are followed by reinforcers. Repeated phrases in the conversation of some people, such as "you know," may furnish us with another example.

Cooperation

One of the problems in social psychology consists of finding the variables which control the behavior of cooperation, i.e., where positive reinforcement is not forthcoming unless one organism learns to postpone his own reinforcement in return for the other organism doing the same later. An experiment along these lines was performed by Daniel (1942), using rats as subjects. The experimental apparatus consisted of the following: In the middle of a grid floor, which was wired in such a way as to deliver shock, a food crock was placed. At one end of the apparatus was a platform which functioned as a switch. When one rat sat on the platform, the shock circuit could be interrupted so that the other rat could reach the food to eat in the absence of shock. If both rats went to the food at the same time, both would receive shocks. The criterion behavior which they had to learn was to alternate feeding and sitting on the platform.

Preliminary training consisted of the following: Rats were first trained to feed individually, without shock; then the individual rats were satiated and placed on the electrified grid. When they had learned to escape the shock by staying on the platform for 30 seconds, the rats, still run individually, were given a random sequence of 20 trials, some with shock and some without shock, food always being available. After 13 days of this preliminary training the rats learned to go to the food crock in the absence of shock and to the platform in the presence of shock within one second.

At this stage, the animals were paired, putting rats of approximately the same weight together. The grid was electrified and both rats were placed on it. Only when one rat remained on the platform could the other rat eat; when both were off, the shock was on, and if both continued to try to leave the platform to feed at the same time, the shock was increased. This procedure of putting both rats on the electrified grid was continued for 40 days with 12 120-second trials per day. The rats received food only during the course of these experimental sessions.

The results of the experiment were quite clear. The animals learned to alternate. For the six pairs of rats, from 94 to 99 per cent of the times when one member of a pair left the food crock to return to the platform, the other rat went to the food crock. Since the animals received all their food during the course of the experimental sessions, it is of interest to note whether the requirement of cooperation allowed them to eat enough. The weight of all the rats in the experiment increased, the increases varying from 24 to 140 grams, with the original weights varying from 96 to 182 grams. It is also of interest to see how efficient the animals were with respect to the amount of time they spent feeding as opposed to being on the platform together. Table 10-1 presents these data for each pair. Considering the fact that the rats had a total of 1,440 seconds available in all for feeding, they obviously learned to cooperate quite well. In addition to the quantitative findings, it is of some interest

Table 10-1. Length of Time Spent Feeding and on the Platform (Data from Daniel, 1942-Table 4)

Pair	Mean Feeding Time (Secs.)	Mean Time Together On the Platform (Secs.)
1-2	1425	15
3-4	1410	30
5-6	1358	82
7-8	1407	33
9-10	1407	33
11-12	1397	43

to report some of the descriptions which Daniel gave of the behavior of the animals. The animal on the platform frequently would get off almost completely, holding the platform down with one foot, and nudge the feeding animal, sometimes biting and pulling the feeding rat's tail. Furthermore, such behavior was often followed by the feeding rat's return to the platform and the platform rat's move to the food. Finally, it should be pointed out that the alternation of positions of the two rats eventually resulted in such a smooth exchange that shock was avoided.

This experiment shows quite clearly at least one set of variables involved in the acquisition of cooperation; although the food and electric shock are provided by the experimenter, the rats themselves make use of their own, perhaps more natural, aversive stimuli, such as biting and nudging. In any case, the more complicated behavior of 2 animals also appears to be amenable to experimental analysis.

Psychophysical Studies

Another basic question posed by social psychologists concerns the way in which a person's view of his environment is influenced by the views expressed by others. One of the classic experiments in this area was performed by Sherif (1935). For his experiment, he made use of the autokinetic effect as the basic stimulus situation. The autokinetic effect consists of exposing a subject to a pinpoint of light in an otherwise dark room. After a short period, during which subjects fixate upon the light, they report seeing it move and, upon instruction, make estimates of the extent of movement. It seemed to Sherif, since the light did not really move, that the judgments of the extent of movement ought to be particularly subject to being influenced by the judgments of others. He therefore tested subjects under conditions in which they judged the extent of movement alone and in which they judged it with another individual. The interesting effect which emerged was that, as the subjects made more and more judgments in each other's company, their estimates became more similar. Typically, their judgments stabilized at some point between the distances originally estimated by each subject. This kind of experiment, of course, immediately raises an entire set of questions. For example, is such a shift in judgment to be expected only when the stimulus is quite unstructured and the response induced? What are the variables which influence the extent to which a given subject changes his judgment in the direction of the other person's judgments?

These questions were investigated by Mausner (1954a, 1954b) and by Asch (1955). Mausner's stimulus material consisted of lighted lines, the length of which the subjects had to judge both under "alone" and "together" (in the presence of another judging subject) conditions. The stimulus can be thought of as being more structured than the pinpoint of light, since the lengths of the lights in the Mausner experiment actually varied. Thus, one would expect the psychophysical stimulus to exert more control in this situation than in Sherif's experiment. Mausner also added one other variable to his experiment, namely, reinforcement history. Instead of making an attempt to measure reinforcement history, he instated it experimentally. Subjects in the alone situation were randomly placed in a positive or negative reinforcement group. Those placed in the former group were told that their judgments were correct in over 80 per cent of the trials and incorrect the rest of the time, while subjects placed in the latter group were told that their judgments were incorrect in over 80 per cent of the trials and correct the rest of the time. Having built into the subjects these different reinforcement histories, the subjects were then combined in all possible pairs (they received no further reinforcement when tested in pairs) to see how they would affect each other's judgments. The results were quite interesting. The only pairs which showed the same effect as Sherif's subjects, i.e., each member shifting his judgments in the direction of his partner, were those in which both members had a negative reinforcement history. When both members of the pair had positive reinforcement histories, their judgments remained stable and uninfluenced by their partner's judgments. Finally, when one partner had a positive, and the other a negative, reinforcement history, the shift in judgment occurred for the negatively reinforced subject, who tended to agree with the positively reinforced subject.

In his next experiment Mausner (1954b) used the same experimental situation to examine another variable in social interaction. The above experiment showed that the discriminative control exerted by the verbal judgment of another person varies with the reinforcement history of the person being influenced. In this experiment he varied the strength of the discriminative control exerted by another person's judgments in a different way. Before the two people were brought together, the subject was given an opportunity to see, in a related task, how good a judge of length of lines his partner was. The partner was, in fact, not a subject but a stooge, instructed to emit judgments quite different from the real subject's. For half the group the stooge gave the impression of being very good in the judgment of length of lines; for the other half he acted quite incompetently. The results showed that a greater change in judgments occurred in the direction of the partner's judgments when the partner gave the impression of competence than when he behaved incompetently.

The experiment performed by Asch (1955) used stimuli even more structured than those used by Mausner. While Mausner's stimuli were more compelling in controlling the response than Sherif's pinpoint of light, Asch's stimuli gave rise to less than 1 per cent error when the subjects were judging alone. In other words, the discriminative control exerted by the stimuli would seem to leave little room for influence (discriminative control) by the judgments of other subjects.

The experimental procedure consisted of the following: Groups of some seven to nine students were brought together for an experiment in vision. Their task was essentially a match-to-sample procedure in which the students were to indicate which of three lines matched a sample line in length. One of the lines matched the sample exactly; the other two were substantially different. At every trial, each of the students announced his response in turn, going around the table at which all were seated. In each group of students, only one was actually a subject, and in 12 out of 18 trials all of the other students, who were instructed on how to behave before the experiment began, chose incorrect matches. Out of 123 subjects, about 25 per cent never agreed with the incorrect judgments of the overwhelming majority; on the other hand, some subjects agreed with the majority almost all of the time. Of some interest is the fact that the subjects who were controlled by the judgments of the majority underestimated the frequency of times on which they conformed. Inspection of Figure 10-4 shows some of the results. The upper left-hand graph shows the per cent of correct estimates when alone and when faced with the opposition of the majority. The upper right-hand graph shows the increase in per cent errors as a function of the number of opponents. Three opponents apparently exerted a maximum effect. The lower left-hand graph illustrates what happened when the subject was given a partner to support him against a majority of opponents. The upper line corresponds to the subject's performance with a partner, the lower line without. Finally, the lower right-hand graph shows the effect on the subject's judgment when the partner leaves him. Two situations were used to examine the effect of losing the partner's support. In the first, after six trials of support, the subject's partner went along with the majority; notice the increase in the error rate of the upper curve. In the second situation, the partner physically left the group after the sixth trial, ostensibly because of a previously arranged appointment. Notice that the effect of losing the support (reinforcement value and discriminative value) of the partner under these circumstances, as shown in the lower curve, does not produce as large an increase in the error rate as when the partner goes over to the majority, or as much as when the subject has had no partner at any time.

All of these studies illustrate the value of taking a rather complex process, such as the influence of people's judgments upon other people, and examining it under the simplified conditions of a precise experiment. Again we find the relevance of behavior theory concepts.

The Direct Application of Behavior Theory to Social Psychological Problems

In the section on animal studies we described an experiment on cooperation in rats. Now we will describe a study of the acquisition of cooperation in children. Azrin and Lindsley (1956) worked with children ranging in age from 7 to 12 years. The cooperative response was defined by the apparatus which is shown in Figure 10-5. Each child had a stylus which he could insert in any of three different holes. Since the two children were separated from each

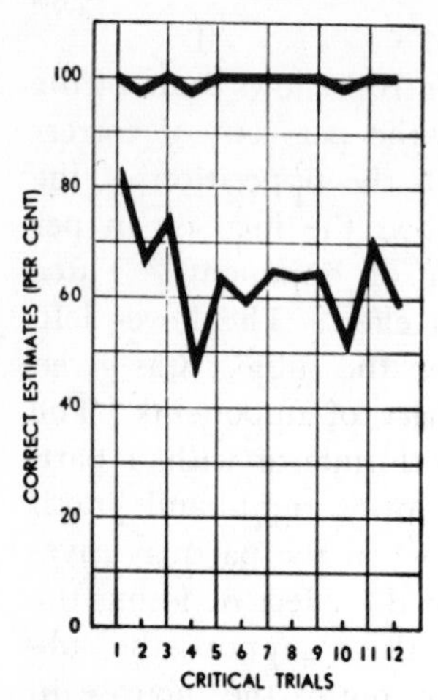

Error of 123 subjects, each of whom compared lines in the presence of six to eight opponents, is plotted in the bottom curve. The accuracy of judgments not under pressure is indicated in the top line.

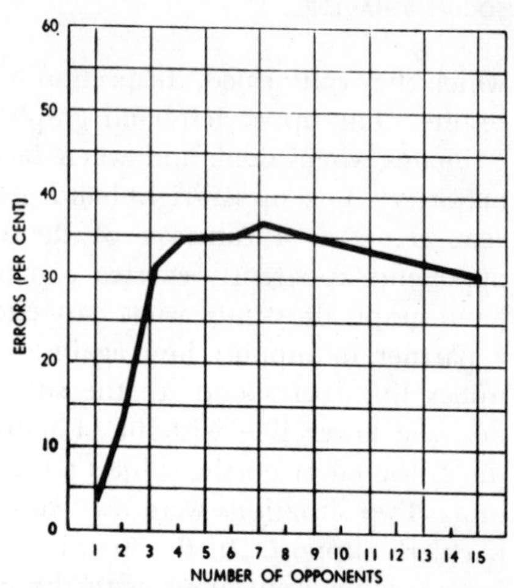

Size of majority which opposed them had an effect on the subjects. With a single opponent the subject erred only 3.6 per cent of the time; with two opponents he erred 13.6 per cent; three, 31.8 percent; four, 35.1 per cent; six, 35.2 per cent; seven, 37.1 per cent; nine, 35.1 per cent; 15, 31.2 per cent.

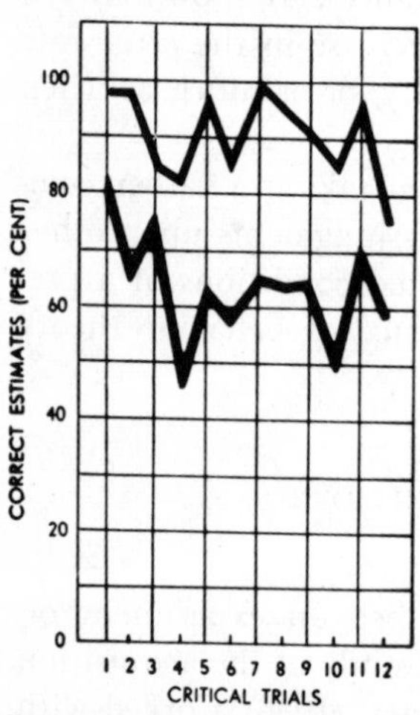

Two subjects supporting each other against a majority made fewer errors (top curve) than one subject did against a majority (bottom curve).

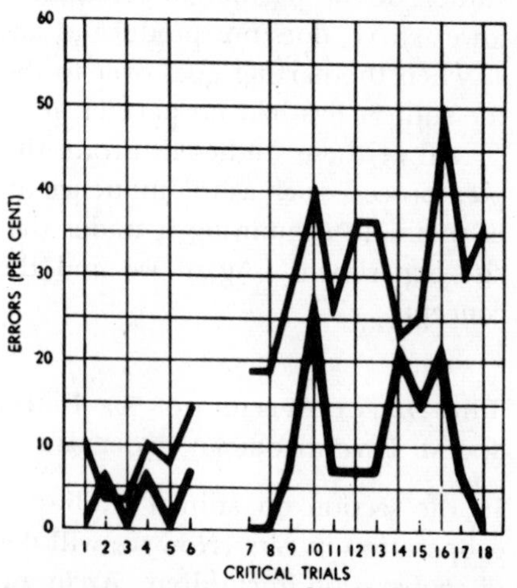

Partner left subject after six trials in a single experiment. The top curve shows the error of the subject when the partner "deserted" to the majority. The bottom curve shows error when partner merely left the room.

Fig. 10-4. (Asch, 1955.)

Fig. 10-5. Apparatus used for the reinforcement of cooperation between children. (Azrin and Lindsley, 1956, Fig. 1.)

other by a screen, each of them had to manipulate his own stylus. Whenever the children placed their styli in similar holes within .04 second of each other, a cooperative response was considered to have been made. During conditioning each such cooperative response was followed by a red light flash and the dropping of a single jelly bean into a cup to which both children had access. The conditioning, extinction, and reconditioning of cooperative responses is illustrated for three different teams with high, median, and low rates (Fig. 10-6). It is of interest to note that each team worked out a scheme for dividing the jelly beans by means of some verbal agreement. The fact that the children had to work out a way of dividing the reinforcers between them meant that, like Daniel's rats, they had to postpone getting the reinforcers part of the time. This study differs from Daniel's, however, in that no experimenter-provided negative reinforcer had to be employed.

In an experiment by Lott and Lott (1960) all the children in a group were instructed to select, on a sociometric questionnaire, two other children from the group with whom they would want to share some activity. Groups of three children each were then composed of children who had *not* selected each other. These groups were then allowed to play a game. On a random basis, some children were positively reinforced and some were not. After the game the children were again asked to select other children with whom they would want to share an activity, such as going into outer space. The children who had been positively reinforced selected a larger number of children from their own game group than did children who had not been reinforced. These results can be interpreted in

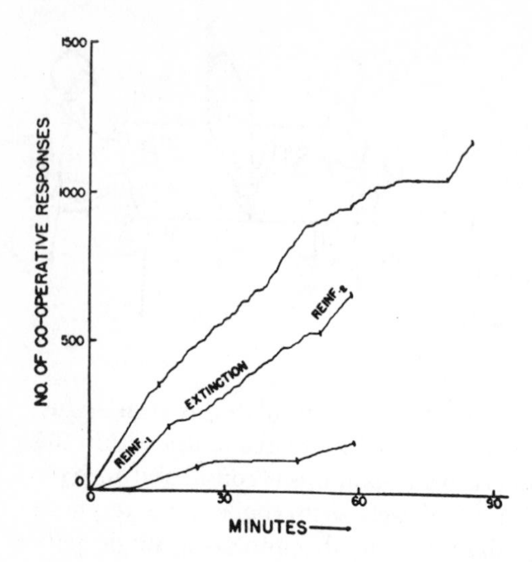

Fig. 10-6. Cumulative response records for the teams with the highest, median, and lowest rates of cooperation. (Azrin and Lindsley, 1956, Fig. 2.)

terms of behavior theory in the following way: The children who were present while a given child was being positively reinforced came to be established as S^D's, just as the inanimate environment does in other studies, and therefore as S^{+r}'s. Hence, they were chosen more frequently. In the case of the unreinforced children, the same argument can be made, namely, that the other children established themselves as S^{Δ}'s, therefore as S^{-r}'s and hence were not chosen frequently.

There are many other examples of the direct application of behavior theory to social behavior problems, some of which we have already described (e.g., cf. Baer and Sherman, 1964 in Chapter 3). Our analysis of the verbal interactions taking place during the course of the interview (cf. Chapter 9) provides another example.

Verbal Behavior

It is undoubtedly true that of all the response classes which man emits in the course of a waking day, verbal behavior exhibits close to the highest, if not the highest, frequency of occurrence. Verbal behavior is, of course, a very important example of social behavior. It is behavior for which the sole source of reinforcement is another organism. With the exception of such consequences to the emission of speech as the feedback to one's own ears, the development and maintenance of speech are determined by other organisms. In addition to the importance of verbal behavior in its own right, it has also been used by social psychologists as a method of obtaining data about nonverbal behavior.

The Measurement of Attitudes

Many studies in social psychology deal with the measurement of behavioral dispositions, i.e., attitudes. The reason for studying attitudes is to be able to predict what behavior an individual will emit. The basic assumption behind an attitude scale is that expression of certain attitudes constitutes a prediction on the part of the subject about his own behavior, or at least might serve as an index of that behavior. It will be instructive in this context to describe a study by DeFleur and Westie (1958) who made an attempt to relate responses on an attitude questionnaire to what the authors term an "overt action opportunity." The attitude test consisted of a series of statements about Negroes and whites, to which the subject had to respond on a five-point scale ranging from "strongly agree" to "strongly disagree." The same items were put about Negroes and whites and an attempt was made to separate such items from each other so that a subject would not remember how he had responded to one while he was responding to the other. The differences between a large number of white and Negro items were then summed for each of 250 undergraduate students. Two groups of 23 students each were selected, representing the two extremes of attitude toward Negroes. Each of these students was subjected to an experimental procedure which included measuring his GSR (cf. Chapter 2) in response to pictures of a Negro and a white of the opposite sex seated in what appeared to be a dormitory lounge or living room. After the experiment each subject was asked if he would pose for a photograph of the kind he had seen (with Negroes and whites posed together) and was requested to sign a release for the photograph to be used, having been given a choice of attaching one of the following stipulations: only to be viewed by professional sociologists in a laboratory experiment; to be published in a technical journal; to be viewed by a few dozen university students in a laboratory setting; to be used as a teaching aid in sociology classes; to be printed in the student newspaper; to be published in the student's home town newspaper to publicize the research; or finally, to be used in a nation-wide campaign advocating racial integration. The signing of this document was considered the overt action opportunity. The relationship of the score on the attitude questionnaire to the level of agreement to use the photograph was presumed to reflect the degree to which attitude tests predict behavior. Although there was a significant relationship between the attitude scale and the level of agreement for showing a photograph taken with a Negro, as many as five students indexed to be highly prejudiced on the attitude scale went above the average level of photograph endorsement, and as many as 9 who were indexed as relatively unprejudiced were found to be below the average level of photograph endorsement. The authors interpreted these findings to be at least partly due to the reference groups (peers, parents, etc.) which the students consider when signing permission for the photographs to be used. The students' expectation of the way the reference groups would react to what they had done was important in determining the signing of the permission. In terms of behavior theory, the discrepancy between attitude scales and behavior is due to the S^D's and reinforcement contingencies which go along with them. The extent to which one can predict from an attitude scale to behavior would seem to depend upon the investigator's ability to ensure that the same reinforcement contingencies are in effect in both situations.

Verbal Behavior and Linguistics

The study of language is by no means the exclusive interest of psychology. Language is studied by communication engineers, mathematicians, philosophers, biologists, sociologists, anthropologists and, of course, linguists. In recent years the influence of linguistics on the field has been so great that the study of verbal behavior in psychology has been named psycholinguistics. The scope of the area is so wide that we will only be able to take up a few issues. The reader who is interested in pursuing this field should look at Carroll

(1964), Ervin-Tripp and Slobin (1966), and Salzinger and Salzinger (1967) among others.

It is probably fair to say that there have been 3 major new developments in the psychological study of language in recent years. One is information theory, one is linguistics, and the last is operant conditioning. The information theory approach to language was started by Shannon and Weaver (1949) and has been employed in such experiments as those by Miller and Selfridge (1950) and Salzinger, Portnoy and Feldman (1962) on statistical approximations to English. Essentially, "information" is a measure of the rarity of a given message among all the possible messages. Recently, information theory has been employed primarily for its usefulness in generating descriptive statistical measures, akin to the variance measure, and has been largely displaced by transformation grammar in linguistics as a theory of language.

In linguistics, the one man whose ideas have had the greatest impact upon psychology is Chomsky (1957). His work was brought into psychology, in large part, through the efforts of George Miller (1962b).

Chomsky's work has concentrated on the development of a kind of grammar called generative grammar, which differs from other grammars in that it is not only a scheme for *describing* the structure of utterances in a language, but it also posits a set of constructs which *determine* the structure of any native speaker's utterances. The grammar assumes that human beings are born with a "knowledge" of some basic, universal, deep linguistic structures. It then goes on to specify a set of constructs, called "rules," which are applied to the deep structures in order to produce an utterance having a surface structure which conforms to the language in which it is spoken. Although the form of an individual's speech is determined by the deep structures and the rules of the grammar, neither the structures nor the rules can be directly observed, but rather are inferred from the speech behavior itself. How does the linguist make these inferences? He does so by two means, the first by virtue of the fact that he is a native speaker of the language for which he is attempting to construct rules, and secondly by the fact that he claims to find certain linguistic forms occurring universally. The rules are to be constructed in as economical and elegant a way as possible. They must satisfy the conditions of being able to generate all the possible word combinations that would be characterized as sentences by a competent native speaker and they must generate no combinations of words that would not be accepted as a sentence. The generative model of grammar has been tested in a variety of ways. To take but one example, Mehler (1963) compared the memory for sentences which for their production required the application of different numbers of rules, the number being specified by the generative model of grammar. He found that the sentences requiring more rules did in fact result in a larger number of errors than those requiring fewer rules for generation. In a recent paper, Miller (1965) made another important point about rules (p. 17):

> Rules are not laws, however. They can be broken, and in ordinary conversation they frequently are. Still, even when we break them, we usually are capable of recognizing (under appropriate conditions) that we have made a mistake; from this fact we infer that the rules are known implicitly, even though they cannot be stated explicitly.

What does behavior theory say about the generative model of grammar? Although a full critique of this model would require more space than can be reasonably allotted to it in a general psychology text, a few points can be made. To begin with, the reader will probably remember some of the difficulties inherent in a model of behavior which has as its major explanatory apparatus unobservable concepts such as (cf. Chapter 1) structure and rules. Furthermore, when a model depends upon a set of rules, validation is ordinarily achieved by means of observing whether or not the rules are complied with. However, in this case, in observations of speech, both following the rules and not following the rules are considered acceptable. The latter does not call the validity of the model into question due to the fact that "knowledge" of the rules need not result in the speaker actually following the rules, but merely in "knowing" when he has made a mistake. Some followers of this model point out that the generative model was never meant to predict speech but rather to explain the structure of language. On this basis, the generative model should not be used to describe verbal behavior at all.

There remains another argument for the usefulness of the model and that is that somehow it describes the physiological basis for language—that some neurophysiological process corresponding to the rules takes place. From this point of view Mehler's experiment would seem to supply some evidence for the usefulness of the model. However, the experiment suffers from a number of difficulties. First, the differences in memory for the various types of sentences could possibly be attributed to differences in frequency of occurrence. Those sentences which require a greater number of rules for generation also appear to be the sentences which occur less frequently in our speech. (Unfortunately, we do not yet have frequency of occurrence data for sentences.) Of more immediate importance, perhaps, is the fact that some of the sentences which require more rules were also represented, in Mehler's experiment, by a larger number of words, which might thereby account for the different numbers of errors which occur in the memory task. For that reason, and in order to use unfamiliar material, Salzinger and Eckerman (1967) did a similar experiment, making use of sequences of combinations of nonsense syllables with appropriate word endings and function words to give them the appearance of sentences—"And the piqy kews were behoving the nazer zumaps dygly." The only effect, if any, that the experiment on different sentence types showed, was an equivocal one, and that only early in learning. After a number of trials even these small differences between sentences, types which presumably varied in the number of rules necessary for their generation, disappeared. Instead, performance on the sentence learning task could be explained by an important and familiar behavior theory variable, namely, frequency. An interesting article by Gampel (1966) recently argued, from data in a variety of different behavioral systems, for the unifying nature of such basic variables. Thus, in sum, and without going into further discussion of this model in the detail which the research it has stimulated deserves, we can say that, at this time, the model in no way preempts the behavioral analysis of language.

Application of behavior theory to language has for many years been most tentative. Even the early behaviorists apparently looked upon speech as a verbal report, suggesting that what is important is not the verbal behavior itself, but the behavior it "describes." The most general and strongest statement about speech as behavior in its own right, comes from Skinner (1957b) in a book in which he maintained that verbal behavior is multiply determined and where he made an attempt to describe the classes of stimuli and responses that might logically be derived from such analysis. Actual experiments using operant conditioning paradigms were first reviewed by Krasner (1958) and Salzinger (1959) and most recently by Holz and Azrin (1966). These reviews showed that a great variety of response classes could be conditioned, and that such conditioning was similar indeed to conditioning in animals. We have already described the conditioning of verbal behavior in connection with the interview (Chapter 9) and as it relates to the development of the child (Chapter 7). Although it is by no means true that the problems of the operant conditioning of verbal behavior have been solved, the relevance of behavior theory to an understanding of language has been firmly established.

Among the problems which must be faced in the operant conditioning of verbal behavior is the fact that, with the exception of very young children or children who are initially speech deficient, the verbal behavior which is being manipulated has a very long reinforcement history. This means that in experiments the response class upon which the delivery of reinforcement is made contingent by the experimenter may not be the same as the response class which is actually conditioned. An experiment by Salzinger, Portnoy, Zlotogura and Keisner (1963) is a case in point. The experimenters reinforced subjects for the emission of plural nouns while they were talking about topics of their own choosing. In order to reinforce the plural nouns accurately, the speech rate was slowed down by having subjects talk in time to a metronome, which was set at the rate of 1 beat per second. The results for three subjects are pictured in terms of six successive 5-minute periods for operant level, three conditioning periods, and two extinction periods in Figure 10-7. Although there was a gradual increase in the response class of plural nouns and no change in the word rate, further analysis of the reinforced response class showed that only a subclass of the total response class in which the experimenters were interested was actually changed, and that in fact only those plural nouns which ended in a /z/ sound were modified. Further analysis of the problem of response class has been undertaken recently by Salzinger (1967). In

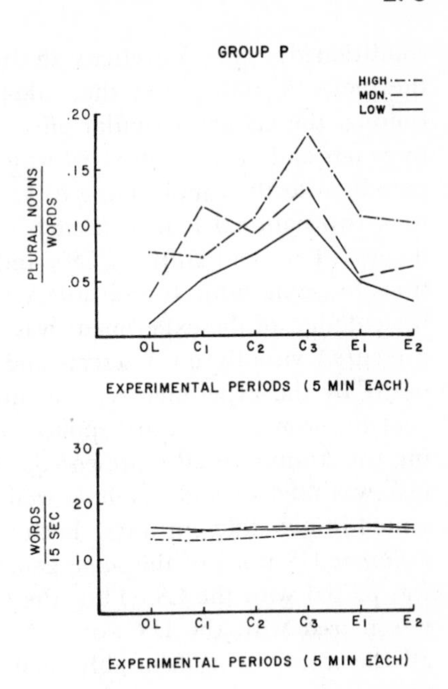

Fig. 10-7. Proportion of plural nouns (upper graph), and word rate per 15 sec (lower graph), for Operant Level (OL), three consecutive Conditioning Periods (C_1, C_2, C_3), and two consecutive Extinction Periods (E_1, E_2), of three Ss reinforced for plural nouns. (Salzinger, Portnoy, Zlotogura, and Keisner, 1963, Fig. 1.)

that paper, the importance of the concept of response class in the acquisition of speech was emphasized in view of the fact that acquisition takes place not in terms of specific responses, but rather, as we have already indicated (Chapter 3), in classes. The fact that classes of responses are conditioned makes clear why children use words in novel combinations which they had not seen or heard used before. Thus, if the response class conditioned consists of furniture words, it is not surprising if a child uses the word "table" in the same word sequence as the word "desk," having been specifically reinforced only for the latter.

The acquisition of meaning is another very important aspect of the study of language. Several approaches, based on behavior theory, have been explored with regard to this topic. Staats (1967) used Osgood, Suci, and Tannenbaum's (1957) measure of meaning, i.e., the semantic differential, to demonstrate that the respondent conditioning model could be used to instate meaning in nonsense syllables. The model was applied by assuming that the nonsense syllable was the CS and the already meaningful words which were systematically paired with it, the US (or at least a stimulus already conditioned). The US elicits an autonomic response which affects the semantic rating, i.e., the index of the meaning. After conditioning, the CS has a similar effect. Let us look at an experiment by Staats and Staats (1958) in which the authors applied the same paradigm to the conditioning of attitudes. In this experiment they took two national names (Dutch and Swedish) and two personal names (Tom and Bill) as CS's and conditioned favorable evaluations for some subjects and unfavorable evaluations in others. The basic design of the experiment was as follows: The CS words were presented visually on a screen and the US words were presented orally by the experimenter; the subjects were also required to repeat the words they heard spoken by the experimenter while viewing the stimuli visually presented. The subjects were told that the task was used to find out how well they could learn material presented in two different ways. Each CS was presented 18 times and a *different* US word of the *same* general class as the other US words was paired with the CS. Thus the CS, "Dutch," presented visually, was paired with the US words, "pretty," "sweet," "healthy," etc., all the words being favorably inclined. When the CS's were later rated with respect to how pleasant or unpleasant the stimuli seemed to the subjects, the results showed quite clearly that those names which were linked with favorable words were subsequently rated as being more pleasant than those which were associated with the series of unfavorable words. Even words to which subjects had already learned a meaning, in this case an evaluational one, were shown to be susceptible to the conditioning effect.

Still another area of research in verbal behavior where behavior theory has proved to be useful is speech perception. Liberman (1957), on the basis of some fascinating and original research, including the production of human sounds on the basis of visual presentations of such sounds (using spectrographic patterns to produce sounds by way of a special instrument called the pattern playback), arrived at the motor theory of speech perception. This theory states essentially that the perception of speech depends upon a matching process, according to which the hearer makes some kind of articulatory movement (ostensibly below the threshold of the subject's ability to discriminate it), which in turn, by means of its feedback, controls the ability to perceive. This theory about the perception of speech placed speech in a special category, i.e., in a class of stimuli quite different from other stimuli. More recently, Lane (1965, 1967) was able to demonstrate that at least some of the special characteristics of speech perception could be reproduced, using non-speech continua, simply by employing a special procedure for conditioning the discrimination. The conditioning procedure which Lane posits as the basis for speech perception can be described as follows: Two stimuli and two responses are involved; Stimulus 1 is an S^D for Response 1 but S^Δ for Response 2, while Stimulus 2 is an S^D for Response 2 but S^Δ for Response 1. Using this training paradigm, Lane is able to demonstrate "categorical perception" in which a particular sound is labelled one way when it has one set of physical properties, and another way when it has a different set of physical properties, rather than showing the more typical psychophysical function, namely, a gradual shift in the proportion of the two labels in response to gradual physical changes in the stimuli.

In general, we can say that behavior theory has proved itself to be quite relevant to the analysis of verbal behavior. With respect to the influence of linguistics on the psychological study of language, it might be well to quote from a critical reappraisal of the two areas (Osgood, 1963, p. 751): "The thing we must avoid, I think, is 'explaining' sentence understanding and creating by simply putting a new homunculus in our heads—in this case, a little linguist in every brain."

Applications of the Knowledge of Psychology to the Problems of Society

As one becomes better acquainted with the behavioral techniques, it becomes clear that they can be applied to practical problems. They include education, therapy, and space exploration using trained animals to report changes as a function of interstellar travel. Still other potential areas of application include such problems as inter-ethnic and international conflict. Work in the latter two areas has hardly been touched by behavior theory as outlined in this book. Appropriate techniques for analyzing, predicting, and controlling human behavior need to be investigated and used, however, before our physical technology irreversibly surpasses our behavioral technology.

Let us look at one experiment which utilized behavior theory as a model for group interaction and then examine some of its implications. Sidowski, Wyckoff, and Tabory (1956), in an early experiment on the use of behavior theory in elucidating social interaction, made use of the following design: Two subjects, each isolated and unaware of the other's presence, were placed in an experimental situation such that each was able to press one of two buttons, one delivering a positive reinforcer, the other a negative reinforcer to the other person but not to himself, except through the indirect effect of his reinforcing behavior on the other. The positive reinforcer consisted of a score on a counter; the subject was told that the object was for him to respond in such a way as to accumulate the highest score possible. The negative reinforcer consisted of electric shock. There were two groups—one group received a strong shock, the other a weak shock as the negative reinforcer. The results showed no evidence for learning, i.e., an increase in responses which would yield higher scores in the group receiving weak shocks as negative reinforcers. The group which received strong shocks as negative reinforcers showed a significant amount of learning in the very first five minutes of the experiment and maintained approximately 65 per cent responding on the button which gave the other person a score (positive reinforcer) rather than a shock (negative reinforcer). After as many as 25 minutes on this procedure, 35 per cent of the responses still produced the negative reinforcers for the unknown partner. The point may be made that had the subjects known the effects of their responses they would have come up with the optimum solution almost immediately. The important point, it seems to this author, is that in many negotiations the effects of one party's responses upon that of the other remains unknown, which might well explain why negotiations between presumably well-intentioned people cause so much misery before an accommodation is actually reached. We obviously need more experiments along this line to apply behavior theory to the bigger problems of the day.

SUMMARY

After defining social behavior as behavior which varies as a function of other organisms, and noting duly the central importance of verbal behavior in this area, Festinger's dissonance theory was described as a social psychological theory in use in the field. This theory suggests that organisms are motivated by a drive to keep their cognitions consistent. It was shown, however, that no special theory is necessary to explain the data engendered by the idea of dissonance, since behavior theory appears to explain it at least as well and, of course, has the advantage of greater generality than the dissonance theory.

Animal studies were next described with respect to the phenomena of social facilitation, cooperation, and superstitious behavior (behavior controlled only by the fact that there is a temporal relationship between responses and reinforcement, as opposed to the causal relationship between response and reinforcement in regularly conditioned behavior).

The use of psychophysical techniques for the elucidation of social psychological studies was presented in the section that followed. These techniques illustrate quite clearly that the influence of the verbal judgment of one person can act as a powerful S^D (and S^{+r}) for the judgment of another person even in the face of conflicting S^D's from physical objects.

Discussion then turned to the application of the above results to the study of the same phenomena in human subjects under more applied conditions. This section discussed the measurement of attitudes (behavioral dispositions) and described, in particular, the problem of divergence between the attitude and the behavior to which the attitude statement refers. The relationship between linguistics and verbal behavior was then taken up, demonstrating the differences in theory between the two areas and the differences in the degree to which the data agree with the theories. Studies using the techniques of operant conditioning, respondent conditioning, and perception were then described as avenues toward understanding language as behavior.

The final section of the chapter dealt with the application of behavior theory to the complex interaction engendered by a seemingly simple experiment as a model of social interaction. In this experiment, one response of a subject positively reinforces the responses of another person, and another response negatively reinforces that other person's responses. The second person's responses have exactly the same effect on the first person. Although neither subject knows that his behavior is controlled by the behavior of another person, yet, at least under conditions of high shock as a negative reinforcer, each person's behavior *is* controlled by the other.

REFERENCES

Aiba, T. S. Can the absolute threshold be conditioned? *Journal of Experimental Psychology,* 1963, *65,* 233-239.

Airapetyantz, E., & Bykov, K. Physiological experiments and the psychology of the subconscious. *Philosophy and Phenomenological Research,* 1945, *5,* 577-593.

Aldrich, C. A., & Norval, Mildred A. A developmental graph for the first year of life. *Journal of Pediatrics,* 1946, *29,* 304-308.

Allport, F. H. *Social psychology.* Boston: Houghton Mifflin, 1924.

Anrep, G. V. Pitch discrimination in the dog. *Journal of Physiology,* 1920, *53,* 367-385.

Antonitis, J. J. Response variability in the white rat during conditioning, extinction, and reconditioning. *Journal of Experimental Psychology,* 1951, *42,* 273-281.

Asch, S. E. Opinions and social pressure. *Scientific American,* 1955, *193,* 31-35.

Ash, P. The reliability of psychiatric diagnoses. *Journal of Abnormal and Social Psychology,* 1949, *44,* 272-276.

Ayllon, T., & Michael, J. The psychiatric nurse as a behavioral engineer. *Journal of the Experimental Analysis of Behavior,* 1959, *2,* 323-334.

Azrin, N. H., & Holz, W. C. Punishment. In W. K. Honig (Ed.), *Operant behavior: areas of research and application.* New York: Appleton-Century-Crofts, 1966.

Azrin, N. H., & Lindsley, O. R. The reinforcement of cooperation between children. *Journal of Abnormal and Social Psychology,* 1956, *52,* 100-102.

Baer, D. M. Effect of withdrawal of positive reinforcement on an extinguishing response in young children. *Child Development,* 1961, *32,* 67-74.

Baer, D. M. Laboratory control of thumbsucking by withdrawal and re-presentation of reinforcement. *Journal of the Experimental Analysis of Behavior,* 1962, *5,* 525-528.

Baer, D. M., & Sherman, J. A. Reinforcement control of generalized imitation in young children. *Journal of Experimental Child Psychology,* 1964, *1,* 37-49.

Bandura, A., & Walters, R. H. *Social learning and personality development.* New York: Holt, Rinehart & Winston, 1963.

Barker, R. G. Explorations in ecological psychology. *American Psychologist,* 1965, *20,* 1-14.

Baughman, E. E. A comparative analysis of Rorschach forms with altered stimulus characteristics. *Journal of Projective Techniques,* 1954, *18,* 151-164.

Békésy, G. von. A new audiometer. *Acta Ota-laryngology,* 1947, *35,* 411-422.

Bem, D. J. Self perception: an alternative interpretation of cognitive dissonance phenomena. *Psychological Review,* 1967, *74,* 183-200.

Bijou, S. W., & Baer, D. M. Operant methods in child behavior and development. In W. K. Honig (Ed.), *Operant behavior: areas of research and application.* New York: Appleton-Century-Crofts, 1966.

Bitterman, M. E. The CS-US interval in classical and avoidance conditioning. In W. F. Prokasy (Ed.), *Classical conditioning.* New York: Appleton-Century-Crofts, 1965.

Blough, D. S. Dark adaptation in the pigeon. *Journal of Comparative and Physiological Psychology,* 1956, *49,* 425-430.

Blough, D. S. A method for obtaining psychophysical thresholds from the pigeon. *Journal of the Experimental Analysis of Behavior,* 1958, *1,* 31-43.
Blough, D. S. The study of animal sensory processes by operant methods. In W. K. Honig (Ed.), *Operant behavior: areas of research and application.* New York: Appleton-Century-Crofts, 1966.
Boren, J. J. The study of drugs with operant techniques. In W. K. Honig (Ed.), *Operant behavior: areas of research and application.* New York: Appleton-Century-Crofts, 1966.
Boring, E. G. A new ambiguous figure. *American Journal of Psychology,* 1930, *42,* 444.
Brackbill, Yvonne. Extinction of the smiling response in infants as a function of reinforcement schedule. *Child Development,* 1958, *29,* 115-124.
Brady, J. P., & Lind, D. L. Experimental analysis of hysterical blindness. *Archives of General Psychiatry,* 1961, *4,* 331-339.
Brady, J. V. Operant methodology and the experimental production of altered physiological states. In W. K. Honig (Ed.), *Operant behavior: areas of research and application.* New York: Appleton-Century-Crofts, 1966.
Brady, J. V., Porter, R. W., Conrad, D. G., & Mason, J. W. Avoidance behavior and the development of gastroduodenal ulcers. *Journal of the Experimental Analysis of Behavior,* 1958, *1,* 69-72.
Braun, H. W., & Geiselhart, R. Age differences in the acquisition and extinction of the conditioned eyelid response. *Journal of Experimental Psychology,* 1959, *57,* 386-388.
Breland, K., & Breland, Marian. The misbehavior of organisms. *American Psychologist,* 1961, *16,* 681-684.
Breland, K., & Breland, Marian. *Animal behavior.* New York: MacMillan, 1966.
Bridger, W. H. Contributions of conditioning principles to psychiatry. In *Pavlovian conditioning and psychiatry,* 1964. Symposium No. 9, 181-198.
Bridgman, P. W. *The logic of modern physics.* New York: Macmillan, 1928.
Brody, N., & Oppenheim, P. Tensions in psychology between the methods of behaviorism and phenomenology. *Psychological Review,* 1966, *73,* 295-305.
Brown, R. T., & Wagner, A. R. Resistance to punishment and extinction following training with shock or nonreinforcement. *Journal of Experimental Psychology,* 1964, *68,* 503-507.
Bruner, J. S., & Goodman, C. C. Value and need as organizing factors in perception. *Journal of Abnormal and Social Psychology,* 1947, *42,* 33-44.
Burtt, H. E. An experimental study of early childhood memory: final report. *Journal of Genetic Psychology,* 1941, *58,* 435-439.
Butler, R. A. Discrimination learning by Rhesus monkeys to visual-exploration motivation. *Journal of Comparative and Physiological Psychology,* 1953, *46,* 95-98.
Carroll, J. B. *Language and thought.* Englewood Cliffs, N. J.: Prentice-Hall, 1964.
Catania, A. C. Concurrent operants. In W. K. Honig (Ed.), *Operant behavior: areas of research and application,* New York: Appleton-Century-Crofts, 1966.
Chapman, L. J. Illusory correlation in observational report. *Journal of Verbal Learning and Verbal Behavior,* 1967, *6,* 151-155.
Chomsky, N. *Syntactic structures.* The Hague: Mouton, 1957.
Clark, F. C. The effect of deprivation and frequency of reinforcement on variable interval responding. *Journal of the Experimental Analysis of Behavior,* 1958, *1,* 221-228.

Daniel, W. J. Cooperative problem solving in rats. *Journal of Comparative Psychology,* 1942, *34,* 361-369.

Darwin, C. *The expression of the emotions in man and animals.* London: Murray, 1872.

Deese, J., & Hulse, S. H. *The psychology of learning.* New York: McGraw-Hill, 1967.

DeFleur, M. L., & Westie, F. R. Verbal attitudes and overt acts: an experiment on the salience of attitudes. *American Sociological Review,* 1958, *23,* 667-673.

Delgado, J. M. R. Cerebral heterostimulation in a monkey colony. *Science,* 1963, *141,* 161-163.

Dollard, J., & Miller, N. E. *Personality and psychotherapy.* New York: McGraw-Hill, 1950.

Dukes, W. F. N=1. *Psychological Bulletin,* 1965, *64,* 74-79.

Ebbinghaus, H. *Memory,* Educational Reprint No. 3. New York: Teachers College, Columbia Univ., 1913.

Ebner, F. F., & Myers, R. E. Corpus callosum and the interhemispheric transmission of tactual learning. *Journal of Neurophysiology,* 1962, *25,* 380-391.

Eldridge, L. Respiration rate change and its relation to avoidance behavior. Unpublished doctoral dissertation, Columbia Univ., 1954.

Eriksen, C. W. Subception: fact or artifact? *Psychological Review,* 1956, *63,* 74-80.

Erlenmeyer-Kimling, L., & Jarvik, Lissy F. Genetics and intelligence: a review. *Science,* 1963, *142,* 1477-1479.

Ervin-Tripp, Susan M., & Slobin, D. I. Psycholinguistics. *Annual Review of Psychology,* 1966, *17,* 435-474.

Estes, W. K., & Skinner, B. F. Some quantitative properties of anxiety. *Journal of Experimental Psychology,* 1941, *29,* 390-400.

Eysenck, H. J. *The dynamics of anxiety and hysteria: an experimental application of modern learning theory to psychiatry.* London: Routledge & Kegan Paul, 1957.

Eysenck, H. J. (Ed.) *Behaviour therapy and the neuroses.* New York: Pergamon, 1960.

Ferster, C. B. Intermittent reinforcement of a complex response in a chimpanzee. *Journal of the Experimental Analysis of Behavior,* 1958, *1,* 163-165.

Ferster, C. B. Classification of behavioral pathology. In L. Krasner and L. P. Ullmann (Eds.), *Research in behavior modification.* New York: Holt, Rinehart & Winston, 1965.

Ferster, C. B., & Hammer, Jr., C. E. Synthesizing the components of arithmetic behavior. In W. K. Honig (Ed.), *Operant behavior: areas of research and application.* New York: Appleton-Century-Crofts, 1966.

Ferster, C. B., & Skinner, B. F. *Schedules of reinforcement.* New York: Appleton-Century-Crofts, 1957.

Festinger, L. *A theory of cognitive dissonance.* Stanford: Stanford Univ. Press, 1957.

Festinger, L., & Carlsmith, J. M. Cognitive consequences of forced compliance. *Journal of Abnormal and Social Psychology,* 1959, *58,* 203-210.

Fitzgerald, R. F. The effects of partial reinforcement on the classically conditioned salivary response in dogs. Unpublished doctoral dissertation, Indiana Univ., 1962.

Fowler, W. Cognitive learning in infancy and early childhood. *Psychological Bulletin,* 1962, *59,* 116-152.

Fox, L. Effecting the use of efficient study habits. *The Journal of Mathetics,* 1962, *1,* 75-86.

Free, J. B. The stimuli releasing the stinging response of honey bees. *Animal Behavior,* 1961, *9,* 193-197.

Fuller, J. L., & Thompson, W. R. *Behavior genetics.* New York: Wiley, 1960.

Gampel, Dorothy H. Data parallels across behavioral systems. *Psychological Bulletin,* 1966, *66,* 499-510.

Garner, W. R., Hake, H. W., & Eriksen, C. W. Operationism and the concept of perception. *Psychological Review,* 1956, *63,* 149-159.

Geiss, G. L., Stebbins, W. C., & Lundin, R. W. *Reflex and operant conditioning. The study of behavior.* Vol. 1. New York: Appleton-Century-Crofts, 1965.

Gesell, A., & Ilg, Frances L. *Infant and child in the culture of today.* New York: Harper, 1943.

Gewirtz, J. L., & Baer, D. M. Deprivation and satiation of social reinforcers as drive conditions. *Journal of Abnormal and Social Psychology,* 1958, *57,* 165-172.

Giedt, F. H. Comparison of visual, content, and auditory cues in interviewing. *Journal of Consulting Psychology,* 1955, *19,* 407-416.

Gilbert, T. F. Mathetics: the technology of education. *The Journal of Mathetics,* 1962, *1,* 7-74.

Goldiamond, I. Stuttering and fluency as manipulatable operant response classes. In L. Krasner and L. P. Ullmann (Eds.), *Research in behavior modification.* New York: Holt, Rinehart & Winston, 1965.

Goldiamond, I., & Hawkins, W. F. Vexierversuch: the log relationship between word-frequency and recognition obtained in the absence of stimulus words. *Journal of Experimental Psychology,* 1958, *56,* 457-463.

Graham, C. H. Sensation and perception in an objective psychology. *Psychological Review,* 1958, *65,* 65-76.

Graham, C. H., & Gagné, R. M. The acquisition, extinction, and spontaneous recovery of a conditioned operant response. *Journal of Experimental Psychology,* 1940, *26,* 251-280.

Gray, P. H. *The comparative analysis of behavior.* Dubuque, Iowa: Wm. C. Brown, 1966.

Grünbaum, A. Causality and the science of human behavior. *American Scientist,* 1952, *40,* 665-676.

Gunn, D. L. The humidity reactions of the wood louse, *Pocellio scaber. Journal of Experimental Biology,* 1937, *14,* 178-186.

Guttman, N., & Kalish, H. I. Discriminability and stimulus generalization. *Journal of Experimental Psychology,* 1956, *51,* 79-88.

Hailman, J. P. Pecking of laughing gull chicks at models of the parental head. *Auk,* 1962, *79,* 89-98.

Hake, D. F., & Laws, D. R. Social facilitation of responses during a stimulus paired with electric shock. *Journal of the Experimental Analysis of Behavior,* 1967, *10,* 387-395.

Hall, J. F. *The psychology of learning.* Philadelphia: Lippincott, 1966.

Harlow, H. F. Mice, monkeys, men and motives. *Psychological Review,* 1953, *60,* 23-32.

Harlow, H. F. The nature of love. *American Psychologist,* 1958, *12,* 673-685.

Harlow, H. F., & Harlow, Margaret K. The effect of rearing conditions on behavior. *Bulletin of the Menninger Clinic,* 1962, *26,* 213-224.

Haughton, E., & Ayllon, T. Production and elimination of symptomatic behavior. In L. P. Ullmann and L. Krasner (Eds.), *Case studies in behavior modification.* New York: Holt, Rinehart & Winston, 1965.

Hearst, E. Resistance-to-extinction functions in the single organism. *Journal of the Experimental Analysis of Behavior,* 1961, *4,* 133-144.

Hebb, D. O. *A textbook of psychology.* Philadelphia: W. B. Saunders, 1966.

Hefferline, R. F., & Keenan, B. Amplitude-induction gradient of a small human operant in an escape-avoidance situation. *Journal of the Experimental Analysis of Behavior,* 1961, *4,* 41-43.

Helson, H. *Adaptation level theory.* New York: Harper & Row, 1964.

Hernández-Peón, R., Scherrer, H., & Jouvet, M. Modification of electric activity in cochlear nucleus during "attention" in unanesthetized cats. *Science,* 1956, *123,* 331-332.

Heron, W. The pathology of boredom. *Scientific American,* 1957, *196,* 52-56.

Herrick, R. M., Myers, J. L., & Korotkin, A. L. Changes in S^D and S^Δ rates during the development of an operant discrimination. *Journal of Comparative and Physiological Psychology,* 1959, *52,* 359-363.

Herrnstein, R. J. Stereotypy and intermittent reinforcement. *Science,* 1961, *133,* 2067-2069.

Herrnstein, R. J. Superstition: a corollary of the principles of operant conditioning. In W. K. Honig (Ed.), *Operant behavior: areas of research and application.* New York: Appleton-Century-Crofts, 1966.

Herrnstein, R. J., & Boring, E. G. *A source book in the history of psychology.* Cambridge: Harvard Univ., 1965.

Herrnstein, R. J., & Loveland, D. H. Complex visual concept in the pigeon. *Science,* 1964, *146,* 549-551.

Herrnstein, R. J., & Morse, W. H. Some effects of response-independent positive reinforcement on maintained operant behavior. *Journal of Comparative and Physiological Psychology,* 1957, *50,* 461-467.

Herrnstein, R. J., & van Sommers, P. Method for sensory scaling with animals. *Science,* 1962, *135,* 40-41.

Hess, E. H. Ethology: an approach toward the complete analysis of behavior. In R. Brown, E. Galanter, E. H. Hess, and G. Mandler (Eds.), *New directions in psychology.* New York: Holt, Rinehart & Winston, 1962.

Hilgard, E. R., & Bower, G. H. *Theories of learning,* New York: Appleton-Century-Crofts, 1966.

Hirsch, J. Behavior genetics and individuality understood. *Science,* 1963, *142,* 1436-1442.

Hirsch, J., & Boudreau, J. C The heritability of phototaxis in a population of *Drosophila Melanogaster. Journal of Comparative and Physiological Psychology,* 1958, *51,* 647-651.

Hoffman, H. S. The analysis of discriminated avoidance. In W. K. Honig (Ed.), *Operant behavior: areas of research and application.* New York: Appleton-Century-Crofts, 1966.

Holland, J. G. Human vigilance. *Science,* 1958, *128,* 61-67.

Holland, J. G. Teaching machines: an application of principles from the laboratory. *Journal of the Experimental Analysis of Behavior,* 1960, *3,* 275-287.

Holland, J. G., & Skinner, B. F. *The analysis of behavior* New York: McGraw-Hill, 1961.

Holz, W. C., & Azrin, N. H. Conditioning human verbal behavior. In W. K. Honig (Ed.), *Operant behavior: areas of research and application.* New York: Appleton-Century-Crofts, 1966.

Honig, W. K. (Ed.) *Operant behavior: areas of research and application.* New York: Appleton-Century-Crofts, 1966.

Howes, D. H., & Solomon, R. L. A note on McGinnies' "Emotionality and perceptual defense." *Psychological Review,* 1950, *57,* 229-234.

Hughes, J. L., & McNamara, W. J. A comparative study of programmed and conventional instruction in industry. *Journal of Applied Psychology,* 1961, *45,* 225-231.

Hull, C. L. *Principles of behavior.* New York: Appleton-Century-Crofts, 1943.

Hunt, H. F., & Brady, J. V. Some effects of electro-convulsive shock on a conditioned emotional response ("anxiety"). *Journal of Comparative and Physiological Psychology,* 1951, *44,* 88-98.

Inglis, J. *The scientific study of abnormal behavior.* Chicago: Aldine, 1966.

Jones, Mary C. The elimination of children's fears. *Journal of Experimental Psychology,* 1924, *7,* 382-390.

Kallmann, F. J. The genetic theory of schizophrenia. *American Journal of Psychiatry,* 1946, *9,* 309-322.

Kanfer, F. H., & Matarazzo, J. D. Secondary and generalized reinforcement in human learning. *Journal of Experimental Psychology,* 1959, *58,* 400-404.

Kanfer, F. H., & Saslow, G. Behavioral analysis: an alternative to diagnostic classification. *Archives of General Psychiatry,* 1965, *12,* 529-538.

Kaplan, M. (Ed.) *Essential works of Pavlov.* New York: Bantam Books, 1966.

Katz, M. S., & Deterline, W. A. Apparent learning in the paramecium. *Journal of Comparative and Physiological Psychology,* 1958, *51,* 243-248.

Kelleher, R. T. Chaining and conditioned reinforcement. In W. K. Honig (Ed.), *Operant behavior: areas of research and application.* New York: Appleton-Century-Crofts, 1966.

Keller, F. S., & Schoenfeld, W. N. *Principles of psychology.* New York: Appleton-Century-Crofts, 1950.

Kellogg, W. N. Auditory scanning in the dolphin. *Psychological Record,* 1960, *10,* 25-27.

Kellogg, W. N., & Kellogg, L. A. *The ape and the child.* New York: McGraw-Hill, 1933.

Kendler, H. H., & Kendler, Tracy S. Vertical and horizontal processes in problem-solving. *Psychological Review,* 1962, *69,* 1-16.

Keppel, G., & Underwood, B. J. Proactive inhibition in short-term retention of single items. *Journal of Verbal Learning and Verbal Behavior,* 1962, *1,* 153-161.

Kimble, G. A. *Hilgard and Marquis' conditioning and learning.* New York: Appleton-Century-Crofts, 1961.

Kimble, G. A. *Foundations of conditioning and learning.* New York: Apppleton-Century-Crofts, 1967.

Kimmel, H. D. Instrumental conditioning of autonomically mediated behavior. *Psychological Bulletin,* 1967, *67,* 337-345.

Kish, G. B. Studies of sensory reinforcement. In W. K. Honig (Ed.), *Operant conditioning: areas of research and application.* New York: Appleton-Century-Crofts, 1966.

Krasner, L. Studies of the conditioning of verbal behavior. *Psychological Bulletin,* 1958, *55,* 148-170.

Krasner, L., & Ullmann, L. P. (Eds.), *Research in behavior modification.* New York: Holt, Rinehart & Winston, 1965.

Lambert, W. W., Solomon, R. L., & Watson, P. D. Reinforcement and extinction as factors in size estimation. *Journal of Experimental Psychology,* 1949, *39,* 637-641.

Lane, H. L. Control of vocal responding in the chicken. *Science,* 1960, *132,* 37-38.

Lane, H. L. The motor theory of speech perception: a critical review. *Psychological Review,* 1965, *72,* 275-309.

Lane, H. L. A behavioral basis for the polarity principle in linguistics. In K. Salzinger and Suzanne Salzinger (Eds.), *Research in verbal behavior and some neurophysiological implications.* New York: Academic Press, 1967.

Lazarus, R. S., & McCleary, R. A. Autonomic discrimination without awareness: a study of subception. *Psychological Review,* 1951, *58,* 113-122.

Liberman, A. M. Some results of research on speech perception. *Journal of the Acoustical Society of America,* 1957, *29,* 117-123.

Lindgren, H. C. *Educational psychology in the classroom.* New York: John Wiley, 1967.

Lindsley, O. R. Operant behavior during sleep: a measure of depth of sleep. *Science,* 1957, *126,* 1290-1291.

Lindsley, O. R. Geriatric behavioral prosthetics. In R. Kastenbaum (Ed.), *New thoughts on old age.* New York: Springer, 1964. Pp. 4-60.

Lissman, H. W. Electric location by fishes. *Scientific American,* 1963, *208,* 50-59.

Lott, Bernice E., & Lott, A. J. The formation of positive attitudes toward group members. *Journal of Abnormal and Social Psychology,* 1960, *61,* 297-300.

Luria, A. R. *The role of speech in the regulation of normal and abnormal behaviour.* New York: Pergamon Press, 1961.

Luria, A. R. The regulative function of speech in its development and dissolution. In K. Salzinger and Suzanne Salzinger (Eds.), *Research in verbal behavior and some neurophysiological implications.* New York: Academic Press, 1967.

Maier, N. R. F. Reasoning in humans: II. The solution of a problem and its appearance in consciousness. *Journal of Comparative Psychology,* 1931, *12,* 181-194.

Maltzman, I. On the training of originality. *Psychological Review,* 1960, *67,* 229-242.

Maltzman, I. Individual differences in "attention": the orienting reflex. In R. M. Gagné (Ed.) *Learning and individual differences.* Columbus, Ohio: Merrill, 1967.

Mandler, G., & Kessen, W. *The language of psychology.* New York: Wiley, 1959.

Mausner, B. The effect of prior reinforcement on the interaction of observer pairs. *Journal of Abnormal and Social Psychology,* 1954, *49,* 65-68. (a)

Mausner, B. The effect of one partner's success in a relevant task on the interaction of observer pairs. *Journal of Abnormal and Social Psychology,* 1954, *49,* 557-560. (b)

McConnell, J. V. Memory transfer through cannibalism in planarians. *Journal of Neuropsychiatry,* 1962, *3,* 542-548.

McGinnies, E. Emotionality and perceptual defense. *Psychological Review,* 1949, *56,* 244-251.

Mednick, S. A. A learning theory approach to research in schizophrenia. *Psychological Bulletin,* 1958, *55,* 316-327.

Mehler, J. Some effects of grammatical transformations on the recall of English sentences. *Journal of Verbal Learning and Verbal Behavior,* 1963, *2,* 346-351.

Melzack, R., & Scott, T. H. The effects of early experience on the response to pain. *Journal of Comparative and Physiological Psychology,* 1957, *50,* 155-161.

Miller, G. A. *Psychology.* New York: Harper & Row, 1962. (a)

Miller, G. A. Some pyschological studies of grammar. *American Psychologist,* 1962, *17,* 748-762. (b)

Miller, G. A. Some preliminaries to psycholinguistics. *American Psychologist,* 1965, *20,* 15-20.

Miller, G. A., Galanter, E., & Pribram, K. H. *Plans and the structure of behavior.* New York: Henry Holt, 1960.

Miller, G. A., & Selfridge, Jennifer A. Verbal context and the recall of meaningful material. *American Journal of Psychology,* 1950, *63,* 176-185.

Miller, N. E. Experimental studies of conflict. In J. McV. Hunt (Ed.), *Personality and the Behavior Disorders.* Vol. I. New York: Ronald, 1944.

Miller, N. E. Learning resistance to pain and fear: effects of overlearning, exposure, and rewarded exposure in context. *Journal of Experimental Psychology,* 1960, *60,* 137-145.

Miller, N. E., & DiCara, L. Instrumental learning of heart rate changes in curarized rats: shaping, and specificity to discriminate stimulus. *Journal of Comparative and Physiological Psychology,* 1967, *63,* 12-19.

Miller, N. E., & Dollard, J. *Social learning and imitation.* New Haven: Yale Univ., 1941.

Moltz, H., & Stettner, L. J. The influence of patterned-light deprivation of the critical period for imprinting. *Journal of Comparative and Physiological Psychology,* 1961, *54,* 279-283.

Morse, W. H. Intermittent reinforcement. In W. K. Honig (Ed.), *Operant behavior: areas of research and application.* New York: Appleton-Century-Crofts, 1966.

Mowrer, O. H., & Mowrer, Willie M. Enuresis: a method for its study and treatment. *American Journal of Ortho-psychiatry,* 1938, *8,* 436-459.

Murphey, R. M. Instrumental conditioning of the fruit fly. *Drosophila melanogaster. Animal Behaviour,* 1967, *15,* 153-161.

Notterman, J. M. Force emission during bar pressing. *Journal of Experimental Psychology,* 1959, *58,* 341-347.

Notterman, J. M., & Mintz, D. E. Exteroceptive cueing of response force. *Science,* 1962, *135,* 1070-1071.

Notterman, J. M., Schoenfeld, W. N., & Bersch, P. J. Partial reinforcement and conditioned heart rate response in human subjects. *Science.* 1952, *115,* 77-79.

Olds, J. Pleasure centers in the brain. *Scientific American,* 1956, *195,* 105-116.

Osgood, C. E. On understanding and creating sentences. *American Psychologist,* 1963, *18,* 735-751.

Osgood, C. E., Suci, G. J., & Tannenbaum, P. H. *The measurement of meaning.* Urbana: Univ. Illinois Press, 1957.

Ost, J. W. P., & Lauer, D. W. Some investigations of classical salivary conditioning in the dog. In W. F. Prokasy (Ed.), *Classical conditioning.* New York: Appleton-Century-Crofts, 1965.

Penfield, W. The interpretive cortex. *Science,* 1959, *129,* 1719-1725.

Peterson, L. R., & Peterson, Margaret J. Short-term retention of individual verbal items. *Journal of Experimental Psychology,* 1959, *58,* 193-198.

Pettigrew, T. F. *A profile of the Negro American.* New York: Van Nostrand, 1964.

Prokasy, W. F. (Ed.) *Classical conditioning.* New York: Appleton-Century-Crofts, 1965.

Ramsay, A. O., & Hess, E. H. A laboratory approach to the study of imprinting. *Wilson Bulletin,* 1954, *66,* 196-206.

Ratner, S. C., & Denny, M. R. (Eds.) *Comparative psychology: research in animal behavior.* Homewood, Illinois: Dorsey Press, 1964.

Razran, G. H. S. The observable unconscious and the inferable conscious in current Soviet psychology: interoceptive conditioning, semantic conditioning, and the orienting reflex. *Psychological Review,* 1961, *54,* 81-147.

Razran, G. H. S. Russian physiologists' psychology and American experimental psychology: a historical and a systematic collation and a look into the future. *Psychological Bulletin,* 1965, *63,* 42-64.

Rescorla, R. A., & Solomon, R. L. Two-process learning theory: relationships between Pavlovian conditioning and instrumental learning. *Psychological Review,* 1967, *74,* 151-182.

Rheingold, Harriet L., Gewirtz, J. L., & Ross, Helen W. Social conditioning of vocalizations in the infant. *Journal of Comparative and Physiological Psychology,* 1959, *52,* 68-73.

Russell, W. A., & Jenkins, J. J. *The complete Minnesota norms for responses to 100 words from the Kent-Rosanoff Association Test.* Technical Report No. 11, Contract N80NR-66216 between Office of Naval Research and University of Minnesota, 1954.

Salzinger, K. Techniques for computing shift in a scale of absolute judgment. *Psychological Bulletin,* 1956, *53,* 394-401.

Salzinger, K. Experimental manipulation of verbal behavior: a review. *The Journal of General Psychology,* 1959, *61,* 65-94.

Salzinger, K. The problem of response class in verbal behavior. In K. Salzinger and Suzanne Salzinger (Eds.), *Research in verbal behavior and some neurophysiological implications.* New York: Academic Press, 1967.

Salzinger, K., & Eckerman, Carol. Grammar and the recall of chains of verbal responses. *Journal of Verbal Learning and Verbal Behavior,* 1967, *6,* 232-239.

Salzinger, K., Feldman, R. S., Cowan, Judith E., & Salzinger, Suzanne. Operant conditioning of verbal behavior of two young speech-deficient boys. In L. Krasner and L. P. Ullmann (Eds.), *Research in behavior modification.* New York: Holt, Rinehart & Winston, 1965.

Salzinger, K., & Pisoni, Stephanie. Reinforcement of affect responses of schizophrenics during the clinical interview. *Journal of Abnormal and Social Psychology,* 1958, *57,* 84-90.

Salzinger, K., & Pisoni, Stephanie. Reinforcement of verbal affect responses of normal subjects during the interview. *Journal of Abnormal and Social Psychology,* 1960, *60,* 127-130.

Salzinger, K., & Pisoni, Stephanie. Some parameters of the conditioning of verbal affect responses in schizophrenic subjects. *Journal of Abnormal and Social Psychology,* 1961, *63,* 511-516.

Salzinger, K., & Portnoy, Stephanie, Verbal conditioning in interviews: application to chronic schizophrenics and relationship to prognosis for acute schizophrenics. *Journal of Psychiatric Research,* 1964, *2,* 1-9.

Salzinger, K., Portnoy, Stephanie, & Feldman, R. S. The effect of order of approximation to the statistical structure of English on the emission of verbal responses. *Journal of Experimental Psychology,* 1962, *64,* 52-57.

Salzinger, K., Portnoy, Stephanie, & Feldman, R. S. Experimental manipulation of continuous speech in schizophrenic patients. *Journal of Abnormal and Social Psychology,* 1964, *68,* 508-516. (a)

Salzinger, K., Portnoy, Stephanie, & Feldman, R. S. Verbal behavior of schizophrenic and normal subjects. *Annals of the New York Academy of Sciences,* 1964, *105,* 845-860. (b)

Salzinger, K., Portnoy, Stephanie, & Feldman, R. S. Verbal behavior in schizophrenics and some comments toward a theory of schizophrenia. In P. Hoch and J. Zubin (Eds.), *Psychopathology of schizophrenia,* New York: Grune & Stratton, 1966.

Salzinger, K., Portnoy, Stephanie, Zlotogura, Phyllis, & Keisner, R. The effect of reinforcement on continuous speech and on plural nouns in grammatical context. *Journal of Verbal Learning and Verbal Behavior,* 1963, *1,* 477-485.

Salzinger, K., & Salzinger, Suzanne (Eds.) *Research in verbal behavior and some neurophysiological implications.* New York: Academic Press, 1967.

Salzinger, K., & Waller, M. B. The operant control of vocalization in the dog. *Journal of the Experimental Analysis of Behavior,* 1962, *5,* 383-389.

Salzinger, Suzanne. Rate of affect response in schizophrenics as a function of three types of interviewer verbal behavior. Paper presented at the Eastern Psychological Association, Atlantic City, 1956.

Salzinger, Suzanne, Salzinger, K., & Hobson, Sally. Memory for verbal sequences as a function of their syntactical structure and the age of the recalling child. *The Journal of Psychology,* 1966, *64,* 79-90.

Salzinger, Suzanne, Salzinger, K., Portnoy, Stephanie, Eckman, Judith, Bacon, Pauline M., Deutsch, M., & Zubin, J. Operant conditioning of continuous speech in young children. *Child Development,* 1962, *33,* 683-695.

Schafer, R., & Murphy, G. The role of autism in a visual figure-ground relationship. *Journal of Experimental Psychology,* 1943, *32,* 335-343.

Schneider, A. M. Control of memory by spreading cortical depression: a case for stimulus control. *Psychological Review,* 1967, *74,* 201-215.

Schoenfeld, W. N. An experimental approach to anxiety, escape, and avoidance behavior. In P. H. Hoch and J. Zubin (Eds.), *Anxiety.* New York: Grune & Stratton, 1950.

Scott, J. P. The analysis of social organization in animals. *Ecology,* 1956, *37,* 213-221.

Shannon, C., & Weaver, W. *The mathematical theory of communication.* Urbana, Ill.: Univ. Illinois Press, 1949.

Shapiro, M. M., & Miller, T. M. On the relationship between conditioned and discriminative stimuli and between instrumental and consummatory responses. In W. F. Prokasy (Ed.), *Classical conditioning.* New York: Appleton-Century-Crofts, 1965.

Shaw, Evelyn. The development of schooling behavior in fishes. *Physiological Zoology,* 1960, *33,* 79-86.

Sherif, M. A study of some social factors in perception. *Archives of Psychology,* New York, 1935, *27,* No. 187.

Sidman, M. A note on functional relations obtained from group data. *Psychological Bulletin,* 1952, *49,* 263-269.

Sidman, M. Avoidance conditioning with brief shock and no exteroceptive warning signal. *Science,* 1963, *118,* 157-158.

Sidman, M. Stimulus generalization in an avoidance situation. *Journal of the Experimental Analysis of Behavior,* 1961, *4,* 157-169.

Sidman, M. Avoidance behavior. In W. K. Honig (Ed.), *Operant behavior: areas of research and application.* New York: Appleton-Century-Crofts, 1966.

Sidman, M., & Stebbins, W. C. Satiation effects under fixed-ratio schedules of reinforcement. *Journal of Comparative and Physiological Psychology,* 1954, *47,* 114-116.

Sidman, M., & Stoddard, L. T. The effectiveness of fading in programming a simultaneous form discrimination for retarded children. *Journal of the Experimental Analysis of Behavior,* 1967, *10,* 3-16.

Sidowski, J. B., Wyckoff, L. B., & Tabory, L. The influence of reinforcement and punishment in a minimal social situation. *Journal of Abnormal and Social Psychology,* 1956, *52,* 115-119.

Simmons, Mae W., & Lipsitt, L. P. An operant-discrimination apparatus for infants. *Journal of Experimental Analysis of Behavior,* 1961, *4,* 233-235.

Skinner, B. F. The generic nature of the concepts of stimulus and response. *Journal of General Psychology,* 1935, *12,* 40-65.

Skinner, B. F. *The behavior of organisms.* New York: Appleton-Century-Crofts, 1938.

Skinner, B. F. "Superstition" in the pigeon. *Journal of Experimental Psychology,* 1948, *38,* 168-172.

Skinner, B. F. Are theories of learning necessary? *Psychological Review,* 1950, *57,* 193-216.

Skinner, B. F. *Science and human behavior.* New York: Macmillan, 1953. (a)

Skinner, B. F. Some contributions of an experimental analysis of behavior to psychology as a whole. *American Psychologist,* 1953, *8,* 69-78. (b)

Skinner, B. F. The science of learning and the art of teaching. *Harvard Educational Review,* 1954, *24,* 86-97.

Skinner, B. F. Freedom and the control of men. *American Scholar,* 1955-1956, *25,* special issue, 47-65.

Skinner, B. F. A case history in scientific method. *American Psychologist,* 1956, *11,* 221-233.

Skinner, B. F. The experimental analysis of behavior. *American Scientist,* 1957, *45,* 343-371. (a)

Skinner, B. F. *Verbal behavior.* New York: Appleton-Century-Crofts, 1957. (b)

Skinner, B. F. *Cumulative record.* New York: Appleton-Century-Croft, 1961.

Sluckin, W. Early experience. In B. M. Foss (Ed.), *New horizons in psychology.* Middlesex, England: Penguin, 1966.

Small, W. S. Experimental study of the mental processes of the rat, II. *American Journal of Psychology,* 1901, *12,* 206-232.

Spelt, D. K. The conditioning of the human fetus *in utero. Journal of Experimental Psychology,* 1948, *38,* 338-346.

Spence, K. W. *Behavior theory and conditioning.* New Haven: Yale Univ., 1956.

Sperry, R. W. The great cerebral commissure. *Scientific American,* 1964, *210,* 42-62.

Staats, A. W. Emotions and images in language: a learning analysis of their acquisition and function. In K. Salzinger and Suzanne Salzinger (Eds.), *Research in verbal behavior and some neurophysiological implications.* New York: Academic Press, 1967.

Staats, A. W., & Staats, Carolyn K. Attitudes established by classical conditioning. *Journal of Abnormal and Social Psychology,* 1958, *57,* 37-40.

Staats, A. W., & Staats, Carolyn, K. A comparison of the development of speech and reading behavior with implications for research. *Child Development,* 1962, *33,* 831-846.

Staats, A. W., & Staats, Carolyn K. *Complex human behavior.* New York: Holt, Rinehart & Winston, 1963.

Staats, A. W., Staats, Carolyn K., Schutz, R. E., & Wolf, M. The conditioning of textual responses using "extrinsic" reinforcers. *Journal of Experimental Analysis of Behavior,* 1962, *5,* 33-40.

Staudt, Virginia M. & Zubin, J. A biometric evaluation of the somatotherapies in schizophrenia. *Psychological Bulletin,* 1957, *54,* 171-196.

Stevens, S. S. (Ed.) *Handbook of experimental psychology,* New York: Wiley, 1951.

Stevens, S. S., & Galanter, E. H. Ratio scales and category scales for a dozen perceptual continua. *Journal of Experimental Psychology,* 1957, *54,* 377-411.

Sutton, S., Braren, Margery, Zubin, J. & John, E. R. Evoked-potential correlates of stimulus uncertainty. *Science,* 1965, *150,* 1187-1188.

Swets, J. A., Tanner, Jr., W. P., & Birdsall, T. G. Decision processes in perception. *Psychological Review,* 1961, *68,* 301-340.

Taylor, W. L. Cloze procedure: a new tool for measuring readability. *Journalism Quarterly,* 1953, *30,* 415-433.

Teitelbaum, P. The use of operant methods in the assessment and control of motivational states. In W. K. Honig (Ed.), *Operant behavior: areas of research and application.* New York: Appleton-Century-Crofts, 1966.

Terrace, H. S. Stimulus control. In W. K. Honig (Ed.), *Operant behavior: areas of research and application.* New York: Appleton-Century-Crofts, 1966.

Thompson, T. I. Visual reinforcement in fighting cocks. *Journal of the Experimental Analysis of Behavior,* 1964, 7, 45-49.

Thorndike, E. L. Animal intelligence: an experimental study of the associative processes in animals. *Psychological Review Monograph Supplements 2,* 1898, No. 4 (Whole No. 8).

Ullmann, L. P., & Krasner, L. (Eds.), *Case studies in behavior modification.* New York: Holt, Rinehart & Winston, 1965.

Ulrich, R. E., Stachnik, T. J., & Stainton, N. R. Student acceptance of generalized personality interpretations. *Psychological Reports,* 1963, *13,* 831-834.

Ulrich, R. E., Stachnik, T. J., & Mabry, J. (Eds.) *Control of human behavior.* Glenview, Ill.: Scott, Foresman, 1966.

Verhave, T. (Ed.), *The experimental analysis of behavior.* New York: Appleton-Century- Crofts, 1966.

Verplanck, W. S. The control of the content of conversation: reinforcement of statements of opinion. *Journal of Abnormal and Social Psychology,* 1955, *51,* 668-676.

Verplanck, W. S. A glossary of some terms used in the objective science of behavior. *Psychological Review,* 1957, *64,* 1-42.

Wann, T. W. (Ed.), *Behaviorism and phenomenology.* Chicago: Univ. Chicago Press, 1964.

Watson, J. B. Psychology as the behaviorist views it. *Psychological Review,* 1913, *20,* 158-177.

Watson, J. B. *Behavior.* New York: Holt, Rinehart & Winston, 1914.

Watson, J. B., & Rayner, Rosalie. Conditioned emotional reactions. *Journal of Experimental Psychology,* 1920, *3,* 1-14.

Weiner, H. Some effects of response cost upon human operant behavior. *Journal of the Experimental Analysis of Behavior,* 1962, *5,* 201-208.

Wenzel, Bernice M. Changes in heartrate associated with responses based on positive and negative reinforcement. *Journal of Comparative and Physiological Psychology,* 1961, *54,* 638-644.

Wike, E. L. *Secondary reinforcement.* New York: Harper & Row, 1966.

Wike, E. L., & Barrientas, G. Secondary reinforcement and multiple drive reduction. *Journal of Comparative and Physiological Psychology,* 1958, *51,* 640-643.

Williams, S. B. Resistance to extinction as a function of the number of reinforcements. *Journal of Experimental Psychology,* 1938, *23,* 506-521.

Wolpe, J., Salter, A., & Reyna, L. J. *The conditioning therapies.* New York: Holt, Rinehart, & Winston, 1964.

Woodworth, R. S., & Schlosberg, H. *Experimental psychology.* New York: Holt, Rinehart, & Winston, 1954.

Wunderlich, R. A. Strength of a generalized conditioned reinforcer as a function of variability of reward. *Journal of Experimental Psychology,* 1961, *62,* 409-415.

Yerkes, R. M. The formation of habits in the turtle. *Popular Science Monthly,* 1901, *58,* 519-525.

Zajonc, R. B. Social facilitation. *Science,* 1965, *149,* 269-274.

Zajonc, R. B., & Nieuwenhuyse, B. Relationship between word frequency and recognition: perceptual process or response bias? *Journal of Experimental Psychology,* 1964, *67,* 276-285.

Zeaman, D., & House, Betty J. The relation of IQ and learning. In R. M. Gagné (Ed.), *Learning and individual differences.* Columbus, Ohio: Merrill, 1967.

Zeaman, D., & Smith, R. W. Review of some recent findings in human cardiac conditioning. In W. F. Prokasy (Ed.), *Classical conditioning.* New York: Appleton-Century-Crofts, 1965.

Zubin, J. Classification of the behavior disorders. *Annual Review of Psychology,* 1967, *18,* 373-406.

SUBJECT INDEX

C

D

K

L

M

N

O

P

AUTHOR INDEX

A

B

C

D

E

F

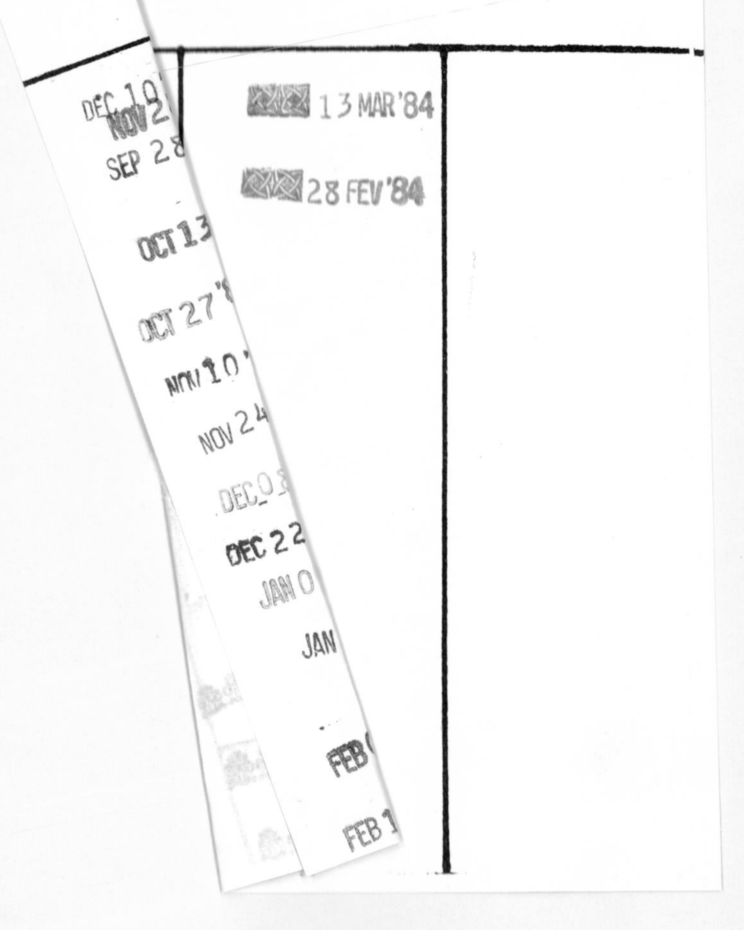

La bibliothèque
Université d'Ottawa
Échéance
The Library
University of Ottawa
Date Due
13 MAR'84
28 FEV'84